Man's Origin, Man's Destiny

Man's Origin, Man's Destiny

A Critical Survey of the Principles of Evolution and Christianity

A. E. Wilder-Smith

BETHANY HOUSE PUBLISHERS

MINNEAPOLIS, MINNESOTA 55438

A Division of Bethany Fellowship, Inc.

Published by Bethany Fellowship, Inc.
6820 Auto Club Road
Minneapolis, Minnesota 55438

Printed in the United States of America

Library of Congress Cataloging in Publication Data:

Wilder-Smith, A   E
    Man's origin, man's destiny.

    Reprint of the 1968 ed. published by H. Shaw, Wheaton,
Ill.
    Translation of Herkunft und Zunkunft des Menschen.
    Bibliography: p.
    Includes index.
    1. Bible and evolution. 2. Man—Origin. 3. Human
evolution. I. Title. [DNLM: 1. Christianity.
2. Evolution. 3. Religion and science. QH366 W675h]
BS659.W5413   1975   213   74-28508
ISBN 0-87123-356-8

CONTENTS

5

PROLOGUE

There is always hope if we keep an unsolved problem fairly in view; there's none if we pretend it's not there.

> C. S. LEWIS
> in *Letters to Malcolm*

In his own subject every man knows that all discoveries are made and all errors corrected by those who ignore the "climate of opinion."

> C. S. LEWIS
> in *The Problem of Pain*

If the universe is a universe of thought, then its creation must have been an act of thought.

. . . The universe begins to look more like a great thought than like a great machine. Mind no longer appears as an accidental intruder into the realm of matter; we are beginning to suspect that we ought rather to hail it as the creator and governor of the realm of matter. . . . We discover that the universe shews evidence of a designing or controlling power that has something in common with our own individual minds . . . with . . . the tendency to think in the way which, for want of a better word, we describe as mathematical. . . . We are not so much strangers or intruders in the universe as we at first thought.

> SIR JAMES JEANS
> in *The Mysterious Universe*

9

ACKNOWLEDGMENTS

The help and constructive criticism of the following friends in preparing the German manuscript and its English translation are gratefully acknowledged:

Pastor W. Gottwaldt, Professor at the Bible Seminary, Bad Liebenzell, Black Forest, Germany, who went through the entire German manuscript.

Dr. Henry M. Morris, Professor and Head of Department of Civil Engineering, Virginia Polytechnic Institute, Blacksburg, Virginia, who gave permission to use a number of photographic plates and with whom the author carried on a lengthy correspondence on some aspects of evolutionary thought.

Dr. John C. Whitcomb, Jr., with whom certain aspects of evolutionary theory were discussed during the author's stay at Winona Lake School of Theology, giving the Dr. G. Campbell Morgan Lectures for 1967, and again in October, 1967. Dr. Whitcomb worked through the English manuscript and made valuable suggestions.

Dr. Clifford L. Burdick, Tucson, Arizona, who gave permission to use a number of photographic plates and to quote his correspondence with the author.

Dr. P. V. Glob, Professor at the University of Aarhus, Denmark, the Prehistoric Museum, Aarhus, Denmark, and the National Museum in Copenhagen, Denmark, who allowed the use of their photographic plates of the Borremosemanden, the Tollundmanden, and the Grauballemanden.

Dr. R. Budde, Physicist, CERN, Geneva, Switzerland, who checked certain physical, linguistic, and other aspects of the German manuscript.

Dr. Wolfgang Saur, Argonne National Laboratories, University of Chicago, who checked particularly the chapters on metabolism. Dr. Saur has since returned to Switzerland.

Dr. A. Grau, Professor of Mathematics, Northwestern University, Evanston, Illinois, who read the entire English manuscript and with whom the author discussed the chapter on probability in some detail.

Dr. John J. Davis, Professor of Archaeology, Grace Theological Seminary, Winona Lake, Indiana, who worked through the English manuscript and made valuable suggestions.

Dr. K. Kantzer, Dean of Trinity Theological Seminary, Deerfield, Illinois, who painstakingly worked through the English manuscript and gave the author the benefit of many constructive suggestions and much wisdom.

Wheaton College Library afforded the author its valuable facilities during the translation of this volume.

Finally, my wife who helped with textual criticism and the preparation of the German and English text and prepared the index.

INTRODUCTION

In August, 1957, an event of great importance took place in the scientific world. Under the auspices of the International Union of Biochemistry, and with the collaboration of the Academy of Sciences of the U.S.S.R., a symposium on the "Origin of Life on the Earth" was held at Moscow. Professor A. I. Oparin, whose book *The Origin of Life*,[1] has become a world classic on the subject, gave the inaugural address. The proceedings of this important series of scientific meetings were published in 1959 in English, French and German.[2] It was the first time that such an illustrious and international team of scientists had come together with the specific purpose of threshing out this important question of the origin of life on the earth.

The symposium attracted contributing scientists from seventeen countries, most of them outstanding investigators in the various disciplines connected with the problem of biogenesis on the earth. It is instructive to examine the varied modern approaches to this ancient problem which has stimulated man's mind from the dawn of history. The transactions of the Muscovite symposium provide a first-class

[1]A. I. Oparin, *The Origin of Life* (New York: Macmillan Co., 1938).
[2]*The Origin of Life on the Earth*, International Union of Biochemistry Series, Vol. I, F. Clark and R. L. M. Synge (eds.). Edited for Academy of Sciences of the U.S.S.R. by A. I. Oparin, A. G. Pasynskii, A. E. Braunshtein, T. E. Pavlovskya. (New York: Macmillan Co., 1959).

opportunity for reviewing the various modern efforts at the solution of an age-old problem.

In his introductory address, Professor A. I. Oparin pointed out that at the end of the nineteenth century scientists had proved that the spontaneous generation of life from nonliving matter did not take place today under any known laboratory conditions. He then commented logically enough: "This [finding] took away the ground from under the feet of those scientists who saw in spontaneous generation a scientifically credible way in which life could have originated [on earth]."[3] Dr. Oparin continued by saying, "They were, thus, without any possibility of an experimental approach to the problem, which led to a very pessimistic conclusion, namely, to the belief that the problem of the origin of life was 'proscribed,' that it was an insoluble problem and that to work on it was unworthy of any serious investigator and was a pure waste of time."

After this historical approach to the problem, the line of thought followed by Dr. Oparin corresponded closely to that followed by a majority of modern scientists active in this field today. In spite of what Dr. Oparin said about the known facts of science proscribing the concept of spontaneous generation today, nearly all scientists assume it to have occurred in the past. Dr. Oparin himself postulated that the development of life from nonliving matter took place spontaneously by stages along the following general chemical pathway: First, simple organic compounds such as hydrocarbons and their close derivatives arose spontaneously under the influence of various radiations on the lifeless earth. That is, spontaneous chemical evolution up to simple organic compounds occurred. There is, of course, some evidence that this can occur. Professor S. L. Miller[4] of the College of Physicians and Surgeons, Columbia University, has reported successful experiments in this field, in which amino acids and other simple

---

[3]Oparin, Introductory Address, *The Origin of Life on the Earth,* p. 1.
[4]S. L. Miller, "Formation of Organic Compounds on the Primitive Earth," *The Origin of Life on the Earth,* p. 123.

substances arose on passing an electric spark or a silent discharge through an atmosphere containing the gases of which the primitive atmosphere on earth was thought to be composed. However, F. Cedrangolo[5] suggests that bacteria infiltrating the unprotected system used by Miller may have been the source of the amino acids produced in the experiment, and he thinks that repetition of the experiments reported by Miller is mandatory. Be that as it may, there are few theoretical difficulties in assuming spontaneous synthesis of simple amino acids. The difficulties begin later in the proposed spontaneous synthesis.

R. M. Kliss and C. N. Matthews[6] report obtaining peptides directly from ammonia and methane without the presence of water and without the intermediate formation of amino acids. Matthews and R. E. Moser[7] developed this line of research further and obtained peptides directly from hydrocyanic acid and anhydrous ammonia. By raising the concentration of hydrogen in their reaction mixtures they obtained adenine, an essential constituent of DNA.

It is often overlooked that Darwin himself, especially in his later years, was inclined to believe in a spontaneous generation of life from nonliving simple chemicals and not as the direct result of a Creator's activity. Especially in his earlier works Darwin often referred with reverence to a Creator as having been responsible for the formation of a restricted number of original forms of life, from which all the varieties of life we know today branched out by natural selection as laid down in his famous The Origin of Species.[8] This is the position taken by some Christian colleges in North America today. But Darwin's thinking, at least in 1871, left the possibility open for spontaneous generation to have been the

   [5]F. Cedrangolo, "The Problem of the Origin of Proteins," The Origin of Life on the Earth, p. 281.
   [6]R. M. Kliss and C. N. Matthews, Proceedings of the National Academy of Science (1962), XLIII, 1300.
   [7]C. N. Matthews and R. E. Moser, Nature (London, 1967), CCVX, 1230.
   [8]Charles Darwin, The Origin of Species, ed. Charles W. Eliot (New York: P. F. Collier & Son, 1909).

basic mechanism of biogenesis. For Darwin wrote in 1871:

> We could conceive in some warm little pond, with all
> sorts of ammonia and phosphoric salts, light, heat and
> electricity, etc., that a protein compound was chemically
> formed ready to undergo still more complex changes. At
> the present day such matter would be instantly devoured
> or absorbed, which would not have been the case before
> living creatures were formed.[9]

Darwin's personal development away from orthodox Christianity is described later.

Dr. Oparin conceives the second stage in the general evolutionary pathway upward to life as having occurred abiogenically also. The lithosphere, atmosphere and hydrosphere are
considered to have been the theater of operations, and the
general laws of chemistry and physics, as we know them today,
are thought to have been responsible for this second stage
of development. Again, no outside influences controlling
the syntheses of the second stage are conceived. Chance is
supposed to have been operative over long time spans. Oparin
postulates that this second stage leads to very complicated
molecules, such as proteinlike substances of high molecular
weight, nucleic acids and other compounds characteristic of
contemporary protoplasms.

Commenting on Dr. Oparin's conception of the second
stage, F. Cedrangolo[10] believes, with many other scientists,
that the postulated spontaneous formation of these larger
molecules is open to serious doubt. The ordinary laws of
probability would make the production of even a single complex protein so rare that, after it had formed, huge time intervals would have to be inserted before a second such molecule could arise spontaneously. And even then, the second
molecule might arise thousands of miles away from the first,

[9]Francis Darwin, *The Life and Letters of Charles Darwin* (New York:
D. Appleton, 1898), Vol. II, p. 202, n., as cited by Garrett Hardin in *Scientific Monthly* (1950) LXX, 178. See also Sidney W. Fox, "A Chemical Theory of Spontaneous Generation," *The Origin of Life on the Earth*, p. 281.
[10]Cedrangolo, *loc. cit.*

and thus would not be able to "collaborate" in forming a living aggregate necessary to produce a living organism.

In order to overcome this grave difficulty in the second stage proposed by Dr. Oparin, Dr. Cedrangolo proposes that the simple molecules of the first stage be considered to possess the property of autoduplication: "These molecules would have lived, so to say, in close association with themselves and with other organic substances in fluid masses and in microscopic drops, inside some particular system that Oparin, using Bungenberg de Jong's terminology, called 'coacervate.' "[11]

But surely it is well to note here that we have no evidence to date that the simple molecules postulated could autoduplicate themselves. To propose this is to pose a problem as difficult as that of life itself. Dr. Cedrangolo's hypothesis is also quite outside the realm of any experimental evidence. For energy would be needed to operate such a duplicative process, which the heat or light of the sun could not supply without the mediation of a complex metabolic motor. A complex association of matter would be indispensable to arrive at autoduplication, yet Dr. Cedrangolo is postulating simple molecules as carrying on this process. We have no evidence for such an hypothesis. Viruses, in duplicating themselves, use the metabolic support of their complex host cells, but the host cells are lacking under the conditions on earth before biogenesis.

According to Dr. Oparin's widely recognized scheme, the third stage in the spontaneous evolutionary process up to life was reached when the complex molecules formed during the second stage were acted upon and changed under the influence of the external medium and which then underwent selection. Thus arose the most primitive primary organisms under the influence of nothing but chance, time, a suitable environment and simple chemicals.[12] Oparin concedes that up to the present, we have been able to realize experimen

[11]*Ibid.*, p. 284. Cf. Oparin, *The Origin of Life*, and H. G. Bungenberg de Jong, *Colloid Science*, reviewed by H. R. Kruyt (New York, 1949), Vol. II.
[12]Oparin, *op. cit.*, *The Origin of Life on the Earth*, p. 2.

only stage one of his scheme. No details are proposed on the problem of how the external medium changed the reaction products of stage two or what precise meaning the word "selection" carries when used by Dr. Oparin.

Oparin's conception of life's origin, as outlined above, is probably the most generally accepted one in scientific circles today. But a perusal of the transactions of the symposium will convince the reader that some of the scientists present could not accept this somewhat facile concept of the problem of biogenesis. Dr. N. W. Pirie[13] of the Rothamstead Experimental Station at Harpenden, England, rejects this whole concept of spontaneous biogenesis simply on the well-founded fact that complicated molecules such as proteins do not, in our scientific experience, arise spontaneously even by stages. But again, in common with practically all scientists—at least those taking part in the symposium—Dr. Pirie rejects the idea of accounting for life on the earth as a result of occult or supernatural intervention. He points out, however, that no less a person than Dr. J. B. S. Haldane was driven to believe that the laws of chemistry and physics must have been different in the Precambrian from what they are now, since the ordinary laws of chemistry and physics, as we know them today, do not allow complex proteins to arise spontaneously even by stages. Therefore, such is Haldane's logic, since life did in his view arise spontaneously, the laws of chemistry must have been different when it arose![14]

Dr. Kurt Felix of the Institut für Vegetative Physiologie der Universität Frankfurt am Main, Western Germany, writes: "Nur eins ist sicher: es kommt in unseren Zeitläufen niemals vor, dass Eiweiss aus einem Haufen loser Aminosäuren, der für sich und isoliert von anderem lebenden Material daliegt, gebildet wird."[15] ("Only one thing is certain:

---

[13]N. W. Pirie, "Chemical Diversity and the Origins of Life," *The Origin of Life on the Earth*, p. 76.
[14]*Ibid.*, p. 78.
[15]Kurt Felix, "Die Kontinuitaet des Eiweisses," *The Origin of Life on the Earth*, p. 248.

it never happens in our time that protein is formed out of a mass of uncombined amino acids if the latter are left alone and kept separate from any living matter.") Dr. Felix refers to his paper on this subject.[16]

We are therefore not surprised that Dr. Pirie also is convinced that proteins did not arise spontaneously from nonliving matter. The statistical difficulties are too formidable to wash away by wishful thinking and bold statements. Therefore Dr. Pirie suggests that life did not arise on spontaneously formed proteins but on much simpler substances. Even though life as we know it today is absolutely dependent on protein matter, this does not mean that life was always dependent on protein. According to Dr. Pirie, the fact that all forms of life known today do use protein

> . . . will have no more relevance [to primitive life being dependent on protein] for a discussion about the origins of life than the now almost universal use of paper has for the origin of writing or the use of matches for the original making of fire. The first metal frying pan was probably made of gold because that metal was available and usable, though later ousted. The point is worth laboring, because very many people have written as if the problem of the origin of life was the same as the problem of the spontaneous synthesis of proteins, and some, having realized that the latter involves difficulties [in thermodynamics] have concluded that God or some similar agency must be involved.[17]

In spite of what Dr. Pirie says, probably most scientists, including the dean of this field, Dr. Oparin, do think that the origin of life is bound up with the origin of proteins. If one cannot explain the spontaneous formation of proteins, a large percentage of scientists would believe that the origin of life was not explicable either.

In view of this impasse, Dr. Pirie postulates life as having arisen spontaneously on a nonprotein basis in a very simple

---

[16]Felix, *Angewandte Chemie* (1948) LX, 231.
[17] Pirie, *op. cit.*, p. 78.

spontaneously produced organic medium. Certain metal ions,[18] thiourea or other simple substances, are postulated to have acted as nonprotein oxidases. It is known that the rare earth elements can function as esterases. Put all these simple catalytic systems together on mud or clay and you have the basis of a simple functioning organism! Dr. Pirie remarks that such a simple organism (eobiont) working on this kind of metabolic motor "might be a little sluggish, but it would be conceivable."

Dr. J. D. Bernal, speaking on "The Problem of Stages in Biopoiesis,"[19] quotes Lippmann's claim[20] that carbamyl phosphate ($OC.NH_2.O.PO._3$) could have functioned as a first type of living molecule or at least as the first step in the evolution of biochemistry.

As soon as it was realized that there are insuperable problems of a theoretical nature blocking the way to the assumption that proteins or other similar complex molecules were formed spontaneously before biopoiesis, scientists were forced to this type of far-out speculation on the origin of life. Certainly no form of life, as we know it today, could be supported by carbamyl phosphate. We need to keep clearly before us the fact that we are trying to explain the origin of life as we know it today and are not trying to conceive of other simpler forms of a kind of life borne on such simple molecules as carbamyl phosphate, the very existence of which, as life units, is highly hypothetical.

Dr. Erwin Chargaff of Columbia University makes some pertinent comments on these and other theories on the origin of life:

> Our time is probably the first in which mythology has penetrated to the molecular level. I read, for instance, in a recent article by a very distinguished biologist: "In the early phases of the molecular stage of evolution, only

[18]Ibid., p. 79.
[19]J. D. Bernal, "The Problem of Stages in Biopoiesis," The Origin of Life on the Earth, p. 44.
[20]M. E. Jones, L. Spector and F. Lippmann, Journal of the American Chemical Society (1955), LXXII, 819.

simple molecules were formed. . . . Later more complex molecules, such as amino acids and perhaps simple peptides, were formed.

"In the more advanced phases of this period it is believed that there appeared a molecule with two entirely new properties: the ability systematically to direct the formation of copies of itself from an array of simpler building blocks, and the property of acquiring new chemical configurations without loss of ability to reproduce. The properties, self-duplication and mutation, are characteristic of all living systems and they may therefore be said to provide an objective basis for defining the living state. . . ." Thus, what started cosmically with beautiful and profound legends has come down to a so-called "macromolecule." If poetry has suffered, precision has not gained. For we may ask ourselves whether a model that merely provides for one cell constituent continually to make itself, can teach us much about life and its origins. We may also ask whether the postulation of a hierarchy of cellular constituents, in which the nucleic acids are elevated to a patriarchal role in the creation of living matter, is justified. I believe there is not sufficient evidence for so singling out this particular class of substances.[21]

Dr. Chargaff comments a little later in his article:

It is not likely that we could learn much about the "origin of the automobile" from an inspection of the parts of a present-day car; nor could such an examination help us decide whether there did not once exist an automobile made of glass. . . . In my opinion it would be more honest to confess that we know very little indeed about these things and to say that the road to the future should not be uselessly cluttered up with shoddy, and often entirely baseless, hypotheses.
. . . Is the cell really nothing but a system of ingenious stamping presses, stencilling its way from life to death?

[21]Erwin Chargaff, "Nucleic Acids as Carriers of Biological Information," *The Origin of Life on the Earth*, pp. 298-99.

Is life only an intricate chain of templates and catalysts and products? My answer to these and many similar questions would be "No"; for I believe that our science has become too mechanomorphic, that we talk in metaphors in order to conceal our ignorance, and that there are categories in biochemistry for which we lack even a proper notation, let alone an idea of their outlines and dimensions.[22]

Thus we have now reached the point where leading scientists acknowledge the fact that biopoiesis cannot be explained on the assumption that complex proteins and other similar molecules were formed by chance spontaneously over immense time spans. J. D. Bernal has suggested, however, yet one more way to get around the difficulties. He, like Oparin, suggests that proteins and other complex molecules were spontaneously formed *by stages*. He cannot bring himself to believe that a drop of a solution of unorganized amino acids could suddenly and spontaneously deliver a perfect synthetic protein. So that the main thesis of Dr. Bernal's paper before the Muscovite symposium runs as follows: "The probability of formation of a highly complex structure from its elements is increased or the number of possible ways of doing it diminished, if the structure in question can be broken down in a finite series of successively inclusive substructures."[23]

What Dr. Bernal is saying is that it is unlikely that a molecule can increase in complexity spontaneously and suddenly like a man falling in one fell swoop up a ladder from bottom to top! But a molecule could "fall up the ladder" (rise in complexity) by falling up it "rungwise." This precise proposition is examined later in this book and is found to be unconvincing from energy considerations. For the energy required to raise from the bottom to the top of the ladder is the same, regardless of whether it is raised in one "fell swoop" or in stages, rungwise. So, neither Dr. Bernal nor Dr. Oparin re-

[22]*Ibid.*
[23]Bernal, "The Scale of Structural Units in Biopoiesis," *The Origin of Life on the Earth*, p. 388.

solve the real problems by postulating their stages.

If biopoiesis cannot be conceived of as the result of the spontaneous synthesis even by stages of complex molecules or as the result of simple molecules assuming the properties of living entities (autoduplication), what alternatives are left for explaining life's origin on a scientific basis? We submit that the assumption of creation is the only reasonable alternative, and it is an unpalatable one for most scientists, who consider it to be sterile. Personally I do not think that any true idea is likely to remain sterile for long. For a recent work on the whole problem of biogenesis, see Dr. J. D. Bernal's exhaustive work.[24]

But why should the whole idea of creation be so unpalatable to most scientists? In the first place, many phenomena thought in earlier times to be supernatural have since been explained on a perfectly natural basis. But surely this ought not lead us to extrapolate too far and assume that therefore *every* phenomenon can be explained on a purely material basis. But that is just what has happened. The pendulum has swung too far toward materialism in biology. Second, it is unacceptable for a scientist to have to reckon with the entirely unpredictable, with a God who might do anything, and whom we cannot "investigate." In science we like to explain everything possible on the basis of known natural law. But, as things stand, modern scientists have explored countless avenues in an endeavor to explain life's origin and man on a purely material basis in the dimensions of time and space known to us. We have repeatedly found that this explanation cannot be arrived at without trespassing against certain well-known material basic laws, particularly those of thermodynamics, which are examined in this book. If we cannot explain things on the basis of the laws of our three-dimensional world (four dimensions, counting time!), why hesitate at introducing another dimension (that of supranature) if we find

[24]Bernal, *The Origin of Life* (London: Weidenfeld & Nicolson, 1967), p. 345.

it unavoidable? Let us rather do this than trespass against the laws of physics and chemistry which we do know about!

Surely, if we see plan, is it not natural to postulate a planner? It is clear to me that Darwinists deny just this point of logic in maintaining that natural selection and random variation simulate plan in living nature without a planner. Darwin himself regularly used examples of adaptation to show that they originated by natural selection without purposive design.[25] In the order of animal and plant adaptation, Darwinists see therefore no designed program or fulfillment of a predetermined aim such as would result from final causes or a creator.[26]

We investigate this logic later when dealing with Darwin's evolution of mind and thought. If natural selection were in a position to neutralize the argument from design in living nature, this same argument does not neutralize the argument from design in nonliving nature, such as in the structure of matter. For here, in nonliving nature, no natural selection and variation can play any role. Since nonliving nature occurs in the universe much more often than living matter, Darwinists have solved little of the problem of design by their theory, for nonliving design still remains untouched by Darwin's selection theories. Thus the argument from design stands in its full force in nonliving nature.

But if we cannot find the planner in our three dimensions (or four, counting time), then the planner must be assumed to reside outside our four dimensions. Admittedly no scientist likes doing this. The method has often proved to be wrong in explaining simpler phenomena! So we must be careful indeed and search our four dimensions painstakingly before resorting to anything outside them in providing ourselves with an explanation of the origin of life. But while we go on actively searching in the dimensions known to us, we should not close our minds to the other possibilities outside our system of time and matter. *The honest searcher is the*

[25]Gavin de Beer, *Charles Darwin* (Garden City, N.Y.: Doubleday & Co., Inc., 1964), p. 103.
[26]*Ibid.*, p. 106.

one who is prepared to look—and find—everywhere. The prejudiced searcher is the one who makes up his mind before-hand where to look and where not to look.

But how are we to take this latter possibility seriously into account? How can a scientist, or any thoughtful person, look for anything outside time and space? His mind cannot deal with such eventualities. How can he search intelligently in these matters? The following example, which is developed more fully later, may help: If a scientist is planning a syn-thesis, he prepares his flow sheets, his formulae, his reagents, test tubes, retorts, distillation apparatus and reaction condi-tions very carefully beforehand. He will go to work with a carefully planned scheme in mind, which may only be in his head or may be partly or wholly committed to paper. He knows exactly what his intended end product is and what the yield aimed at is calculated to be. But to carry out this re-action scheme our planning scientist never actually enters the reaction system. He carries it all in his head. He remains exogenous to his retorts, beakers and test tubes. Without en-tering them at any time, he will nevertheless effectively con-trol all that happens in them during the reactions leading to his desired end product.

If now I were capable of residing in and becoming a part of the dimensions of the reaction system (losing my knowl-edge of the outside world at the same time, so as to be able to watch at a molecular level, and inside molecular dimen-sions, the molecules as they combine to form the end prod-uct), I would see nothing happening there but simple, well-known chemical combinations and reactions, all taking place according to laws of chance, chemistry, physics, mass action, affinities, solubilities, etc. These laws operating inside the reaction system and entirely inside molecular dimensions, would account completely for the attainment of the end prod-uct. From within the dimensions of the reaction system, where I reside and of which I am a part, I would be able to see nothing but the purely chemical and physical side of the whole reaction system leading to the end product. I would,

inside my reaction system, be entirely correct in explaining
the whole synthetic operation in terms of what I saw and experienced at a molecular level. From this level I would never
find it necessary to assume notebooks, thought, technical and
theoretical skill on the part of the planning scientist in order
to achieve his ends. I would never be able to begin to imagine the nature of the overall grand concept of the synthesis.
That would be absolutely invisible to me, for the simple
reason that it is outside the dimensions of the reaction system
of which I am a part. Planning, flow sheets, affinities, etc.
(mostly maybe on paper), would be inconceivable to me,
living as I do at the molecular level of the reaction system.
But my comprehension (or incomprehension) will not alter
the reality of the planning of this synthesis.

The only way the scientist operating at the molecular level
could get an idea of the exogenous planning behind his reaction system would be by examining the end product. As an
inhabitant of reaction systems in general he would find that,
within his experience, independent reaction systems would
produce only increasing chaos and not end products showing
signs of design. As an inhabitant of reaction solutions his experience will have shown him in countless cases that equilibrium and increase in entropy tend to be increasingly reached
with increasing time. He is now confronted with a highly organized molecule (showing reduced entropy compared with
other products of reaction and time), which represents an exception to that which he would expect to result from the random interplay of molecules showing affinity for one another.
If now the scientist does find an exception to what he would
expect, judged by his experience of random reaction systems
and their end products, he will not be able to find an explanation for an ordered end product, if he merely searches within the realm of his reaction medium. Nevertheless it is most
likely that he will attempt to account for the planned end
product before him in the same way as he accounts for every
other reaction taking place in his system. That is, he will be
tempted to ascribe everything to the interplay of pure chance

and chemical affinities. And we can understand fully the scientist thinking thus. Anything outside his system of reaction is outside his ken. So he explains everything on the basis of laws within his experience, even though he is uneasy about the evidence of design emerging from systems governed otherwise by randomness.

All this adds up to the following: If God did create and does maintain the universe, life and man by using chemical and physical reactions such as we know in our "system" (and he certainly did and does so) we shall nevertheless be entirely unable to see anything of his planning, "flow sheets" or operation technique. We shall never be able to "see" or "prove" his plan or thought concept in creation, for that is as much outside our ability, tied as we are to time and space, as it was outside the scientist's ability to see the overall synthetic plan while being restricted to life at a molecular level in the retorts. There will be one way only of obtaining an idea of what is really going on in the "reaction flasks" producing the ordered end product (as long as we are restricted to our material world). We must inspect carefully, not simply the reaction system, of which we are a part, but the "end product" which gives evidence of design not stemming alone from our reaction system. Our random reaction system cannot of itself produce design—it is a chance system. The laws of thermodynamics have long shown us that this is the case. But the evidence of random laws producing design (lowering of entropy if we wish) shows us *indirectly* that an exogenous source is controlling our three-dimensional system by thought and plan and by methods we can as well hope to understand as the scientist—who was resident in and part of the reaction system we have discussed—understood the synthetic scientist's grand concepts. In spite of the derision heaped on the "argument from design," it has never been adequately refuted. It alone can account for order apparently arising spontaneously out of chaos—just as apparent spontaneous order arose among our otherwise random molecules during the synthesis by the scientist. The technique he used was completely invisible from within the reaction system. He used apparently only the chemical affinities belonging to that system and evident to it.

Thus, I believe, God's thought controls our three-dimensional world from outside of the three dimensions. It follows that the direct mechanism by which his "hand" works will be invisible to creatures of three dimensions. Only an examination of the "end product" (man, or any of God's creatures or creations) will give us an indirect and faint idea of the overall grand concept. Our very design gives us indirectly and by induction some of his thought concept in forming and molding matter invisibly from outside the realm of matter. Of course, this does not exclude visible, manifest miracles, as in the plagues of Egypt, for example. Here we are not speaking of exceptions but rules.

In the following text I have examined some of the possibilities open to us to explain the origin of man. I have also endeavored to look at the thought concept behind our creation—what God intended in making us. For this reason I have referred to both science and to the Bible in an attempt to arrive at a balanced view on the creation and the meaning of life. All I request of the reader is a fair, careful, patient and unprejudiced reading of all the text that follows, accompanied by an inner willingness to bow before the facts.

MAN'S ORIGIN

1

MAN—AN ANIMAL OF THE HIGHEST INTELLIGENCE?

From earliest times man has been interested in the question of his origin and this interest is still showing no signs of flagging. Today two main types of opposing views are recognizable: First, the generally popular view taught and accepted without contradiction in most universities and colleges of the Eastern and Western worlds, that man has evolved from lower animals to his present state according to the principles first laid down by Charles Darwin, Alfred R. Wallace and their pupils. Thus man is, in this view, nothing more than a highly intelligent animal. Second, the view put forward as revelation by the Bible, which represents man as having been created specially, as he is today. There is a third mediating view, propounded by certain Christians, who try to combine the two above views by compromise. We cannot here go into various views put forward by certain non-Christian religions.

It is well, right at the start of our discussion, to be perfectly clear about the fact that Darwinism and Neo-Darwinism, rightly or wrongly, have been used everywhere in the East and West, in the hands of the atheists and agnostics, as the main weapon against the biblical doctrine of origins. It is well known today that the Communists officially use the "facts" of evolution to destroy or ridicule all theistic or Christian faith. Atheism and Darwinism are official state doctrine in the East, of which Darwinism is the main basis.

Professor Sir Julian Huxley maintains: "After Darwin it was no longer necessary to deduce the existence of divine purpose for the facts of biological adaptation."[1] Compare also Sir Julian Huxley's categorical statement at Chicago on November 26, 1959: "In the evolutionary pattern of thought there is no longer need or room for the supernatural. The earth was not created; it evolved. So did all the animals and plants that inhabit it, including our human selves, mind and soul as well as brain and body. So did religion."[2] This point of view is most widespread in the East behind the Iron Curtain, and in the Anglo-Saxon world. However, on the European Continent (and to a lesser extent in the United States) the intermediate viewpoint mentioned above is fairly common. It proposes that Darwinism, far from making the idea of God untenable or unnecessary, shows us God's creative method used in building our present world. Theistic evolutionists and progressive creationists are found in high concentrations in certain American denominational colleges. The views of Father Pierre Teilhard de Chardin (of the Society of Jesus), which have swept Europe and the United States in the past decade, would also fit into this latter category.

In the following discussion it will be necessary to weigh the following questions: (1) Does Darwinism as such really render the idea of a God superfluous and is it to be viewed as a suitable weapon for the atheists? or (2) Has evolution in the animal and vegetable kingdom been God's method of building the world of life as we know it? That is, does evolution show us God at work and that therefore theistic evolution is true?

Both views concede evolution to be a fact to be acknowledged and reckoned with. However, we shall have to consider a third question in the course of our studies: (3) Is a slow

[1]Julian Huxley, *Rationalist Annual* (1946), p. 87. Cf. L. M. Davies, "The Present State of Teleology," *Transactions* of the Victoria Institute (London, 1947), LXXIX, 70.

[2]Huxley, "Issues in Evolution," *Evolution After Darwin* (Chicago: University of Chicago Press, 1960), III, 252 f., as cited from William J. Tinkle, *Heredity, A Study in Science and the Bible* (Houston, Texas: St. Thomas Press, 1967).

spontaneous evolution of animal and plant life upward from the simple to the complex by chance, as Darwin and the Neo-Darwinists maintain, scientifically feasible or likely?

WHAT DOES EVOLUTION TEACH?

LIFE AROSE FROM ONE CELL?

All animals and plants, as we know them in the living world today, have arisen from a simple original living cell. Thus life now has been continuous with life from the beginning, but has blossomed out spontaneously into complexity from simplicity. Thus all forms of life are postulated as being genetically related and derived from one common source, the simple primitive cell, formed spontaneously at biogenesis by means not fully understood at present.

CONTINUAL CHANGE TOWARD COMPLEXITY

All forms of life have changed from the beginning onward. This change has usually been in the direction of complexity. Variety has developed out of a single "standard simplicity." The theory of evolution seeks not only to explain the origin of life as such, but also the mechanism by which the changes have occurred under natural and known laws or conditions.

The mechanism postulated is one involving modifications arising by chance. These changes may be known as mutations; they occur in the genetic material by chance. The chance mutations, which give the possessor an advantage over organisms not possessing the same, help it to survive in the struggle for existence. As a result, the possessors will become more numerous and leave more offspring than the unsuccessful organisms not possessing the chance mutation in the genetic material. Small or large mutations may take place and may be caused by ionizing radiation or certain chemical compounds. Other mutations may occur without any cause we can at present postulate. The distribution of such mutations is again ascribed to chance. Macromutations are supposed in some circles to be responsible for the sudden appearance of new species in the geological formations.

STRUGGLE FOR EXISTENCE

A struggle for existence is postulated by the Darwinists as existing between living organisms. Peaceful living together (symbiosis) is supposed to be less prevalent than struggle for existence. Only on the supposition that such a struggle is present can Darwinism postulate an upward trend in evolution, for without a struggle there can be no advantage in that struggle which could favor the organisms carrying a new and advantageous mutation over older organisms not carrying such an advantage. So that without struggle there could be no natural selection and no upward trend in evolution. The idea of evolution without the struggle for existence just could not be viable.

MILLIONS OF YEARS NEEDED

Since evolution is postulated as having taken place very slowly, millions of years are considered necessary for the evolutionary process.

On the basis of these four postulates Darwinism seeks to establish that a single primitive living cell could work itself up "automatically" to a complex higher organism. No God or higher Being would be necessary to direct this process. Mutation by chance and struggle for existence (natural selection) would automatically produce this upward trend in complexity of life. It is on just this basis that evolutionists deny the necessity of the God postulate—the whole postulate of design is rendered unnecessary by the automaticity postulated for the evolutionary process.

A majority, perhaps, of Darwinists take one further step. They assume that primitive life, or the primitive cell, was so simple that it, too, arose by pure chance. In some primitive ocean the correct concentrations of inorganic salts, ammonia, carbon dioxide, etc., arose, so that by chance some amino acids were formed. These then polymerized to polypeptides which combined with one another by chance to give the first primitive molecule. Protein is today a prerequisite for life, and once we have a ready-made protein, life could start to "ride" upon it. Thus primitive biogenesis (archebiopoiesis) is postulated to have "occurred." For the thorough-going Darwinist the only creator at work in this whole process is chance variation and selection working over millions of years in a favorable environment.

The evolutionary principles have been applied to the development of areas outside those of life, of course. Though the idea of struggle for existence has not been applicable to the inorganic world, an evolutionary process has been and is postulated to explain the origin of matter, the galaxies, energy, etc., without the idea of a mind behind it all, guiding the various synthetic procedures observed to occur. The evolutionary concept has taken charge of human thinking in areas concerned with biogenesis, political economy, the origin of matter, etc., and is postulated as governing the mechanism of all synthesis.

CHRISTIAN EXPLANATIONS

THE BIBLICAL TEACHING

The Bible professes to be God's revelation, not only on spiritual matters but also on such obviously scientific and material matters as the origin of the universe, our world and life. How do the statements of Scripture on these subjects line up with those taught by the proponents of Darwinism? To treat this subject properly it will be necessary to sketch just what the Bible does teach on these lines, since all kinds of statements are imputed to the Bible, which it never actually makes.

Certain Constancy of Species. The scriptural teaching runs to the effect that in the beginning God created heaven and earth, which were at that point waste and void.[3] After this specific primary creation, seven days are named during which God formed the world, as we know it. All the plants and animals were formed according to their kinds, after which they

[3]Gen. 1:1-2.

then reproduced themselves. This, on the surface, would seem to indicate at least a certain constancy of species, and that the various forms we know today are not *genetically* related. The idea of each form of life being separately created would not lead one to postulate, from the account given in the Bible, that primitive, early, simple forms of life were genetically ancestral to later more complex forms.

Not Absolute Constancy. On the other hand, one could never assume, if one took the Bible as the only source of information, that all species or kinds are absolutely constant. The reason for this statement is, of course, that the Bible account recognizes that Adam's species of man gave rise, after Noah, to the various ethnic strains of man, that is, the Semitic, the Hamitic (black or colored) races and the other white races. So the Scripture certainly teaches an "evolution" or divergence within a species, even though it teaches that all living things were created according to their kinds originally and that one simple kind did not evolve naturally or spontaneously into more complex and higher kinds. That is, the biblical report of origins would not seem to fit into the idea that one primitive cell arose spontaneously by chance from random amino acids or polypeptides and proteins, and that this cell gradually, without any divine or outside guidance, but purely by chance mutation and natural selection, gave rise to all the complex higher forms of life we know today.

Unless one were prejudiced and ready to read things into the text, one would scarcely suppose that statements such as these refer to evolution:

> Let the earth bring forth the living creatures after his kind, cattle, and creeping thing, and beast of the earth after his kind.

> The LORD God formed man of the dust of the ground, and breathed into his nostrils the breath of life; and man became a living soul.

> The LORD God caused a deep sleep to fall upon Adam, and he slept: and he took one of his ribs and closed up

the flesh instead thereof; and the rib, which the LORD
God had taken from the man, made he a woman, and
brought her unto the man.[4]

Such statements would scarcely remind the unprejudiced of
a process of chance mutation and natural selection resulting,
over millions of years, without any outside interference, in
the development of complex organisms from a simple cell,
which was also the result of pure chance. The typical Darwinist
believes in chance working over millions of years, coupled
with natural selection, as the only motive force necessary to
form random molecules into man, whereas the creationist
believes that the same random molecules were formed into
man and other organisms by the mighty divine intelligence.
If the chance processes of evolution really are the motive
force behind the upward surge of nonliving matter to complex life, and if the Bible is really telling us that life originated in this way, all we can ask ourselves, is: Why does the
author of the Bible not speak up and express himself more
plainly in this matter? Why does he not tell us more directly
the truth about the role played by chance in creation? If
Genesis really describes a slow process of upward development by chance over millions of years, why does its author
not say so? Surely these facts could have been expressed more
clearly, even in primitive language and times, if God had
wished to convey to us the idea of chance operating through
millions of years with natural selection as the prime motive
force of creation instead of God Himself. From the Bible
account one gains the impression of the urge of Logos, which
Darwinism replaces by blind chance and natural selection.
The least we would expect of a book purporting to mediate
divine instruction is clarity of expression.

POPULAR EFFORTS AT HARMONIZING DARWINISM WITH
GENESIS 1-3

Professor von Huene's Theories. Since the relationship

[4]Gen. 1:24; 2:7; 2:21-22.

between Genesis 1-3 and Darwinism is not clear on superficial inspection, evangelical Christians have expended a large
amount of time and energy in searching for points of contact
between the two views. On the European Continent one of
the most active and respected geologists who has worked in
this area has been Professor Freiherr von Huene of Tübingen.
Professor von Huene is also a keen evangelical Christian. His
books *Weg und Werk Gottes in der Natur* and *Schöpfung
und Naturwissenschaft*[5] (*Way and Work of God in Nature*
and *Creation and Science*) have been widely circulated and
accepted among Continental Christians.

Professor von Huene is what would be designated in Anglo-Saxon circles as a theistic evolutionist. He teaches:

1. Mankind has been slowly evolved from primitive life
   via unspecialized animal evolutionary stages through
   long ages.
2. There was a race of pre- and para-Adamic men which
   existed thousands of years before Adam and Eve.
3. God selected Adam from among this para-Adamic race,
   probably as a child, breathed the breath of God into
   .him and thus rendered him no longer an animal but
   a man. Thus Adam was spiritually, but not physically,
   the first member of the new human race. Adam was
   then placed in paradise, the Garden of Eden.

Adam was thus, biologically speaking, of pre- or para-
Adamic origin and race, though spiritually he was the first
man. Around Adam, living in paradise, the pre- and para-
Adamic races and their cultures flourished. The Garden of
Eden served the function of protecting Adam, as the first
member of the new spiritual race, from the destructive influences of the older human para-Adamic cultures.

Von Huene advances the view that, since God made use of
an animal body from which to synthesize Adam by breathing

[5]Freiherr von Huene, *Weg und Werk Gottes in der Natur,* Siegen-Leipzig:
Wilhelm Schneider Verlag, n.d.) and *Schöpfung und Naturwissenschaft*
(Stuttgart: Quell-Verlag).

his breath into it, God did still in fact make Adam from the "dust of the earth." Thus the "earth" God took to make Adam was earth already built into the selected animal's body. God used, according to this view, an "indirect" dust, in other words, an animal body.

But could the Bible have intended us to take this view? For Genesis 3 declares: "In the sweat of thy face shalt thou eat bread, till thou return unto the ground [dust, *adamah*]; for out of it wast thou taken: for dust [*'aphar*] thou art, and unto dust [*'aphar*] shalt thou return."[6] Thus, if the dust (*'aphar*) out of which Adam was constructed was really an animal body, the dust to which he returns at death must be just the same, that is, an animal body! Which could only mean, if we take the view Profesor von Huene offers that at death all mankind becomes some kind of lower animal again, maybe a para-Adamite! We assume he would scarcely have meant this. But if the word "dust" is used twice in one sentence, one must interpret it the same way each time, unless one has very good reason not to do so. Surely, in this case, the obvious interpretation involves letting the meaning stand at its face value, that is, as "dust," without introducing unnecessary hidden meanings.

Our own view is that the simple interpretation is confirmed by other passages of Scripture, for example, "All flesh is not the same flesh: but there is one kind of flesh of men, another flesh of beasts, another of fishes, and another of birds."[7] Thus, man's flesh (dust) is not equivalent to a beast's flesh (dust). The two would surely be equivalent if Adam's flesh had been in fact a beast's flesh into which spirit had been merely breathed. The inbreathed spirit would not alter material genes and chromosomes, which the professor thinks for Adam and his race were derived straight from beasts, in that God selected a pre- or para-Adamite and turned him into a man spiritually, though he remained a beast biologically. Under

[6]Gen. 3:19.
[7]I Cor. 15:39.

these circumstances man's and beast's flesh must have been equivalent and not different. First Corinthians 15:39 maintains, however, that *biologically* man is different from beasts.

Perhaps it would be useful to consider further some consequences of Professor von Huene's views since they throw light on other theistic evolutionary arguments. If Adam was biologically a beast into whom God had breathed his spirit and thus "humanized" him, then Adam was not really the first man *biologically*. For the professor teaches us that Cain took his wife from among the para-Adamic races, thus confirming his view that biologically and racially Adam remained unchanged, even after being breathed into and then placed in Eden. Thus cross-fertilization was possible between Adam's race and the para-Adamites, and yielded highly fertile offspring—a sure indication of racial identity. It follows that the para-Adamites and Adam were biologically truly one *species* of humanity. Which means simply that Adam, biologically, was definitely not the *first* man. The professor goes further, as do others of similar views. He maintains that the city which Cain built[8] can only be explained on the assumption that pre- and para-Adamites were present to cooperate with Cain and supply him with a wife and city builders. But if we take the Bible seriously we cannot go along with such views, for the Scripture maintains expressly that Adam was the first man and that his wife, Eve, was the mother of *all* living humans.[9] If the professor's views are correct, mankind must be derived only partially from Adam and Eve, since the pre- and para-Adamites are also, in this view, ancestors of later mankind. But the Bible maintains that Adam and Eve alone are our total and sole progenitors.[10]

Professor von Huene attempts to explain the whole development of man on the basis of a slow upward evolution through millions of years in accordance with Darwinian principles. At the same time he unequivocally recognizes the

[8]Gen. 4:17.
[9]Gen. 3:20.
[10]See Rom. 5:14; I Cor. 15:22, 45; I Tim. 2:13-14.

Bible as God's inspired Word, which is, of course, rare in a German scholar of Professor von Huene's standing.

But surely it is going to be very difficult to honestly interpret the biblical account of origins in a consistently evolutionary context, in spite of all the heroic efforts of sincere theistic evolutionists. Is not the account of Eve's miraculous surgical origin from Adam's side sufficient to prove that the Bible is not describing here any natural evolutionary chance process modified by natural selection through millions of years? Eve was taken during deep sleep direct from Adam's side, which is surely not, by any stretch of the imagination, a description of evolutionary processes. Why did not the Lord God provide Adam with a suitable para-Adamic wife, if he wished to build the human race from them by "natural" means and processes of reproduction? We know today from tissue culture work that, short of new creation, a good way to rebuild an organism with identical racial and genetic properties, would be to take a vegetative portion of it and reculture it by tissue culture methods, just as the Bible describes in the account of Eve's origin.

The biblical account of Eve's origin from Adam's side may also have a symbolic as well as a purely physical surgical meaning. Every man possesses, psychologically speaking, a shadow feminine part of his personality which compensates for his dominant male nature. Thus, Eve's origin from Adam's side may represent a symbolic separating of the combined two sexes originally present in Adam. We know that Christ taught that in the resurrection there will again be no separation of the sexes, resurrected man will be as the angels, neither male nor female.[11] This means that the end or eternal state of man, in which male and female are combined in one being, may reflect the initial state of man in which the one being, Adam, represented the whole posterity of men and women. This again would reflect the scriptural position that the eternal state will possess factors in common with the para-

[11]See Matt. 22:30.

dise or garden of God at the commencement of creation. The
end reflects the beginning in a similar way to Einstein's concept of curved space—by staring straight ahead of us out into
space we find we are looking at the backs of our heads because the curvature of space leads to everything doubling
back on itself.

The account of Eve's arrival on the scene, if we take the
Bible seriously, surely cuts out the possibility of any "natural"
evolutionary process over millions of years as the total explanation of man's origin. The biblical account is that of a
plainly miraculous and nonuniformitarian origin, of woman
at least. It represents a complete break with normal methods
of reproduction in the whole higher animal kingdom. Evolutionary processes cannot by any stretch of the imagination be
called upon to explain it.

The possibility of building cities quite early in the history
of mankind is explainable without resorting to postulations
on pre- or para-Adamic races. Man lived in those early ages
for much longer periods than at present, and the Bible accounts report 900 years as not unusual. Accounts of nonbibli-
cal origin report much longer lifetimes, some kings being
credited with having reigned thousands of years. It would
almost look as if they had counted days or even weeks or
months as years, in order to arrive at their age figures. But
during the 900 years of life reported by the Bible, the birth
of sons and daughters is mentioned.[12] We are going to assume
that the 900 years mentioned by the Bible are years of the
same length as we know them now, for the same Bible report
reduces the years first from 900 to 120 years and then to threescore years and ten. The threescore years and ten were obviously the same then as now, so we assume that the right proportions, at least, have remained for the greater ages mentioned.

If the gestation period of nine months was the same then
as now, and no reasons are seen at present for doubting this,

---

[12]See Appendix I.

then early man could have had huge families. Cain would have had no difficulty in marrying one of his sisters, as Abraham, much later, married Sarah, his half sister. The consequences of inbreeding would not have been comparable to those of such unions today, since genetic deterioration directly after the creation would have been less prevalent than now.

Today laboratories all over the world practice on a grand scale brother-and-sister mating for producing laboratory animals. As long as no undesirable recessive genes are present in either the brother or the sister, no undesirable consequences can arise, and vigorous races are the result of this practice. Certain Egyptian royal houses apparently used the same technique and produced highly fertile offspring for their dynasties. Today, with the danger of recessives, the practice in the human would be, to say the least, risky. But at the time of Cain, the marrying of one of his many sisters would have presented no difficulties at all from a genetic point of view, there being little or no genetic deterioration to fear in either partner.

"The Seven Days Are to Be Considered as Seven Ages." An effort has been made to overcome some of the difficulties of harmonization by reckoning the seven creative days of Genesis as seven geological ages. It is our own view, however, that the attempt to overcome some difficulties by this method often introduces even greater problems.

According to the biblical account, plants arose on the third day. But the sun is reported as having been made (not "created") on the fourth day. If the third and fourth days are in reality "ages," then the third age, that of plants, was devoid of sun. If the vegetation of the third age was responsible for the coal measures, of which we know today, then the age-equals-day interpretation must be incorrect, for the coal measures arose in powerful tropical sunshine. No cosmic light, such as the light of the first day, could have been responsible for such vegetation. Our present sun must have supplied the energy for the coal measures if the theories of modern astronomy have any weight at all.

Another difficulty arises if one tries to apply the age-equals-day interpretation. The whole important biblical doctrine of the Sabbath is weakened by this view. For God is reported as having rested on the seventh day after working the six days. The implication is that man should also rest on the seventh day as God did. But did God rest for an age, maybe of millions of years? The whole biblical concept of the Sabbath is coupled with six working days and one day of rest in seven.[13] God certainly did not need to rest, but presumably set us a pattern with the Sabbath rest. The idea of jubilee (7 X 7) is, of course, well known to biblical thought (see Lev. 25 and 27).

Still another difficulty arises if one takes the seven days to be seven ages. Sin, according to the Bible account, entered the world with Adam's fall and with this fall, death (presumably also the death of animals) is reported to have entered Adam's realm. The matter is discussed in Romans 5. If this is the case, how does it happen that there was death in the world, according to the seven-days-equal-seven-ages theorists, long before Adam fell and introduced to the world by his fall the phenomenon of death?[14]

Geological formations containing fossils are, of course, witnesses of death in a past age, since fossils are obviously produced only by the death of the organism concerned. So that any fossils geologically older than Adam introduce automatically the difficulty of death having occurred before Adam introduced death by his fall. Yet, according to the Genesis account and that of the Apostle Paul, Adam by his fall was the introducer of the phenomenon of death to the creation. So that death, on this basis, ought not to predate Adam. The theory we are considering makes seven days equal to seven ages and must make death in the creation at large predate Adam by millions of years. Yet the Scripture maintains that death only reigned from Adam,[15] and that as sin was intro-

[13]Cf. Exodus 20:10-11; 31:15-17.
[14]Cf. Appendix I.
[15]Rom. 5:14.

duced into the world by one man, the sin of Adam introduced death.[16] There are therefore considerable difficulties in applying the theory making one day equivalent to one geological age.

One can, of course, argue about the meaning of the word "death" in this context. It may mean spiritual death among Adam's kind, thus indicating the spiritual separation between God and man brought about by Adam's sin. On the other hand, the Bible teaches that if a man trusts in Jesus Christ, that man will never die, meaning that physical death is to be neutralized by eternal life through the resurrection after new birth. So spiritual and physical death are closely linked with one another. Spiritual death is the cause of physical death and spiritual life results in physical death being "swallowed up" at resurrection.

It is thus difficult (not absolutely impossible) to align biblical teaching with death being in power in creation long before Adam was reported to have introduced it by his fall. In any case, the theory under discussion would seem to require this state of things. On the other hand, scientifically from the point of view of the laws of thermodynamics which describe the present behavior of matter, it is impossible to conceive of the present order of creation as existing without the necessity of death. This is discussed later in relation to the question of the resurrection.

The Gap Theory. The Gap Theory offers a third possibility of escaping some of the difficulties we have noticed above.

The Genesis account informs us that in the beginning God created the heavens and earth and that the earth was (or became) waste and void (according to whichever translation one prefers). It is argued that the creation could not have come originally from the Creator's hand in a condition of voidness and waste. Everything that comes directly from his hand must be perfect. What is void, waste, dark or empty, thus indicating a state of incompleteness or chaos, cannot

[16]Rom. 5:12.

have come as such from his hand. Thus, according to the Gap Theory, if the creation could be described at any time as dark, void or waste, it must have *become* thus. The proponents of the Gap Theory argue that it could not have been made so by God without denying God's attributes or character. Of course, God need not have created the perfect world in one fell swoop by necessity. He may have chosen to do so, but He was not forced. He healed the blind man by stages.[17]

It is postulated that just as the total creation at the time of Adam was involved in Adam's fall, so an earlier creation before Adam fell when its prince fell to produce death and darkness before Adam. For God created heaven and earth and installed Lucifer, the lightbearer, as chief prince of his pristine creation. Lucifer was a perfect angel of God with free will and therefore the ability to love and serve God. But he abused this free will and essayed equality with God. This brought about a fall in creation prior to Adam's fall and ruined the original creation before the creation which involved Adam. It is postulated that this original fall made the earth waste, void and dark. The serpent, Satan, was thus in a fallen state before Adam's fall. He seduced Eve into the fallen condition in which he already found himself, thus merely extending his kingdom into Adam's new realm.[18] Thus Satan, Lucifer, was not created as a sinful creature but fell into that state after creation.[19]

On this view, therefore, sin and death had already entered the world before Adam and Eve which, of course, denies the scriptural teaching that sin and death entered the world the first time by Adam's sin.[20] When Adam fell, Satan entered, as it were, merely another corner of unfallen creation. The seven days mentioned in Genesis 1 and 2 become, on this basis, seven literal days of reconstruction and rehabilitation. The geological layers, with their pre-Adamite witness of death

[17]See Mark 8:22-25.
[18]Cf. Isa. 14:12.
[19]Cf. A. E. Wilder Smith, *Why Does God Allow It?* (Eastbourne, England: Victory Press, Evangelical Publishers Ltd., 1960), p. 119.
[20]Rom. 5:12.

before Adam's fall, would thus be merely witnesses of Satan's prior fall and the death this produced before Adam's sin. Adam's creation is thus to be viewed on this theory merely as a part of the re-creation and renewing of a previously fallen universe.

But one further matter must receive attention here. It is a fact that there is no obvious hiatus between Genesis 1:1 and 1:2. Such a gap between verses 1 and 2 would obviously be expected, if the above-suggested interpretation of prehistory is true. However, hidden gaps often do occur in the Bible as, for example, in the prophecies concerning the first and second comings of Christ. Prophecies of the first and second advents often merge into one another, so that the two separate events are not distinguishable prophetically or textually. The long period of time between these events is often not in the least clear in the text. The prophetic view into the past and future is often supratemporal.

Viewed in this way, the earth and life in general could be millions of years older than Adam. The pre-Adamite world is thus thought to have been destroyed by one or a series of catastrophes and to have been restored in seven literal creative days. The view would coincide with the geological finding that man is, relatively speaking, very young compared with the age of the earth, and that he appeared relatively suddenly and late.

These ideas actually represent a development of the theories of Cuvier, who also postulated a series of catastrophes in order to explain the successive geological formations. Cuvier's thoughts on this subject were so popular 100 to 150 years ago that some scientists think they held up the acceptance of Darwinism by a majority for many years. Alcide d'Orbigny (1802-57) developed Cuvier's theories and taught that after each catastrophe a new creation of life took place. It was Dr. Thomas Chalmers of England who first actually postulated the gap between verses 1 and 2 of Genesis 1 in order to place in time the series of pre-Adamite catastrophes. Many of the great geologists of the past century shared Cuvier's views

simply because they thought such an explanation the best interpretation of the known facts of the geological strata.[21]

It will suffice here to mention that one strong point against
the validity of the Gap Theory is brought out in Exodus
20:11, where it is categorically stated: "In six days Jehovah
made heaven and earth, the sea and all that in them is." If,
as the Gap Theory maintains, God made the heavens and the
earth and all that is in them in long ages by processes of evolution before the six days of Genesis 1, then Exodus 20:11
would be highly misleading at its face value. For the word
'asah (made) used of these six days, may show that the earth
was not "refashioned" out of a ruined, judged earth, but
created ex nihilo. Some theologians believe that *'asah* is syn-
onymous with *bara* when used in the creation context.[22]

For further interesting and important conclusions on this
subject, see Dr. Whitcomb's article.

Uniformitarianism. Charles Lyell (1797-1875) in his well-
known textbook *Principles of Geology,* finally rejected the
whole idea of successive catastrophes and replaced them with
the idea of "uniformitarianism." According to Lyell's views,
which today are the universally accepted ones, everything, including the geological strata, has developed slowly, uniformly
and regularly through immense periods of time without catastrophes of any type playing an important part. Lyell adopted
the theories of William Smith (1769-1839), who believed that
all geological formations, no matter where they occurred,
showed the same chronological order and the same classes of
fossils. Thus arose the concept of "index fossils," that is, the
type of fossil a geological formation bears, serves to classify
and identify that formation chronologically and geologically.

But Lyell advanced a step further than his mentor in maintaining that *all* geological formations are the result of slow
uniform processes and are *all* produced without the agency

---

[21]For further information on the implications of the Gap Theory, see the
article by Dr. John C. Whitcomb, Jr., *"The Gap Theory of Genesis 1 and 2"
Annual of the Creation Research Society* (1965).
[22]*Ibid.,* p. 6.

of catastrophes of any type. This philosophy of Lyell is taught in one form or another in all recognized universities of the Eastern and Western worlds. According to these modern ideas, the laws of nature have always been the same as they are today, so that the present state of nature is the explanation of its past state and of its future state too. Thus, geological formations, fossils, etc., arise today in just the same manner as they did millions of years ago. Hence the name "uniformitarianism" for this type of philosophy. And thus the concept arose that catastrophes and acts of God have nothing or little to do with the formation of the geological strata we observe today.

These ideas remind one of the prophecy of the Apostle Peter: "Where is the promise of his coming? For since the fathers fell asleep, all things *continue as they were from the beginning of creation.*"[23] The Apostle Peter was referring to the state of things such as will obtain at the end of this age, when mockers, who live after their own lusts, will jeer at the idea of a second coming of Christ to judge the world and save his own. They will maintain that everything has continued as it was from the time of the Fathers, that is, that history has been uniform. No change has been wrought by a direct non-uniform act of God. Everything has been formed by the forces of natural change which we know about. The spirit of uniformitarianism is certainly in the ascendant in the biological sciences today—perhaps less so in the world of physics— and it may, to judge by the Apostle Peter, be a foretaste of the spirit of the end times.

Surely it is obvious that on principle a Christian can scarcely ever be an absolute uniformitarian. He can scarcely maintain that things have never changed catastrophically and never will, if he believes in the words of the Apostle Peter:

> But the heavens and the earth, which are now, by the same word are kept in store, reserved unto fire against the day of judgment and perdition of ungodly men. But, beloved, be not ignorant of this one thing, that one day

[23]II Peter 3:4.

is with the Lord as a thousand years, and a thousand years as one day. The Lord is not slack concerning his promise, as some men count slackness; but is longsuffering to us-ward, not willing that any should perish, but that all should come to repentance. But the day of the Lord will come as a thief in the night; in the which the heavens shall pass away with a great noise, and the elements shall melt with fervent heat, the earth also and the works that are therein shall be burned up.[24]

This type of biblical expectation is scarcely uniformitarianism.

Thus, a Christian who believes in the Bible can on principle hardly be a uniformitarian. He cannot reject all types of catastrophic occurrences as an explanation of natural phenomena. For he, as a Bible-believing Christian, will be expecting for the warring world the catastrophic nonuniformitarian interference of God in world events at the second coming of Christ. The biblically oriented Christian can never maintain that everything has always remained as it was in the times of the Fathers, that the present is the key to the past and the future. It may be so to a small extent, but certainly not as a principle. The very idea of an act of creation itself lies quite outside the principle of a continuous uniformitarian explanation of life and the world as we know it. The very act of the creation of matter or of life demonstrates a mighty interference of God with time and space, which can never be entirely explained on the basis of the present uniformitarian state of matter. The same applies to the virgin birth of Christ and also to his resurrection, both of which are scarcely uniformitarian.

Progressive Creationism. A number of prominent Evangelicals today do not wish to be classified as theistic evolutionists, nor do they like being classified with creationists who believe that God created everything in seven literal days. For progressive creationists (or "Threshold Evolutionists," as Dr. Bernard Ramm styles this way of thought) believe that God

[24]II Peter 3:7-10.

created first of all the material world and then proceeded stepwise to bring into being the various forms of life, starting at the lowest forms and progressively producing, but by separate acts of creation at each stage, higher forms, ending the whole stepwise creative process in man. Thus the creative activity of God is thought by these Evangelicals to have extended over many ages but to have been restricted to small periods of time during these ages.

Darwin, in his *Origin of Species* poured out his displeasure and sarcasm upon just such beliefs, which were popular in his day, as being, in his view, illogical in their attempt to combine his randomness-orientated theories with the planning of orthodox Christians.

There is little one can comment on concerning these views put forward by the progressive creationists for, from a scientific point of view, there is little tangible evidence to work on. Further, the theories merge by small steps from "frank" seven-day creationist views to convinced theistic evolutionary explanations. The language of progressive creationists is often so ambiguous that one is not really sure whether one is discussing a problem with a creationist or a theistic evolutionist. If the question under discussion is that of the "evolution of the horse," one usually comes away convinced that at heart the "progressive creationist" is in fact a "theistic evolutionist."

As the scope of progressive creationist theories is too large for the present volume, readers are referred to some of the standard works published by those committed to this position, together with some theses which discuss these problems.[25]

[25]Bernard L. Ramm, *The Christian View of Science and Scripture* (Grand Rapids: Wm. B. Eerdmans Publishing Co., 1954); Floyd E. Hamilton, *The Basis of Evolutionary Faith* (London: James Clarke & Co., Ltd., 1931); Wayne Frair and P. William Davis, *The Case for Creation* (Chicago: Moody Press, 1967); H. Enoch, *Evolution or Creation* (Madras: Union of Evangelical Students of India, 1966); Paul A. Zimmerman, John W. Klotz, Wilbert H. Rusch and Raymond F. Surburg, *Darwin, Evolution and Creation* (St. Louis: Concordia Publishing House, 1959); James O. Buswell, "The Origin of Man and the Biocultural Gap," *Journal of the American Scientific Affiliation* (June, 1961), XIII, p. 47; Russell L. Mixter, *Evolution and Christian Thought Today* (Grand Rapids: Wm. B. Eerdmans Publishing Co., 1959).

2

ARE THE MAIN POSTULATES OF DARWINISM SCIENTIFICALLY SOUND?

In this section it is our intention to investigate the main postulates of Darwinism for some of their scientific content and to test their scientific basis.

SIMILARITIES BETWEEN MAN, ANIMALS AND ALL LIVING CELLS

Darwinism postulates that similarities in living organisms predicate common ancestry.

It is perfectly clear that similarities do exist between man, animals and plant life. The resemblances, sometimes very close, between man and ape are simply there; they are facts which are observable and should not be denied, if one wishes to be honest and objective. The theory of evolution explains these resemblances by maintaining that they imply a genetic relationship of common ancestry. Since man is related directly or indirectly to the anthropoid apes, he resembles the ape. All types of life resemble one another in biology and biochemistry, and therefore all life is derived from a common ancestral cell. This is the basis of modern reasoning. The nearer two forms of life are in their common ancestry, the more they will resemble one another.

Thus we have to ask ourselves the fundamental question: "Does resemblance or similarity always require genetic relationship?"

DOUBLE PHENOMENON

The phenomenon of the "double" occurs everywhere, for example, the individual who so much resembles another that the two are continually mistaken for each other. But it would surely be a grave mistake to imagine that the more one resembles another, the more closely they must be related. Similarity may mean genetic relationship, but it certainly does not predicate it. Brothers and sisters may well be more easily distinguishable than relatively unrelated doubles.

OCTOPUS EYE AND HUMAN EYE

It is quite well known that the octopus eye shows many resemblances to the human eye. But, according to the theory of evolution, the ontogenies of the octopus and human eye have little in common with their phylogenies. They are genetically not related, although they certainly closely resemble one another. Again, resemblance is no proof of genetic relationship.

MARSUPIAL-MAMMALIAN DOUBLES

It is quite well known that among the marsupials the thylacinus quite closely resembles the mammalian wolf. Similarly, there are, of course, marsupial "mice" and marsupial "bears," all closely resembling their mammalian opposite numbers. But no one in biological circles would dream of classifying these marsupials as closely related genetically to their mammalian "doubles." The phenomenon is explained on the basis of evolutionary convergence as follows: Because the habitat of these animals "demanded" a "wolf," a "bear" or a "mouse," evolution by convergence brought forth such an organism from any stock available on the spot—in this case from the marsupial stock. Of course, this explanation is no real explanation and is a good deal less than scientific, to say the least. How should evolution, if it is a purely materialistic concept, *know* what is *needed* by a habitat?

COMMON PLAN OR PLANNER

Might not the observed resemblances between animals, men and plants be better explained on the basis of a common plan or planner behind them? It is often possible to identify the artist behind an as-yet-unidentified masterpiece by some common characteristic, some common clue, regularly used by a certain master in his known pictures. May not the similarities between the anthropoid apes and man be similarly explained on the basis that one master planned them both? The same creative thought behind creatures may be betrayed in the same biochemistry, the same physiology, the same optic structure or the same immunochemistry.

MEANING OF SIMILARITIES

Dr. Russell L. Mixter, Professor of Zoology, Wheaton College, Illinois, in a monograph published by the American Scientific Affiliation devotes a chapter to the subject "The Meaning of Similarities between Species." Dr. Mixter writes:

> The white eyes of *Drosophila simulans* did not descend from the white eyes of *Drosophila melanogastor*. The white eyes are homologous. . . . "They are due to corresponding alterations in corresponding parts of the hereditary constitution. . . ."[1]
> ". . . the homology, though perfectly real, no longer implies descent from a common ancestor showing the common feature."[2] It is concluded, then, that some similarities between species may not be the result of their kinship. . . . It is not certain therefore that "similarity can be reasonably attributed to only one cause, namely heredity from a common ancestor."
> Common [physiological] plan may be attributed to descent from an ancient vertebrate *or* to a Creator who uses the same fundamental process for all vertebrates but who varies it at will for specific purposes.[3]

[1]Julian Huxley, *Evolution: The Modern Synthesis* (London: Allen & Unwin, 1942), p. 514, as cited in Russell L. Mixter, *Creation and Evolution* (Mankato, Minn.: American Scientific Affiliation, 1953), Monograph 2.
[2]Huxley, *ibid.*, p. 395.
[3]Mixter, *op cit.*, pp. 8-9, 11.

IS THE POSTULATE OF EVOLUTION UPWARD FROM SIMPLICITY TO COMPLEXITY BY CHANCE THEORETICALLY LIKELY OR POSSIBLE? THE QUESTION OF ENTROPY

It is now necessary to go into a problem of scientific importance which is seldom treated because of its complexity.

THREE LAWS OF THERMODYNAMICS

Today's physical sciences are built on the three laws of thermodynamics which describe the energy relationships of matter for the whole universe as we know it. We need touch on only the first two laws here.

First Law. The first states that energy (matter) today can neither be created nor destroyed. Although Professor Fred Hoyle's views on a pulsating universe without beginning or end are well known to us and might deny this first fundamental law, we will still assume that it is valid. Our position here will be justified by the recent publication by Professor Hoyle[4] in which he refutes his own views on this subject, establishing the first law once more. We are going to restrict ourselves in this discussion, as far as we can, to science verifiable by experiment in the laboratory.

Second Law. The second law of thermodynamics states that, although the total energy in the cosmos remains constant, the amount of energy available to do useful work is always getting smaller.

Third Law. The third law states that, as absolute zero temperature in a perfect crystal is approached, its entropy will also approach zero.

ELABORATION OF SECOND LAW

It is first necessary for our future line of thought to enlarge on the second law a little further.

Energy Constantly Decreases. To make things clearer, let us use water as a symbol for energy. If we have water on top

---

[4]Fred Hoyle, *Science* (Dec. 24, 1965), CL, 1708. Cf. Hoyle, *Galaxies, Nuclei and Quasars* (New York: Harper & Row, 1965), pp. 1-160.

of a mountain, it possesses kinetic energy which we can put
to use as it descends the mountain by passing it through tur-
bines to generate electricity. However, once the water has
reached sea level, no more kinetic energy is available to develop current. The mass of water theoretically remains the
same, whether it is on top of the mountain or at sea level.
But the available kinetic energy does change and diminishes
as the water loses altitude. Thus the *total* energy in the cosmos remains the same, but the available energy is constantly
diminishing. The available energy is continually approach-
ing the position of "sea level," as it were, where nothing more
is obtainable in the way of work.

Neither matter nor energy are today being created as far as
we know (in spite of Dr. Hoyle's former views!). But matter
may be converted into energy, as in the case of the atomic
reactor or the atomic or hydrogen bomb, although the total
quantity of matter plus energy remains constant. Nevertheless, the energy available for work is relentlessly getting less
as time advances, which means that the amount of *unavailable*
energy in the universe is ever increasing. A measure of the
amount of this unavailable energy is known as entropy.

These same facts can be expressed otherwise by saying that
in nature everything is continually moving toward greater
probability. It is improbable that water will stay on the top
of a mountain. If it gets a chance it will move to an area of
greater probability, nearer sea level. Water tends to the position of least available energy, just as everything in nature
tends toward the area of highest entropy or greatest probability.

Thus everything in the physical world tends to the area of
highest entropy or greatest probability. Either expression
means that the area of least orderliness or greatest chaos or
"rundownness" will tend to be reached. Order is improbable
and order tends to disintegrate into disorder, just as water
tends to flow down the mountain rather than up to the mountaintop. Order descends to chaos, just as a city with no cleaning, repair and disposal services descends to chaos with the

passage of time. If one doubts this universal fact, it is only necessary to place one's shiny new car under a tree in a forest and leave it there for twenty years with no attention. Chaos will certainly have overtaken the once orderly car by then.

Randomness and Chaos Increase. This principle of the second law of thermodynamics is so important for our future discussion that we must cite another example. I take a small aircraft and fly at a 6,000-foot altitude over my home in Einigen/Thun in Switzerland. I have with me in the aircraft one hundred thousand unprinted white cards stacked in orderly little piles. When I am over my home I open an escape hatch in the aircraft and push out all these heaps of cards with one mighty heave. The cards flutter down slowly and spread out in the breeze over the shores of the Lake of Thun and Einigen. Some come down over Interlaken and some over Beatenberg.

What would be our reaction, however, if someone were to announce after our landing that all these one hundred thousand cards had landed on the roof of my house in Einigen and precisely in the form of my initials A-E-W-S? The cards ordered themselves in fluttering down through the Alpine breeze to land in neat formation as A-E-W-S on my roof! They were arranged neatly in little heaps in the plane when I pushed them out, and now their order has increased with passage of time while falling to earth. Impossible! Everyone knows that the cards would become more and more disorganized (random) as they fall, until they reach a more or less completely random distribution all over the area. And this is precisely what the second law of thermodynamics predicts and requires: order degenerates with passage of time into increasing randomness and chaos. This is the universal state of things in this universe in any closed (isolated) system, barring certain exceptions with which we deal later.

The theory of evolution teaches, when all the frills are removed, just the opposite to this state of affairs demanded by the second law of thermodynamics. Evolutionists assume that nonliving carbon atoms, hydrogen atoms, nitrogen atoms, etc., as they "fluttered down" through the ages since the beginning of time, have slowly ordered and organized themselves into more complex, more energy-rich, less chaotic forms. They believe that entropy, with respect to biogenesis, has not increased but spontaneously decreased during the passage of the ages. They believe that biogenesis, that is, synthesis of order, took place by *chance* and of its own accord. The degree of ordering of atoms and molecules is immeasurably greater in a "simple" cell than in the ordering of the cards to form my initials. If the spontaneous formation of A-E-W-S out of random cards dropped from an aircraft is incredible and against the laws of thermodynamics, how much less credible is the belief in the spontaneous formation of much more complex life from simple nonliving random molecules?

And yet, this is precisely what Sir Gavin de Beer, my former professor of zoology at Oxford (now London), implies when he maintains that evolution by natural selection is a mechanism for attaining a high degree of improbability.[5] For most evolutionists maintain that that universal force which guided evolution uphill in life also guided nonliving matter upward to life.

It is, of course, possible that some of our cards will by chance so fall that they may, as it were, dot an *i* or form parts of an A or an E, even if they do not form the total A-E-W-S. But the degree of probability of the cards forming a perfect set of A-E-W-S initials under the conditions cited is so small as to be negligible.

In a similar manner molecules may react together to form simple amino acids and even to some extent simple polypeptides, purely on a random basis. They are behaving then like the cards in the chance dotting of an *i*. But as the chances of forming the whole A-E-W-S structure are so small as to be negligible, so the chances of a perfect nucleic acid molecule arising by chance are so small as to be nonexistent. Thus the

[5]*Endeavour* (London: Imperial Chemical Industries Ltd., 1958), Vol. XVII, No. 66.

chance formation of stable amino acids is good, the chances of polypeptide formation less good, while the chances of the random formation of a protein molecule complicated enough to function as an enzyme and bear life are, at our present state of knowledge of mathematical thermodynamics, negligible.

Dr. Harold F. Blum, who is an evolutionist, has endeavored to treat mathematically this whole subject of the origin of life on a chance basis, in his book *Time's Arrow and Evolution.*[6] It would be difficult to find a fairer, mathematically and biologically more correct presentation of the theories and facts of evolution and biogenesis by a scientist. Rightly so, his book has been highly praised by evolutionists, although it stirred up extensive discussion regarding the operation of the second law of thermodynamics in evolution and biogenesis. It can probably be maintained that Dr. Blum's arguments for evolution on Darwinistic principles are among the best that can be found, and we quote some relevant passages to let him speak for himself. Incidentally, it will be noted that the arguments we have advanced up to the present are actually confirmed by Dr. Blum.

Where Did Protein Come From? Many scientists are agreed that life needs proteins to "ride" upon as the basic prerequisite,[7] so that matter in its nonliving state must have become organized into some sort of a protein or substance of similar type capable of catalyzing metabolic processes *before* life appeared. That is, a chemical evolution must have taken place in nonliving matter before life appeared. For life to exist, it must possess a "metabolic motor" for extracting free energy from its environment necessary for life processes to continue once life is present. This means that proteins of some sort must have been formed by chemical evolution in nonliving matter before life appeared, in order to carry and support

[6]Harold F. Blum, *Time's Arrow and Evolution* (2d ed., Princeton, N.J.: Princeton University Press, 1955).

[7]Cf. F. Cedrangolo, "The Problem of the Origin of Proteins," *The Origin of Life on the Earth* (New York: Macmillan Co., 1959), p. 281.

life's processes once it was there. Thus the basic question in discussing biogenesis always is, where did the protein (or other molecule capable of serving the metabolic function of protein) come from before life arose to synthesize it? Many scientists have supposed protein synthesis to have occurred by chance in the first place from chance amino acids. Many of them have seen the absolute necessity on the basis of Darwinistic evolution, of a chemical evolution in nonliving matter leading up to protein synthesis having occurred before life could appear.

Dr. Blum discusses just this problem (of the chemical evolution of nonliving molecules to proteins or similar substances before life could appear) :

> Now let us examine the possibility of the spontaneous formation of protein molecules from a non-living system. We may assume, for purposes of argument, that, in the course of chemical evolution, there had already come into existence a mixture containing a great quantity of various amino acids. As we have seen, the free energy change for formation of the peptide bond is such that, at equilibrium, about one percent of the amino acids would be joined together as dipeptides, granting the presence of appropriate catalysts. The chances of forming tripeptides would be about one hundredth that of forming dipeptides, and the probability of forming a polypeptide of only ten amino acids as units would be something like 10^{-20}. *The spontaneous formation of a polypeptide of the size of the smallest known proteins seems beyond all probability*. This calculation alone presents serious objection to the idea that all living matter and systems are descended from a single protein molecule which was formed as a "chance" act.
>   . . . The riddle seems to be: How, when no life existed, did substances come into being which, today, are absolutely essential to living systems, yet which can only be formed by those systems?
>   . . . A number of major properties are essential to living systems as we see them today, the origin of any of

which from a "random" system is difficult enough to conceive, let alone the simultaneous origin of all.

. . . the fact remains that no appreciable amounts of
polypeptides would form unless there were some factor
which altered the equilibrium greatly in their favor.

. . . If proteins were reproduced as they must have
been, if living systems were to evolve [from nonliving
systems]—free energy had to be supplied. The source of
this free energy is a fundamental problem we must
eventually face. . . .

. . . The quanta in sunlight are inadequate to supply
the energy necessary to forward this endergonic reaction
[photosynthesis], however, and the difficulty in summing
quanta in simple photochemical reactions has already
been discussed.[8]

In the introduction we have already mentioned views such
as those held by N. W. Pirie who rejects the whole hypothesis
of life having spontaneously arisen on randomly formed complex protein molecules on the basis that such spontaneous
synthesis is inconceivable on mathematical statistical grounds.[9]
Dr. Pirie therefore suggests that life arose on much simpler
molecules. This theory introduces more difficulties than it
solves.

The fundamental problem with which Dr. Blum is wres-
tling is that of building a protein metabolic motor to support
life before life was present to build it. *This motor has to be
built under the choking restriction imposed by Darwinism
that it must have been built by chance in a nonliving medium
by chemical evolution.*

In order to pump water up the mountain or to reduce
chaos and randomness to order, a motor to supply the energy
is necessary. To pick up wastepaper in the park, to knit a
sweater, or pick up my cards from random distribution over
the Lake of Thun requires energy. Work must be done. The
living cell or organism possesses a means of supplying this

[8]Blum, *op. cit.*, pp. 163, 170, 178, 164, 166.
[9]N. W. Pirie, "Chemical Diversity and the Origins of Life," *The Origin of
Life on the Earth*, p. 78.

energy for work by extracting it from the environment by oxidative and other processes—oxidation of fats, sugars, proteins, etc. What Dr. Blum is saying is: How was the motor to extract the energy from the environment built before life processes had arisen to build it? Once a motor (enzyme, metabolic system) is present, it can easily supply the free energy necessary to build more and more motors, that is, to reproduce. But the basic problem is: How do we account for the building of the first complex enzymatic protein metabolic motor to supply energy for reproduction and other cell needs? Dr. Blum has shown that it is inconceivable to account even for the building of a simple protein by chance. But chemical evolution taking place before the advent of life could only rely upon chance. Dr. Blum says precisely this and hopes we shall be able to find ways and processes which would explain how nature overcame this otherwise insuperable mathematical problem without invoking extramaterial interference.[10]

The creationist believes that God synthesized nonliving matter into living organisms and thus provided the motors which were then capable of immediately extracting energy from their environment to build more motors for reproduction. This view is thus perfectly sound scientifically and avoids the hopeless impasse of the materialistic Darwinists in trying to account for the design and building of the first necessarily highly complex metabolic motors by random processes. Once the motor has been designed, fabricated and is running, the life processes work perfectly well on the principles of the known laws of thermodynamics. Cell metabolism itself is perfectly in conformity with the second law of thermodynamics. But origins and original biogenesis from nonliving matter pose us great difficulties if we are scientific materialists. And Dr. Blum, one of evolution's most brilliant advocates, admits this in his famous riddle: "How, when no life existed, did substances come into being, which today are absolutely

[10]*Ibid.*, p. 163.

essential to living systems, yet which can only be formed by those systems?"[11]

Effect of Long Time Spans. After a discussion of this problem recently in an article in *Christianity Today*[12] I received some criticism from two Christian graduate students at the Massachusetts Institute of Technology. Their attitude was that, *in an improbable situation or reaction the lengthening of reaction time, if carried sufficiently far, would make an improbable occurrence almost inevitably probable. Is this true?*

On this subject Sir James Jeans writes to the same effect:

> It was, I think, Huxley, who said that six monkeys, set to strum unintelligently on typewriters for millions of millions of years, would be bound in time to write all the books in the British Museum. If we examined the last page which a particular monkey had typed, and found that it had chanced, in its blind strumming, to type a Shakespeare sonnet, we should rightly regard the occurrence as a remarkable accident, but if we looked through all the millions of pages the monkeys had turned off in untold millions of years, we might be sure of finding a Shakespeare sonnet somewhere amongst them, the product of the blind play of chance. In the same way, millions of millions of stars wandering blindly through space for millions of millions of years are bound to meet with every sort of accident, and so are bound to produce a certain limited number of planetary systems in time. Yet the number of these must be very small in comparison with the total number of stars in the sky.[13]

This is, of course, quite in keeping with the mathematical expressions for probability, which demand that the improbable become the expected if time is sufficiently increased. If

[11]*Ibid.*, p. 170.
[12]A. E. Wilder Smith, "Darwinism and Contemporary Thought," *Christianity Today* (May 26, 1967), Vol. XI, No. 17, p. 3.
[13]Sir James Jeans, *The Mysterious Universe* (New York: Macmillan Co., 1930), p. 4.

the probability of success of an event in unit time is p_1, and this is independent of time (that is, constant), we may regard the probability of success in an interval of time T as the probability of success in T independent trials. The probability of success in this interval then is:

$$p_T = 1 - (1 - p_1)^T$$

If p_1 is not null, p_T increases monotonically in T and as T increases without limit, p_T approaches the value 1—just as the M.I.T. graduates maintain.

Although the above type of thought has often been expressed, is it applicable in the case of biogenesis? Dr. Blum[14] does not think so, and many mathematicians agree with him. For, as he points out, biogenetical synthesis, and the probability laws governing it, represents the result of many *reversible* reactions, all in equilibrium with one another, as far as we can see, since they are reactions governed by catalysis biogenetically. The monkeys strumming for millions of years on typewriters produce "compositions" which are "stable end products" as opposed to unstable biological end products in equilibrium with their precursors. The Shakespeare sonnet churned out by the monkey, once turned out, remains fixed on the paper and does not decompose, returning through the keyboard into its constituent words and letters conceived by the monkey's brain. Once typed, it stays as such and does not get further modified to another sonnet nor does it become analyzed into its constituent alphabet. This means that it is *out of equilibrium* with its "precursors" and has no "postcursors."

On the other hand, the new biological product supposed to have been involved in biogenesis does not stay "put," for it is *in equilibrium* with both its precursors and "postcursors." It is *just this fact of equilibrium* which changes the whole mathematical situation with respect to probability and *which invalidates the comparison of the chance of biogenesis taking*

[14]Blum, *op cit.*, p. 178A.

place in long enough time spans with the chance of Shake-
speare sonnets arising by monkeys strumming long enough on
typewriters. Dr. Blum points out that allowing greatly increased time for an *improbable biological equilibrium reac-*
tion will *not* increase the probability of the production of an
improbable end substance (maybe living substance) but, in
equilibrium reactions such as those on which life is dependent, will merely increase the probability that *equilibrium*
will have been reached. This is just another way of saying
that, *in a chain of equilibrium reactions such as those on*
which biogenesis and life depends, increasing time spans will
not increase the attainment of an improbable end product
(life) but will favor the attainment of true reaction equilib-
rium. And this reaction equilibrium will certainly not lie at
the end of the chain of reaction where the highest degree of
improbability will almost certainly be found.

To sum up the situation in a nutshell: Shakespeare sonnets
produced by monkeys strumming for millions of years on
typewriters are irreversible end products which do not break
down reversibly into their constituent alphabets nor do they
develop into more complicated and better sonnets. But the
catalytically conditioned chains of reactions leading to biogenesis and supporting life are not fixed and do not produce
fixed end products. Everything is in equilibrium with the next
stage forward or backward. *This fact leads Blum to assert*
that increased time spans in biological systems will merely in-
crease the probability of equilibrium being set up and not
the probability of improbable reaction products being
formed. The following considerations illustrate this:

If one lets molecules pass down the ages for a long enough
time, can one say, mathematically speaking, that the probable
formation of complex molecules like proteins and nucleic
acids, grows with time, until, when huge time spans are conceded, we shall be forced to *expect* the spontaneous synthesis,
by chance, of otherwise improbable molecules? This is by no
means a mere academic matter, for the evolutionary hypothesis consistently teaches that, in the formation of life from

nonliving material, huge periods of time are a vital necessity. The hypothesis must allow time for the staggering improbables of chemical evolution to become probables and even expecteds, that is, to allow time for the spontaneous synthesis of proteins, etc., syntheses which would be impossible in short periods of time. *The long periods of time postulated by the evolutionists are the conditio sine qua non for the credibility of the whole evolutionary theory of biogenesis without extramaterial influence.* A short consultation with almost any textbook on evolution will confirm this view.

But is this almost universally accepted idea true—that long periods of time alone would make the spontaneous and otherwise improbable synthesis of highly complex molecules from simpler nonliving matter by chemical evolution probable? Is the principle of the whole idea of lengthening of time span to make the improbable probable, scientifically watertight in reversible reactions? This is most important to decide, for the idea is the very basis of most of the evolutionary theories I have read about or discussed with evolutionists. It must be tested fundamentally, if our thinking is to be basically sound.

In order to test the idea simply, we shall have to return to our rather hard-worked example of the packs of cards which we jettisoned from our aircraft over the Lake of Thun. And to test the idea for basic credibility without complicated mathematics, we must do something quite simple in principle. We provide each of our hundred thousand cards with a huge gossamer-light parachute before pushing it out of the aircraft. Thus, with the help of parachutes, we give each of the cards a much longer period of time to flutter down to the earth through the Alpine breezes. Each card, instead of reaching the earth in twenty minutes, for example, now takes twenty years to get down to lake level. *Do we, by the enormously lengthened time span of the card-descent period increase the possibility of the cards landing in the form of my initials A-E-W-S or indeed any other ordered structure?*

To be sure, as we give the cards much more time to fall by the operation of chance into the rightly ordered formation, so we also increase the possibility of this order by increasing the time. If we increase the time enough, the possibility might theoretically at some infinitely remote period become a probability. *But at the same time—a fact consistently forgotten—owing to the well-known laws of physics concerned, by increasing the lengthening of the time period the descent takes, we also increase the chances of additional disorder arising.* Accordingly, instead of the cards being distributed randomly in this new experiment all over the area of the Lake of Thun, they become distributed over an area as large as Europe—just by increasing their descent time! So what we had gained on the roundabouts (merry-go-round)—gain in order-possibility by lengthening descent time—we more than lose on the swings—gain in disorder by increasing the time during which disorder can grow.

Thus, this must also apply with molecular order and ordering in *reversible* reactions. *The longer the molecules are exposed to random forces, the wider will become their random distribution and the fewer chances of forming an ordered protein or nucleic acid molecule out of nonliving random molecules.* Increasing reaction time may increase the chances of synthesis. But, according to the laws we have just been studying, increasing reaction time in reversible reactions will also increase still more the possibility of degradation (randomness) of already synthesized molecules, that is, if their entropy is lower than that of the starting materials. It is so easy to forget that the possibility of decomposition in reversible reactions increases with time just as the chance of synthetic processes does. So our friends at M.I.T. are attempting to introduce, although unwittingly, a fallacy into our system of logic.

Our system of cards fitted with parachutes illustrates the importance of keeping steadily in mind the effect that increasing time allowed to reach equilibrium shows in such reaction systems. Thus our parachuted cards cannot really be compared with nonreversible probability systems (Shakespearian sonnets produced by monkeys strumming on type-writers) . The parachute merely serves the function of increasing the length of time allowed to reach *equilibrium* (or the end product) . Our cards represent in reality a reversible system, for they can be blown up to a higher altitude temporarily by winds or carried out of the way right up to the time of landing or even after that. Thus the ordinary formula for increasing probability with time (the formula quoted) does not apply to biological and chemical systems such as we are considering. In such systems longer time for reaction gives increasing chance of *equilibrium* being established. That is, by increasing the time, the probability of the spontaneous formation of, for example, a hemoglobin molecule from simple organic chemicals, decreases—random equilibrium is favored.

The improbability of the spontaneous formation of proteins, nucleic acids, etc., from simple nonliving molecules without the intervention of prior life or its metabolic energy renders the supposition of the spontaneous appearance of life theoretically highly unlikely. For life is like a baby; it needs a cradle ready for it before it arrives. The cradle is, of course, in this case the system of proteins and enzymes it needs in order to extract energy from its environment for its metabolic and synthetic needs. This cradle must be there for it to use immediately on its arrival if it is to survive. After its arrival, the baby can extract energy by means of its cradle to build bigger and better cradles for extracting more energy! But how was the first cradle made before the baby arrived? Where did the free energy to make it come from? No theory of biogenesis from nonliving matter prior to the appearance of life is complete or even worthy of serious thought, without the solution of this very real and exceedingly precise question. Cradles, capable of extracting energy from the environment (and therefore complex, as motors of this sort have the habit of being) just do not occur spontaneously by cooking up soups or irradiating randomly dilute amino acid solutions with energetic radiation. One might as well expect automobile motors to arise by pounding up scrap iron. And in case one does not believe the theory behind this sort of speculation on origins, scientists have tried in the past, and still are trying now, to do such *syntheses by random methods* yet have uniformly failed to arrive at a *functional "motor"* or "cradle."

Dr. Blum himself has made the discovery that lengthening of time spans in order to increase the possibility of an improbable synthesis from nonliving materials and making it probable (that is, making an unlikely synthesis likely, just by increasing the reaction time available), is theoretically unsound, for he says:

> I think if I were rewriting this chapter [on the origin of life] completely, I should want to change the emphasis somewhat. *I should want to play down still more the importance of the great amount of time available for highly improbable events to occur. One may take the view that the greater the time elapsed the greater should be the approach to equilibrium, the most probable state, and it seems that this ought to take precedence in our thinking over the idea that time provides the possibility for the occurrence of the highly improbable.*[15]

Dr. Blum is saying here, in effect, that increasing time will increase the chances of finding things at equilibrium, that is, randomness or the probability of finding water at sea level or molecules in a random equilibrium state and not water on the mountaintop or molecules ordered into such a complex improbable state that they can support life. In other words, Dr. Blum is saying that huge spans of time will bring likely equilibrium randomness and not unlikely synthesis such as the Darwinians have supposed with impunity for a century. To put things crudely, as infinite time is approached, infinite randomness will be achieved, namely, complete lack of order. And thus Dr. Blum denies in effect the basic concept of his own book.

All this brings us to the conclusion that chemical evolution

[15]*Ibid.*

upward to a state capable of bearing life is highly improbable on theoretical grounds. Why are we then on theoretical grounds afraid to postulate that an extramaterial force (maybe God) synthesized matter upward to life, since we cannot account for life without this supposition?

Free Energy Cannot Upset Applecart. Let us come back again to the illustration of our cards jettisoned from the aircraft. I now declare that my cards did land on my roof and in the form of my initials within twenty-four hours of my throwing them from the plane. Is that thermodynamically possible? Of course! I organized hundreds of Boy Scouts to wait all round the Lake of Thun with boats and jeeps and they picked up every card as it reached the earth or lake and hurried to my house and put each card into position on my roof. Thus arose the gigantic A-E-W-S on my roof. Does this upset any thermodynamic applecart? Not in the least! For these Boy Scouts supplied *free energy and did the "metabolic" work necessary to overcome randomness by order.* They lowered the entropy of the cards, they ordered them by doing work by using their enzymatic motors to supply ordering energy. To accomplish this work they extracted energy from their environment (bread, butter, proteins, etc.) to overcome randomness and chaos. Just as it is necessary to expend energy in pushing water up the mountainside from sea level, so energy must be used to pump molecules up to a higher state of order. If men or life or anything else does work, that is, supplies energy in ordering chaos, no thermodynamic applecart is upset when order is increased locally at the expense of chaos. But this is discussed later.

There have been many attempts to overcome this fundamental problem of how nonliving matter obtained the energy to synthesize the complex molecules necessary for bearing life. Just as our Boy Scouts supplied the energy to organize the fallen cards into my initials on the top of my house, so molecules must be supplied with energy before their entropy can be reduced in increasing complexity. This problem of the source of the energy necessary to carry out this ordering process on a molecular basis in archebiopoiesis is a fundamental one upon which the credibility of any theory in this area must depend.

Solar Energy and Kinetic Energy. It is often airily maintained by evolutionists that the energy for these synthetic processes was obtained from the sun. Nonliving matter is bathed in solar energy, so why not postulate its use in archebiopoiesis? Living matter uses just this supply of solar energy to carry out its syntheses, so why should nonliving matter not do the same in using the same source?

This solution entirely begs the question. For the whole force of Blum's argument on just this problem lies in his emphasis of the fact that solar energy, even though it may bathe nonliving matter, is not available to it for syntheses of the type in which we are interested. A complex metabolic (protein?) motor is a necessary intermediate in making solar energy available. Chlorophyll (chloroplasts) functions as just such a motor, but is far too complex to have arisen by chance processes from nonliving matter.

Proponents of this view of energy sources available for synthesis in nonliving matter may reflect that, as our cards fluttered down over the Lake of Thun, they were, as it were, bathed in the kinetic energy of falling cards. But such kinetic energy, though surrounding them on all sides, was not available for them to supply energy for the synthesis of A-E-W-S. Without the intermediary of some motor or another (a propeller and rudder?), the use of the kinetic energy bathing them was impossible for synthesizing A-E-W-S. In exactly the same way solar energy may surround nonliving matter, but it is not available to it for synthetic purposes without the intermediary of a synthetic motor of some sort. Where did this motor come from before life arrived to synthesize it?

It could perhaps be objected that order may appear spontaneously out of chaos, as when random molecules in a solution crystallize out. But actually the order we see in the appearing crystals was first present in molecules, though in an unseen form. We see something of the same kind of hidden order in chromosomes and genes which determine (in interaction with our environment) our make-up for life. All the information for the functioning of the synthetic apparatus of the body is present in coded chemical form on the genes at fertilization, before any body is present. This highly compressed, and to the naked eye invisible, information on the genes expands to visible dimensions in producing the adult body. Thereby entropy is reduced in the body at the expense of energy taken from the metabolic processes, mostly by oxidation reactions involving sugars, fats, proteins, etc. But the whole process is masterminded by the coded order on the genes and chromosomes of the cells. It is so masterminded that locally work is done and entropy is locally decreased, local order is increased and local randomness decreased.

Different Laws Now in Operation. The second law of thermodynamics seems thus to describe the whole situation of our present material world perfectly and the Bible very clearly confirms this description. For example, Romans 8:22-23 teaches us that the whole creation is subjected to "vanity" or to destruction. Everything tends to go downhill to chaos and destruction as things stand today. When God created the whole world out of nothing, everything, with the act of creation, went uphill, chaos became order, nothing became something, so that during this creative act the law of destruction or "vanity" acted, as it were, in reverse gear and each "day" of creation lowered entropy and increased order. Energy and matter arose. Order appeared. But just at this very point a fundamental error often slips into some scientific thinking today. The effort is made to try to measure and describe the processes of creation with the yardstick of the opposite processes of destruction, or "de-creation." Perhaps we can illustrate this fallacy better than describe it.

Growth-Rate Not Constant. When my eldest son was eight years old he posed me the following problem: "Now I am nearly four-and-a-half feet tall. One year ago, when I was

seven years old, I was three feet ten inches tall. I would like
to know how to figure out how tall I was ten years ago." Perfectly correctly, he extrapolates back step by step as far as he
can remember ages and heights. His scientific reasoning back
to four years old is perfectly sound. He assumes reasonably
steady growth from four to eight years. He could go back
even further to about the time when he was one or two years
old. The growth line would not be quite straight but an idea
could be obtained of approximate heights at one, two and
three years by extrapolating back from eight, six and four
years because growth rates would still be reasonably steady.
But how about extrapolating back to ten years ago in the case
of an eight-year-old boy? Would we arrive at a meaningful
answer by means of such a calculation? What would the negative height we would probably arrive at mean?

The calculation starts to go awry when we extrapolate back
too far into areas of time not governed by the same growth-
rate laws as those obtaining during the normal growth rate of
a healthy eight-year-old. The reason is, that at the beginning
of his existence entirely different laws obtained from those he
now knows about and can use for calculation. But he knows
nothing of the catastrophe of birth, which is never repeated in
life. Nor does he know anything of the mystery of the fertilization of an ovum by a sperm, of the time when "he" was
separately half his mother and half his father and only became "himself" by the union of the two halves. These events
are catastrophic and have a catastrophic effect on his uniformitarian ideas of growth rate. They can never recur and can
never be deduced or calculated from looking at a growth-rate
curve showing his increase in height. The basic laws of
growth are constant enough once we are here and growing
into adolescence, but they never betray the laws governing
conception or birth, and they never can. They are entirely
different worlds governed by different laws. My boy was
making the basic error of trying to calculate, on the basis of
laws obtaining now, events which took place under entirely

different laws. And this just cannot be done, no matter how exactly and conscientiously one works.

We are in a precisely similar situation if we try to calculate back to the beginning of life and creation on the basis of the fairly uniformitarian period in which we find ourselves just now. *Today everything is subject to the law of decay. Entropy in the total cosmos is increasing, chaos is taking the place of order more and more, with the local exceptions produced by local expenditure of energy we have noticed. But the measurement of these processes can never give us information on a process involving creation.*

Thus, on principle, one can never measure back to the beginning, to creation, to conception, to birth, by measuring a growth curve. The laws operating at the beginning were different from those operating now, and by studying the properties of matter while it is subject to decay, one can never hope to find out about creation. It would be just as foolish to hope to find out about the laws of conception and birth by studying growth-rate curves. Creation and its laws are inconceivably different from any laws we encounter now and are therefore not measurable nor understandable until we can get some data which is not merely that supplied by decay. It may even be questionable whether our brains could handle information on true creation, since the very brain and its thought are controlled by the decay described by the second law of thermodynamics.

Study of Decay Rate. Perhaps we may be permitted to use a second illustration of this very vital point of principle, since it is so often overlooked. Let us once more put our brand new car under a tree in the forest and leave it there twenty years or so. From time to time we visit the car and measure the varying signs of increasing entropy—decay. The battery runs down, corrosion begins under the paint, the tires deteriorate and burst, the safety glass gets translucent. After twenty years we can plot a fine decay curve of our car. With time we might even become an expert in predicting the decomposition of a new car. But even by the most exact study of this decay curve we could never gain much authentic information on the car company's internal administrative organization for manufacturing such cars. We could, of course, gather some ideas about the large metal presses necessary for metal bodywork, the fine boring machines for the cylinders, etc. But the complex planning and design organization for such a creation as a new car would not be greatly elucidated by our carefully produced decay curve over twenty years.

Scientists are diligently studying the universe which is everywhere subjected to the laws of decay described by thermodynamics. We should be perfectly clear about the fact, however, that such studies may give us very little light on events which took place under laws of nature entirely different to those we now know, namely, those of creation, be it of life at biogenesis or of matter and energy themselves. But we can know from our own experience that the lower the entropy, the more complex the structure, the more ordered matter is, the greater the "planning energy" expended in creating it. To put it popularly, the greater the complexity of an object, the greater the mind or spirit behind it.

Logical Conclusion: A Creator. For this reason the Apostle Paul in Romans 1 says that whoever can look at the order in creation and not revere the Maker of it, is a fool. Observing the creation must lead us to reverence the Creator if we follow the normal course of logic.[16]

In fact Sir James Jeans writes:

> Nature seems very conversant with the rules of pure mathematics, as our mathematicians have formulated them in their studies, out of their own inner consciousness and without drawing to any appreciable extent on their experience of the outer world. . . . In the same way, a scientific study of the action of the universe has suggested a conclusion which may be summed up, though very crudely and quite inadequately, because we have no language at our command except that derived from our

---

[16]Cf. A. E. Wilder Smith, *Why Does God Allow It?* (Eastbourne, England: Victory Press, Evangelical Publishers Ltd., 1960), p. 119.

terrestrial concepts and experiences, in the statement that *the universe appears to have been designed by a pure mathematician.*

. . . the universe can be best pictured, although still very imperfectly and inadequately, as consisting of pure thought, the thought of what, for want of a wider word, we must describe as a mathematical thinker.

There must have been what we may describe as a "creation" at a time not infinitely remote. *If the universe is a universe of thought, then its creation must have been an act of thought. Indeed the finiteness of time and space almost compels us, of ourselves, to picture the creation as an act of thought;* the determination of the constants such as the radius of the universe and the number of electrons it contained imply thought, whose richness is measured by the immensity of these quantities. . . . *Modern scientific theory compels us to think of the creator as working outside time and space, which are part of his creation, just as the artist is outside his canvas "non in tempore, sed cum tempore, finxit Deus mundum."*[17]

The natural consequence to Sir James' line of logic is, of course, that, if the material world was the result of thought, then why should the further synthesizing of the material, once created by thought, toward life not be attributed to the Creator's thought too—instead of to chance and natural selection? The mathematical physicists have come to the conclusion that the universe bears the indelible marks of a creator's thoughts, *which thought is outside time and space and is therefore supernatural in the strict sense of the word.* Why then should Oparin and Shapley, among others,[18] maintain that "any resort to supernaturalism is a humiliating retreat?"

Why should a resort to supernaturalism be represented as a humiliating retreat when so great a scientist as Sir James Jeans regarded the universe as the pure thought of a mathematical thinker outside time and space? Sir James did not

[17]Jeans, *op. cit.*, pp. 138-39, 146, 154.
[18]A. I. Oparin and V. Fesenkov, *Life in the Universe* (New York: Twayne, 1961), foreword by Harlow Shapley.

think of this pure thought as residing in any *material* or natural being, so that we can only ask ourselves why thought such as that of Sir James can ever be regarded as a "humiliating retreat," for strictly speaking Dr. Jeans was thinking at least *supranaturally*. One can only conclude that Dr. Shapley feels himself humiliated in having to reckon with anything beyond matter, namely, God, for some purely personal reasons.

If Not Evolution, What Then? At this stage it may well be asked what the creationist scientist *does* believe in regard to the mechanism of the creation of the universe and of life on it, if he rejects the evolutionary doctrines. What has he better to offer? First, it is obvious that creation of matter *ex nihilo* must be incomprehensible to our finite mechanism of thought, as knowledge stands at present. For such creation of matter *ex nihilo* must be infinite, which to the finite mind must be incomprehensible. Thus, on the face of things, what objective scientist is going to deceive himself into believing he understands the infinite?

But the creative synthesis *of life* from nonliving matter is an entirely different proposition—if life consists of ordered matter and that alone, with no "spiritual" component. For we *can* conceive of putting atoms and molecules together to arrange a form of matter capable of bearing life. The synthesis of nucleic acids and the genetic code is already being conceived in thought. How then does the thinking creationist visualize the synthesis of life from nonliving matter if he rejects the Darwinistic postulates? What has he as a scientist to replace the evolutionary concept? Such a question is a perfectly fair one which is being asked the creationists, who have, up to present, only blandly repeated that creation replaces evolution. This can amount to obscurantism and begging the question on the part of the creationist.

The author's personal conception of the origin of life from nonliving matter can perhaps best be illustrated by the following rather simple example. Some years ago Dr. F. Sanger of Cambridge conceived and carried out a brilliant analysis of the structure of insulin[19] from which its synthesis ensued. If we had been capable of observing the progress of this synthesis, the marshaling of the chemical groups, *from inside the reaction medium* (i.e., within the dimension of the reaction medium), from inside the solutions used, we would have seen the radicals and groups marshaling themselves into position in time and space according to the known chemical affinities of these groups. In the reaction media themselves there would have been little to have been seen of Dr. Sanger's overall grand concept of insulin structure, but only perfectly well-known chemical combinations according to the familiar laws of chemical affinities, mass action, etc., would have been visible. Viewed from *inside the reaction system and solutions* everything would have been strictly governed by the known laws of matter and chemistry—statistics, mass action, solubilities, affinities, etc., within three dimensions and time. And yet the chemist used in his thought concept of the overall synthesis just these natural laws to achieve his own ends, namely, the synthesis of insulin.

Again, let it be emphasized, *from inside* the chemical system used to achieve his end, Dr. Sanger's exogenous overall thought concept was not visible. Only the familiar laws of chemistry would be observed and not the exogenous grand thought concept governing the total synthesis. That lies in an entirely different dimension exogenous to the reaction system and is therefore invisible in it. Only the end product showed the breadth of the chemist's thought in employing perfectly ordinary natural chemical affinities to reach his goal.

It is my conviction that inside the dimensions of our "reaction system," that is, our "test tube," our universe governing our life, we can only observe the ordinary laws governing this universe in the three dimensions of space enduring

---

[19]A. P. Ryle, F. Sanger, L. F. Smith and R. Kital, *Biochemistry Journal* (1955), LX, 541, 556, and F. Sanger, *Bulletin de la Societé chimique biologique* (Paris, 1955), XXXVII, 23.

through time (as the fourth dimension). We—restricted to the three dimensions of our system, as we are—are *not capable* of observing the great concept of pure thought creating life and matter, which governs these processes from outside our system. *This great concept can only be guessed at by viewing the end product of the synthesis (life).* But neither life nor insulin could have ever been arrived at solely by ordinary chemical reaction undirected by exogenous thought, even though internal observation of the reacting molecules showed only ordinary chemical forces at work. Thus the guiding exogenous thought concept outside any material system *must be invisible from within that system.* Though the creator may be at work marshaling molecules up to life here on earth, we can, on principle, only see ordinary chemical forces at work. Only the finished synthetic product (in our example, insulin) lets us see his guiding from outside during the formation process, but the formation processes themselves show us nothing but material forces at work. It really means that a five-dimensional force, for example, carrying out a job in a three-dimensional system will be seen in that three-dimensional system as consisting of only three dimensions. Thus if God, who is multidimensional, is going to direct synthesis up to life in our three-dimensional world (four-dimensional, counting time), his work will only be *visible* as a three-dimensional activity within the normal laws of a three-dimensional system. *It follows that we shall see only "natural" forces at work when he does a supernaturally conceived work.* This affords no thinking scientist a brief to deny the possible existence of other dimensions. Even though these three-dimensional forces are all "natural," it would be wrong to "explain" them entirely on the basis of "chance" and infinite time spans within a three-dimensional system only, as the Darwinist and most modern scientists attempt to do. For it is still the Creator, working in the multidimensional sphere, who is guiding the synthesis, within the three dimensions, by the grand concept, even though we see only a minute part of this concept, namely, that part which coincides with our three dimensions. Of course, synthesis in multi-dimensional phases is impossible for us to visualize outside mathematical formulae.

It all amounts to this: we can observe nature and its processes with ease, but we are quite unable, with our natural senses, of observing the Logos behind it. Which all adds up to the teaching of Hebrews 11:1 to the effect that "faith is the substance of things hoped for, *the evidence of things not seen.*" We possess no natural means of seeing directly behind nature to the Logos, this being outside our natural ken. We can only argue from design, just as the fact of insulin being synthesized in fact points to Dr. Sanger's otherwise invisible activities in elucidating the insulin structure.

MORE OBSERVATIONS ON THE SECOND LAW OF THERMODYNAMICS

Evolutionists Ignore Known Laws. About one hundred years ago when Carnot, Clausius and Kelvin were working out thermodynamic generalizations on their steam engines, Darwin's book *The Origin of Species* was scarcely written. Today the thermodynamic laws we have examined are known to every student of physics, and many other people besides. But in Darwin's time things were different. Nobody knew anything about these principles. Even Kelvin and his friends scarcely dreamed how their experiments would change physics and our views on the cosmos itself. For Kelvin's and his colleagues' views have been applied to terrestrial and cosmic problems, as well as to those of life and metabolism. But one approached these problems in those days much more empirically than one does today and, all the same, often arrived at the correct answer without the theory.

Ideas of Pasteur. Pasteur is an example of this. No one had seen in those days why it was theoretically unlikely for flies to arise *de novo* by spontaneous generation in dunghills. At that time people believed that flies could so arise. Today scientists can easily give a reason for the unlikeliness of such spontaneous generation, and, indeed, on grounds we have discussed. But even without this theoretical background,

Pasteur, on empirical experimental grounds, gave us the correct answer: that spontaneous generation does not occur. This answer was entirely in agreement with theory after it had been worked out much later. There was a huge amount of vituperation against Pasteur on the part of the adherents of the spontaneous generation theory, just as today there is vituperation against those creationists who maintain that *spontaneous* generation by chance in the past is just as unlikely an explanation of biogenesis as it is at present.

In former times it used to be thought that the normal laws of chemistry and physics, as one encounters them in the laboratory, did not apply to the chemistry and physics of living organisms. But it has been discovered today that it is not necessary to postulate a special "vital" chemistry and physics to account for cell metabolism, the functioning of which is known to remain inside the prescribed limits of known "laboratory" laws. The Darwinists have rightly insisted that we reject the idea of special "vital" laws for life processes and stick to the "laboratory" laws of biochemistry and enzymology to govern our theories about life processes and origins.

Why Not Have the Courage of One's Convictions? The question we must now ask is: Why do the Darwinists not take the same step they are requiring others to take? The normal laws of thermodynamics, physics and biochemistry explain the functioning of the world, as we know it, quite well. As we have pointed out before, chemical and physical properties of the chemical elements must have remained unchanged from the beginning, if life has been continuous from the beginning. This being the case, why does the Darwinist not bow to these known laws of thermodynamics in his theories about the origin and development of life on this planet? If the laws of thermodynamics make the Darwinist's explanation of biogenesis and evolution by chance untenable, why does he not reject his views and admit that he has been wrong on sound theory all the time? For the Darwinist is losing at his own game here. He demanded that the creationist give up his ideas on vital chemistry, for example, because they are no longer true or necessary. And the creationist has long since done this, thus bowing to his increasing scientific knowledge. But when the creationist demands that the Darwinist give up his ideas that chance is the creator (which the second law will not allow) the Darwinist balks and refuses. We know, and any scientist will confirm, that entropy in an isolated system increases, and that time in a reversible system brings equilibrium and not endless synthesis, on which the Darwinist insists.

Earth Is Isolated System in Regard to Life. It is of no use saying that this planet is not an isolated system with respect to life, on the basis that sunlight reaches it from outside and that therefore entropy could be reduced at the expense of sunlight and cosmic radiation. For, as Dr. Blum has shown, quanta of sunlight acting on nonliving matter (without chlorophyll—a life product) will not suffice, on theoretical grounds, to explain synthesis from nonliving matter by sunlight. The quanta of sunlight cannot be summated. Why does the Darwinist not bow to the theoretically founded fact that, if this planet is isolated with respect to life, life will not arise *spontaneously* from nonliving molecules on it—sunlight or no sunlight?

Let us take another example to illustrate the situation more clearly. A sardine can full of sardines hermetically sealed illustrates the nature of a closed system pretty well. As long as it is sealed, the "sardine molecules" will only slowly decompose and off-tastes will only slowly develop. Entropy will increase with time, the "sardine molecules" will decompose. If one now opens the can and inoculates the contents with *penicillium notatum,* for example, then something new will happen, if the conditions of temperature and moisture are right. The "sardine molecules" will be broken down by the *penicillium notatum* organism to supply energy and raw materials for new "penicillium molecules." Although, in general, overall entropy will have been increased (more molecular order is *in toto* destroyed than synthesized) , locally in the organism entropy will have been decreased and order increased.

So the second law is only valid for isolated systems. As soon as outside energy exchanges (introduction of a living organism to the sterile sardines) are permitted, local decreases in entropy are possible at the cost of an overall general increase in disorder.

But if we increase the sardine can to the size of Switzerland and still keep it hermetically sealed and full of sardines, will new life appear in this sealed system? The answer is, of course, no, for the laws of thermodynamics are not dependent on the size of the isolated system (the can) concerned. We go one step further. We increase the can size to the size of our planet, still keeping it hermetically sealed and full of sardines. Will life appear in this large can spontaneously? The answer is, of course, again no—as long as the system really is isolated.

It is important to realize in using this example that the penetration of our "sardine can" (the whole isolated planet) by sunlight and cosmic radiation does not "open" it in the same way as we "opened" the sardine can to introduce *penicillium notatum*. For, as Dr. Blum has mentioned, the energy of sunlight cannot be used directly for molecular synthesis without the medium of a "motor." Sunlight cannot work on nonliving molecules of matter to yield organic synthesis, owing to the difficulty of summating its quanta. Just as the energy of petroleum cannot be conveniently used and harnessed without the intermediary of a properly designed internal-combustion or steam engine, neither can sunlight quanta be used without a properly constructed photosynthetic motor, which is not present in nonliving matter, for reducing carbon dioxide to sugars and starch. Once more, the problem of providing a complex motor to utilize solar energy has to be solved. And such complex motors do not arise by chance from nonliving matter. *This is basically the problem which Darwinists avoid or beg.*

Thus we have a sterile can of sardines on our hands as big

as our planet, just waiting to spring into life. Maybe our planet was just like this before life appeared; Father Teilhard de Chardin, whose views we shall examine, thinks so anyway. Basically there are two ways in which we can imagine life to have arisen under such circumstances:

1. One could have inoculated life in from the outside, as we did with the *penicillium notatum* culture and the sardine can. We could inoculate the sterile medium with men (and women), or tomatoes. This would correspond to having brought in life from elsewhere, for example, from another planet. But this gives us no fundamental insight into the origin of life processes. It merely pushes back the problem outside this planet, so that the question would then be: How did life arise outside this planet?

2. We could today, theoretically at least (or maybe in twenty to thirty years to be conservative), arrange for a team of expert biochemists to get down to synthetic biochemistry using the proteins and nucleic acids of the dead sardines as raw materials. Their intellectual synthetic technique would work on these materials, degrade them and then resynthesize them until they arrive at, for instance, the genetic material of *penicillium notatum,* tomatoes, or even the physical bodies of men. From our point of view, what they arrive at is not so important as the principle that theoretically a new form of life might be arrived at. The means of doing this is simple and vastly important, for it involves a "biochemical intelligence" technique, which we will not attempt to define for the moment, which "combines" with nonliving matter, with the result that a new form of life is produced.

What would be proved by this or a similar feat of biochemistry? Simply that something we call human intelligence, combined with advanced biochemical technique, is capable of "reacting" with nonliving matter, so as to reorder it and raise it to a state capable of bearing life processes. One could shake the constituent "sardine molecules" up in a test tube for an indefinite period of time (i.e., act without intelligent technique) if one wished to prove that order does not spontaneously arise out of chaos, and on theoretical grounds we may rest assured that it will not. But "open" matter to suitable "biochemical intelligence" (whatever that may be defined as being), and we know immediately what the answer may be: reduced entropy, higher order arising out of chaos, more energetic molecules, maybe even life from the nonliving.

Now Christians maintain just this, that Intelligence (which they call God) did "react," according to laws now becoming known, with nonliving matter (molecules), and life from the dead resulted. The "system" was opened to intelligence. This upsets no thermodynamic applecart. The system is "open" (to "outside" influence) here, whereas the Darwinist assumption that order in a system closed to "outside" influence resulted spontaneously, does conflict with known laws of nature. Which side is being obscurantist here?

Local Decrease of Entropy in Isolated Areas. The objections of the two graduate students at M.I.T. to these ideas have been quoted already but perhaps it would be well, for absolute clarity's sake, to cite them again: They write,

> First of all, a system that is closed to life-from-the-outside and to intelligent technique is not necessarily closed thermodynamically: a particular case of this is a lifeless earth continuously receiving energy from the sun. Secondly, even in a system which *is* closed, the entropy (disorder, simplicity) of one section or component may actually decrease, provided only that the total entropy of the system increase—and an example of this might well be the laboratory synthesis of highly complicated molecules from the juxtaposition (at ordinary temperatures) of molecules which are less complex. What this means to the argument in question is just this: the putting-together of molecules which are complicated enough to reproduce themselves is indeed very improbable and hence would take a *very long time; but given this long time, and the right environment for the survival of the species, the event is almost likely.*

Our graduate students are saying, in effect, two things: First, that even though a system is closed, locally—in some corner or other of it—synthesis may take place as long as the general entropy of the whole system, as such, is increased. Is this the case? Second, one must have a long time to produce the likelihood of the unlikely reaction. We have already dealt with the second fallacy by fitting parachutes to our cards and jettisoning them over the Lake of Thun. Thus, we have only to deal with the first problem, which is that of local decreases of entropy taking place in odd corners of an otherwise closed system. I have seen no experimental evidence for this on a scale which would lead to life-size molecules. But the real refutation comes of course from the matter I have emphasized above and which has been dealt with before. Namely, even for this odd-corner hypothesis, long time spans are introduced to make even it at all likely. So that if only in odd corners of a system, otherwise closed, life is assumed to have been produced spontaneously, the long time spans required even for this local generation idea neutralize it effectively on grounds we have already discussed, namely, that long time spans favor equilibrium and not improbabilities even in odd corners. *It would seem to be time that this ancient red herring were obliterated from the textbooks.*

Would Conditions of Yesteryear Produce Life? The Darwinist endeavors to escape some of the above difficulties by postulating that there were conditions in nature at original biogenesis that we have not yet been able to reproduce in our laboratories. If one could repeat in the laboratory, they say, these conditions of yesteryear, then life would again "arise spontaneously." Dr. Harlow Shapley[20] of Harvard, for example, states what amounts to just that. Is this possible?

Of course, conditions at creation (or biogenesis) must have been vastly different from present conditions, for the simple reason that the world was being "wound up" then, whereas now it is "running down"—with all that that implies. The

[20]Harlow Shapley, *Science News Letter* (July 3, 1965), p. 10.

difficulty here is that the creationist wants to admit that the chemical and physical world at the time of the creative act was definitely different from what it is now, but that the Darwinist for some purposes wants to maintain that it was the same then as now, that it was and is in fact uniform in conditions and properties! And yet the latter maintains that we have *not* been able to repeat the biogenetic conditions in the labs! He wants to maintain this, when it suits him, while at the same time maintaining things were *not* uniform, when it suits him, in his efforts to explain biogenesis. This whole matter of dealing with Darwinism reminds me uncommonly of my efforts to deal with eels in the Thames, near Wallingford, when I was a boy! When dealing with *biogenesis* then, the Darwinist wishes to maintain that conditions were different (not uniform) from what they are today, in fact, so different that we have not been able to produce the same conditions in our laboratories. But at other times he insists on uniformitarianism!

Let us briefly consider this proposition. Life today, as we have already mentioned, consists of exactly the same material elements as at biogenesis. The hydrogen, oxygen, sulphur, phosphorus, carbon atoms, etc., must be exactly the same today as they were at the beginning. For, if their chemical or physical properties had changed in the passage of time since biogenesis, then life could not have remained the same or been continuous since biogenesis. That is, the properties of carbon must always have been the properties of carbon as we know it today. One cannot even change oxygen for sulphur in the body or even carbon for silicon without endangering life. Even the exchange of deuterium (heavy hydrogen) for hydrogen has far-reaching consequences in some cases. So the physical and chemical properties of the elements making up the physical basis of life now must have been constant from the beginning.

But this simple piece of reasoning has important consequences. It means that *the conditions necessary for chemical reactions between the same elements and leading to life, must be the same now as at biogenesis.* The conclusion we must obviously draw, then, is that life, if it is going to arise today, must do so under the same chemical and physical laws as at biogenesis yesteryear. For, the life-bearing elements and their reaction properties have remained the same today as yesteryear.

The consequences of this for biogenesis are twofold:

1. The same laws of thermodynamics had to be followed at biogenesis as are followed now. These laws can easily be summed up in assuming that spontaneous order never occurs out of chaos in a closed system.

2. *Today we have already discovered at least some experimental conditions necessary for synthesis of life, which conditions the Darwinists profess still to be looking for!* For we have already discovered that only if thought or a "technical intelligence" (however we like to define this, be it in the form of a God or man), gets to work on synthesis ("forming") of molecules, can we expect a higher order capable of bearing life to arise out of chaos! That is, life results only if we "open" a nonliving, previously "closed" system either to technical intelligence (thought) or to living matter. If this is true today, it must also have been true at biogenesis, for the properties and laws of matter must have remained unchanged since biogenesis. We conclude, then, that life can appear in a closed system only when we open it to outside intelligence or living influence.

The True Position of the Darwinists. These considerations reduce the position of the Darwinists to the following:

Nonliving matter behaves creatively. They are maintaining that nonliving matter is capable in itself, under conditions now unknown, of behaving creatively, that is, in the reverse sense to that demanded by the known laws of thermodynamics. Or one may put the matter differently: they are maintaining that nonliving molecules and nonliving matter are capable of producing results we can only ascribe to "technical intelligence" or to life. Now, in the eyes of the Darwinists, "nonliving nature" has itself become creative; non-

living nature has ordered simple molecules to more complex
ones capable of bearing life. Nonliving nature, according to
this scheme, has assumed the properties of "intelligence" or
of life itself, which reduces the Darwinist to ascribing creative properties to nonliving matter; that is, nonliving matter
is quite simply a kind of creative god to them. But the laws
of thermodynamics demand just that nonliving nature be
not creative but subject to decay. *This is the true impasse
between creationism and Darwinism.*

Matter has upward surge of psychic pressure. Father Teilhard de Chardin, whose Darwinistic writings have swept
Europe in the last decade, has recognized this impasse as few
Darwinists do and ascribes boldly to all matter the property
of an upward surge of "psychic pressure." He postulates an
"irresistible" urge to upward development and consciousness
of matter. Primitive molecules, according to Teilhard, have
an innate tendency to psychic pressure build-ups ending
"inevitably" in man or the noosphere and Point Omega.
Although Teilhard does mention sketchily the laws of thermodynamics,[21] he never makes a real effort to apply them, but
is content to repeat that "our earth is an unbelievable acci-
dent."[22] "Nothing new ever burst forth from earth—all was
originally there."[23] "Ultra-microscopic grains of protein are
thickly strewn over the surface of the earth . . . our imaginations boggle at the mere thought of counting the flakes of
this deposit [of proteins]."[24] Teilhard evidently believes that
this spontaneous deposit of spontaneously formed proteins
all over the earth was formed by spontaneous polymerization.
The author has been called over the coals for not taking
Teilhard's thermodynamics very seriously. Frankly, such
statements of Teilhard's and the following ones take one's
breath away, scientifically speaking: "Everything, in some
extremely attenuated extension of itself has existed from the

[21]Cf. Pierre Teilhard de Chardin, *The Phenomenon of Man,* (New York:
Harper & Row, 1964), p. 51.
[22]*Ibid.,* p. 67.
[23]*Ibid.,* p. 71.
[24]*Ibid.,* p. 73.

very first. Then, at a given moment, after a *sufficient lapse of time,* these same waters here and there must unquestionably have begun writhing with minute creatures."[25] "Here and there, at the base of nervous systems, psychic tension is doubtless increased. Outside the *vegetative kingdom, which does not count.* . . ."[26] If all evolution upward is simply another way of saying evolution of the nervous system upward toward the mind—nothing else counts—how do we explain the obviously important complexity in the plant kingdom with complex flowering plants at its apex but no nervous system? For the plants are not psychic nor do they possess a nervous system. Their "evolution" must be nonsense, if we accept Teilhard's views on the *sole importance* of the upward surge of psychic pressures. But we have not time to go more completely into Teilhard's views just now.

Of course, many other thinkers besides Teilhard have attributed primitive psychic and conceptual properties to matter itself—apart from matter which is a part of living systems. They have attributed such properties partly to avoid the difficulties encountered in explaining the upsurge of order from the primeval chaos of nature without postulating the helping agency of divine thought. The stumbling block appears to be nearly always the idea of a God exogenous to our three-dimensional nature. A God in nature, a thinking nature, does not cause much philosophical indigestion. But a God "out there," outside our system of dimensions, does.

Richard Overman, for example, grapples with this problem of explaining the evolutionary upsurge of order out of the natural chaos surrounding us when he writes: ". . . how are we to express this in the face of evidence that indicates man appeared on the planet as a result of a 'make-do' process with no intrinsic long-term goals?"[27] "Design, we might say, was somehow thwarted by the swarming, purposeless New-

---

[25]*Ibid.*, p. 78.
[26]*Ibid.*, p. 153.
[27]Richard Overman, *Evolution and the Christian Doctrine of Creation* (Philadelphia: Westminster Press, 1967), p. 156.

tonian atoms."[28] Over against this surging force of disorder, hindering the emergence of higher order out of chaos, stands the "fact of evolution" with its high order in cells and complex organisms.[29]

Overman attempts, together with Whitehead, Teilhard and others, to account for the order observed in nature without invoking an actively ordering God in supernature, by assuming that each basic unit of nature possesses a primitive "mentality." "This provides us with one reason for attributing to electrons some glimmering of mentality. . . ."[30] Rock molecules, likewise, may have "flashes of conceptual novelty," apples may have their "consciousness." An X-ray particle is conceived of as having a "pulse of emotion." Electrons are spoken of as "obedient."[31] With the help of this hypothesis, Overman and his friends try to relate the upsurge of evolutionary processes to the "subjective aims of actual occasions" in the atomic and subatomic world, which would otherwise be offset by the downward tendency toward chaos.

But this line of thought is a very shaky philosophical house of cards. We have no evidence, of course, of any "conceptual inwardness" of any nonliving matter. In fact, the weight of experimental evidence is against any such propositions for the simple reason that mere compositions of matter, left to themselves, show no tendency whatsoever to "conceptual synthesis" or to mounting order leading to increased complexity and reduction of entropy. Decay, loss of complexity, according to the second law of thermodynamics, are the firm observations on which the success of modern science has been built. The only way the down-to-earth scientist knows of obtaining results looking like "conceptual," that is, overcoming the innate trend to increased chaos and entropy, lies, as we have already pointed out, in the intelligent (or conceptual!) application of energy.

On Overman's and similar theories, nonliving matter, left

[28]*Ibid.*, p. 40.
[29]*Ibid.*, pp. 97, 122, etc.
[30]*Ibid.*, p. 178.
[31]Cf. *ibid.*, pp. 180, 183, 208, 284.

to itself, ought to show some sort of primitive conceptual
trend toward higher order even over the short experimental
periods at our disposal. That it does not, discredits all theories of this sort. Indeed, it cannot, for the available energy
is lacking; the sun's energy as such is not available for synthetic purposes, as we have mentioned before. This discredits pantheistic theories involving "conceptual units of
non-living matter." They represent an attempt to avoid the
necessity of the supernatural to account for archebiopoiesis
by attributing creative or conceptual properties to nonliving
matter itself. Like all his colleagues in this field, Overman
invokes huge time periods to allow his postulated conceptual nature of nonliving matter to reveal itself in the upward
upsurge of order.[32] Although these authors do not realize it,
this is a further point in disfavor of their theories.

Surely, since ordering of chaos obviously has occurred to
produce life, it would be more scientific to maintain that,
in view of our thermodynamic experience, an outside "intelligence"—at present maybe unknown to us—did this ordering
originally. And where, in our experience, does intelligence
ever reside, if not in a person, even though here it may be a
superperson?

Would Synthetic Life Disprove God? It seems that in biological circles and in everyday life a catastrophic lapse of logic
often passes as sound currency and is constantly used against
the creationist position. It is commonplace reasoning today
to assume that, because the biochemists are reputedly on the
way toward synthesizing life in the laboratory, therefore God
is explained away. The achievement of synthetic life is being
awaited with gloating as the final nail in God's coffin. But
is this reputable logic?

Every year I publish scientific articles on my synthetical
experiments in leprosy and tuberculosis and report exact
methods of synthesis and biological testing of the products.
Assume now that a colleague reads my articles, finds the results interesting, and decides to repeat the work himself.

[32]*Ibid.*, pp. 122, 129, 149, etc.

After a year or so he finds all my methods exact (I hope!) and the biological activities of the synthetic products correct. He, in turn, reports his results in the scientific literature and in conclusion summarizes that he has repeated my experiments, found them correct and thereby exploded forever the myth of Wilder Smith's existence. I do not really exist at all, for he has been able to repeat my work! The logic is, of course, pretty well inconceivable! But yet it represents the actual position of the Darwinists and Neo-Darwinists today. For, man is on his way to thinking God's thoughts after him, repeating his "experiments" in creation, maybe repeating his work in the laboratory synthesis of molecules capable of bearing life. Man has "read" God's "publications" thoroughly in the study of the cosmos and nature, and is now verifying and repeating to some small degree his creative thoughts. We are coming up with "secondary" publications on results he has already achieved, and therefore the conclusion is drawn that, because of these secondary publications, God is a myth. He does not exist! We are not trying to prove the existence or nonexistence of God here, but merely the falsity of this kind of logic.

The only conclusion, surely, that we can draw from this sort of logic is that the one who did the pioneering work is infinitely greater than the one who later copies, and that he who copies is often the one who gives the first author no acknowledgment; he often ignores the first author entirely!

Significance of Aging. Before leaving this subject it will be necessary to consider one other aspect of increases and decreases of entropy in living systems. When a child is conceived and then born, the level of organization and order of the molecules of which the child consists, materially rises. Entropy is locally lowered by using the metabolic energy of the environment. Taking the total environment of the child into account, entropy is, of course, raised. But locally, in the child, it is lowered at the expense of raising the entropy of the total system in which the child exists.

But as this local reduction of the entropy of the child goes on, another process becomes noticeable and grows stronger with the passage of time, though it is present from the beginning. It is an opposite process to that of growing up, it is that of growing old, aging. The second law of thermodynamics begins to assert itself even in the midst of juvenile growth, and aging ends irrevocably in the death of the adult. Everything goes back to the dust from which it was taken. Total physical dissolution finally takes place and entropy is, in the end, increased more than it was locally reduced by the life processes. Chaos and disorder win over order in the last analysis, which proves that the local reduction of entropy we see in the young organism, is, in fact, only local and temporary.

This principle may be extended. Not only do individuals among men, animals and plants age, it would appear that whole races get senile and die out. This may be connected, of course, with changing environment in some cases. A race also represents, just as an individual does, a lowering of entropy, so that the dying out of a race represents a raising of entropy, an increase of chaos over order.

Thus, although one can work locally against the second law of thermodynamics in the individual and in the race by expending metabolic energy, yet over longer periods of time the second law always wins in both the individual and the race, in that both succumb to total disorder in death. An illustration will serve to make this matter clear. After sunset, when there are no stars shining or moonlight visible, the general darkness rapidly increases. Locally, and for a limited time, one can work against this darkness by lighting candles. Their effect is only local in the general gloom, just as entropy reduction in individuals is only local in the general sea of darkness (chaos). But, in the course of a few hours these little islands go out one after the other and are unable to resist indefinitely in their encroachment on the general night. The ever increasing ocean of darkness after sundown can be compared with the law of increasing entropy and decreasing order all around us. In the sea of increasing disorder tiny oases of life flare up like candles in the night, burn for a time and triumph over the general darkness, whether they are living cells, plants, animals or men. But in the last analysis the night of disorder wins and the candle (life) goes out, and we all pass into dissolution.

Life cannot do more than our candles. It cannot ban the night, just as we cannot ban the second law of thermodynamics. For this very reason scientists, particularly older scientists, used to forecast that our planet will die the "entropy death"—it will run down. They did this more in the past than at present for the very good reason that before atomic energy, the exhaustion of the sun and of fossil fuel was foreseeable. But all the same, our universe, if left to itself and barring accidents, will eventually die the entropy death. The only way of preventing this is to "open the system" and supply it with a new charge of energy. Indeed the biblical message foresees just such an infusion of new energy into the system when it speaks of God making a new heaven and a new earth. And there is nothing unscientific about the idea, for if God infused energy into the present system to wind it up, why should he not be able to repeat this operation in the future?

Spontaneous Upward Evolution of Species. Having looked somewhat into the question of the spontaneous upward *chemical* evolution of nonliving matter to life, we will now turn our attention for a moment to the question of the possibility of the spontaneous upward evolution of the living cell, once we have life, to more complex forms. At first glance this problem would seem to be quite different from our first fundamental question concerning the spontaneous upward development of nonliving molecules in prelife chemical evolution. So the question is: Even if it were not possible for chemical evolution to produce complex proteins without the help of life processes, could a cell, once formed, evolve itself upward to complex multicellular forms by spontaneous self-regulating mechanisms?

It is established that living cells are able, by means of their metabolic processes, to extract energy from their environment and use it to reduce entropy, to increase individual complexity and to build their own highly complex bodies and brains. Why may we not assume then that, over the course of long time spans, such organisms could use their free energy to build up not only their own bodies and brains but also to build up new, better and more complex somatic tissue? That is, why could an organism not be assumed to use its metabolic energy to overcome the ebb of entropy and to mount the evolutionary ladder, thus producing new species? This, on the face of it, would not upset the laws we have been examining. The question of energy requirements for such a process would seem to be easily taken care of. Energy from food metabolism would then be easily available for such an evolutionary route upward.

If one takes the living cell literally as a metabolic machine with no other main functions than those of surviving in a hostile environment and reproducing itself, then the problem is relatively easier to handle. For, it is clear, a chief function of such a machine must be that of mere replication. Molecular biology has shown that the genetic material of a cell is specifically set up to replicate itself and uses the molecular "template" (or algorithm) for this purpose. The synthetic processes of the cell enzyme systems are those of exact replication of genetic and other material pure and simple. If errors in this replication process do arise, as when mutations occur, they are very often what may be described as degenerative changes, which can even be lethal to the organism bearing such changes. These changes may, among other things, be those of switching the position of certain pieces of genetic information, omission of such, or changes resulting in the partial or incomplete development of organs.

In the very large body of experimental material on hand today concerned with cell reproductive processes, it is probably fair to state that the overwhelming evidence is that the normal cell metabolic energy is used up largely in purely *replicative processes*. Very large numbers of generations of

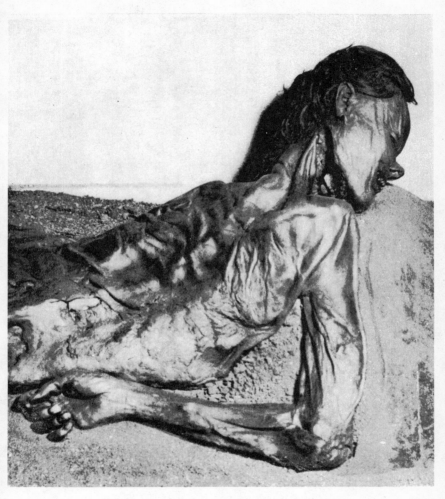

Fig. 1. Grauballemanden (The Grauballe Man).
(Jysk Archeological Society, Denmark)

Fig. 2. Right hand of Grauballe Man.
(Jysk Archeological Society, Denmark)

Fig. 3. Borremosemanden (The Borremose Man) with noose.
(Danish National Museum)

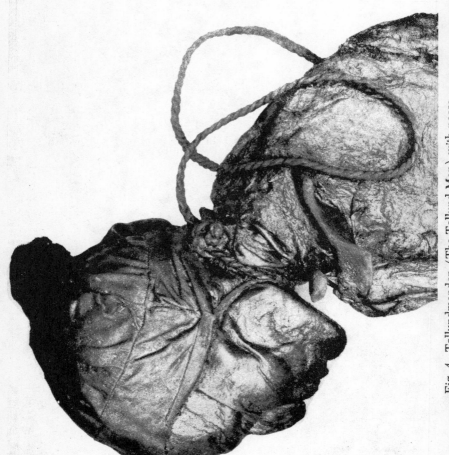

Fig. 4. Tollundmanden (The Tollund Man) with noose

Fig. 5. The Grauballe Man, side view.
(Jysk Archeological Society, Denmark)

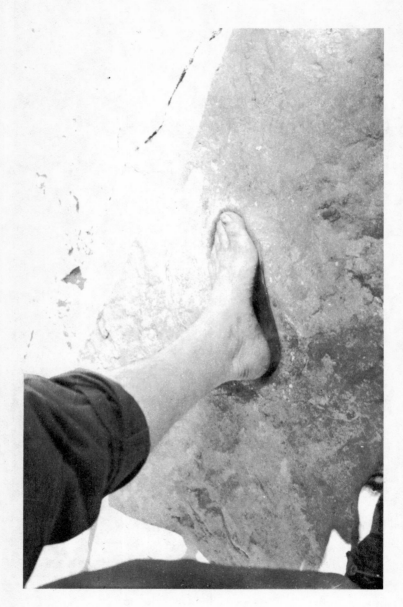

Fig. 6. Ten inch man track on ledge in Paluxy River near brontosaurus tracks.
(Photo: Marian L. Taylor)

Fig. 7. Tyrannosaurus (?) tracks from the Cretaceous. Paluxy
River, Glen Rose, Texas.
(Photo: Dr. C. L. Burdick)

Fig. 8. Four-toed Brontosaurus tracks from the Cretaceous. Paluxy River, Glen Rose, Texas.

(Photo: Dr. C. L. Burdick)

Fig. 9 . Man tracks from the Cretaceous, Paluxy River ledge,
near brontosaurus tracks in Dinosaur State Park.
(Photo: Stanley E. Taylor)

Fig. 10 Several children's tracks, five inches in length, found along Paluxy River ledge near brontosaurus tracks.

Fig. 11. Three-toed Dinosaurus track. Paluxy River bed, Glen Rose, Texas.
(Photo: A. E. Wilder Smith)

Fig. 12. Three-toed Dinosaurus tracks. Paluxy River bed, Glen Rose, Texas.
(Photo: A. E. Wilder Smith)

Fig 13. Brontosaurus tracks, Paluxy River bed, Glen Rose, Texas.
(Photo: A. E. Wilder Smith)

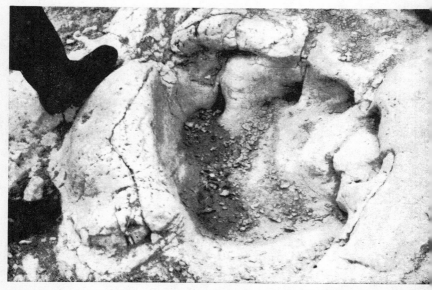

Fig. 14. Brontosaurus tracks. Paluxy River bed, Glen Rose, Texas.
(Photo: A. E. Wilder Smith)

Fig. 15. Brontosaurus tracks. Paluxy River bed, Glen Rose, Texas.
(Photo: A. E. Wilder Smith)

g. 16. A Brontosaurus
ok a walk. Paluxy River
ed, Glen Rose, Texas.
Photo: A. E. Wilder Smith)

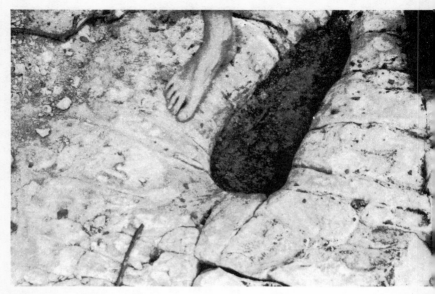

Fig. 17. A large track in the Cretaceous. Paluxy River, Glen Rose, Texas.
(Photo: A. E. Wilder Smith)

Fig. 18. Same large track as in Fig. 17.
(Photo: A. E. Wilder Smith)

Fig. 19. Same large track as in Fig. 17 photographed to show length of
one pace.
(Photo: A. E. Wilder Smith)

Fig. 20. At work in the Paluxy River bed, Fall, 1965.
(Photo: A. E. Wilder Smith)

Fig. 21. Brontosaurus track on ledge in Paluxy River with man track in background. Dinosaur State Park.

bacteria, *drosophila,* mice and rats have been bred, and in the overwhelming majority of cases the previously present genetic and other structures have been merely exactly replicated. This is, of course, not to deny that mutations do take place and new strains are formed. The point to be emphasized here is, that up to the present, it has not been found possible to put the metabolic energy of the cell to work *to generate new kinds of genetic material progressively more complicated,* that is, purely and simply to synthesize in the strict sense of the word, rather than to strictly replicate existing material. It has not been possible to date to do this or demonstrate it, at least, not on a regular or grand scale under controlled laboratory conditions.

Thus the living cell seems to be, by common consent today, primarily a machine for replicating existing materials and not one for upward purposeful synthesis *toward higher complexity and new substances.* The only organisms we know of which do any real *evolutionary* synthesis in the strict sense of the term at all (as opposed to replicative synthesis) are those which have a large brain, namely chemists and biochemists! Thus Teilhard describes the effect which he believes the human brain or spirit will have on the future growth of evolution, that is, on the future of purposeful upward synthesis as opposed to mere replication: "If each of us can believe that he is working so that the Universe may be raised, in him and through him, to a higher level—then a new spring of energy will well forth in the heart of earth's workers."[33] Teilhard maintains that *once the brain and its thought are present on the evolutionary tree the latter will continually perfect itself, that is, extend evolutionary synthesis over mere replicative synthesis.* This development of a brain "turning in" on itself to perfect itself, is Teilhard's view of a new direction in synthetic evolution.[34]

[33]Teilhard de Chardin, *The Future of Man* (New York: Harper & Row, 1964), p. 118.
[34]Teilhard de Chardin, *op. cit., The Phenomenon* . . . , p. 146.

It would seem then, that life without cerebralization or cephalization (to use Teilhard's terminology) is a strictly repetitive, replicating process which uses its metabolic energy largely for just these purposes. But once *cephalization* and *thought* have developed, *then metabolic processes and energy may be used for truly upward synthetic purposes in addition to mere synthetic replicative processes.*

Obviously, man has only recently turned to biochemical synthesis, in particular to that of genetic material, so it is far too early to say how far this new factor will influence the use of metabolic free energy for the upward surge of evolution to more complex forms of life beyond man. Only time will show how far Teilhard's prophecies are valid. But it is obviously clear already that thought and cephalization in man and higher animals have not thus far contributed much to upward evolutionary surges. Our *biochemical* and *synthetic* techniques are even now still far too crude to have had any effect either in the present or past. This means that in the past purely replicative processes will have predominated, which do not produce, however, upward surges of evolutionary syntheses. It does not seem reasonable to suppose that life without cephalization has been capable of perfecting new and apparently purposeful synthetic processes for the complex genetic material that higher organisms need. There are today many references in the literature to the fact that the most complicated syntheses can only be of use when perfect. This means that a slow and nonpurposeful development of such complex purposes could not have taken place. There is, on this score, no difficulty about replication of already planned complex processes. The difficulty arises where an automatic brainless and thoughtless system is supposed to have developed by pure replicative processes a progressive conceptual upsurge of complexity.

To suppose this might be compared to expecting an automatic machine for repetitively making screws to gradually develop itself automatically into a machine for building complete television sets. It has not the *brains* to do this! But obviously once life has attained cephalization, the brain and thought power to do the syntheses (as opposed merely to replicate) is present, as Teilhard so rightly points out. Once *thought* is present, metabolic energy can be used *to fuel thought* for synthesis upward. Thus evolution on this basis could obviously have taken place. It would be more correct to say that this upsurge might take place in the future, for even today our technique would not allow us to make any real contribution by thought to upward evolution.

It is remarkable in connection with the above considerations that the Holy Scripture is perfectly clear in stating that God's *thought* alone is at the back of this creation and universe. He created it by thought in the first place and then maintained it, that is, his thought directed the upward synthesis and also the replicative maintenance processes. This fits in perfectly with the above thesis. But where no thought is, there can be no *synthesis* other than replicating synthesis. And even this latter has to be established by thought programming somewhere. In this we entirely agree with Teilhard, who admits that the advent of thought changes the whole aspect of evolution upward, with the difference that we obviously do not think that man's thought has really changed any postulated evolution synthetically yet. And apart from God's original thought, the evidence that man's thought will be able to effect upward evolution would seem to be rather meager. Teilhard thinks that this aspect of man's thought directing the evolution of man upward to Point Omega lies largely in the future and not in the past. If Point Omega is Christ, as Teilhard thinks, Holy Writ would not support him very much, since it maintains consistently that man in general flees from God and does not follow the way to him.

We are forced to the conclusion that replicative processes replicating the already existing and programmed complexity of animal and plant organisms have been used in the past to maintain life. There is little evidence of thought-based biologically upward synthesis except for that which took place at creation. This helps to explain the constancy of species that has been observed and also the lack of missing links which has so disappointed evolutionists in the past. Upward spontaneous synthetic processes leading to evolution, *unless backed by thought somewhere,* are on the face of things unlikely, seeing that noncephalized or lowly cephalized life seems to be geared to pure replication.

One Species Changing into Another During Evolution. Experience clearly shows that changes within species during the course of time do take place in plants, animals and man. The various strains and races of wheat, barley, dogs, cats, pigeons and man prove that. But is it also clear that one species changes into another, maybe higher, species in the course of time? The doctrine of evolution teaches that this is exactly what does take place and ascribes the whole diversity of life we see around us to this process. To seriously question this postulated change of one species into another is simply not acceptable today. As Teilhard so aptly says: "Excepting a few ultra-conservative groups it would *not occur* to any present day *thinker or scientist*—it would be *psychologically inadmissible and impossible*—to pursue a line of thought which ignores the concept of a world in [biological] evolution."[35]

This reflects present-day thought pretty closely. One is considered to be neither a scientist nor capable of being a thinker if one even calls these matters into question. The concept of evolution by one species changing into another in the course of time is for the majority today a fact to be attacked on pain of scientific excommunication. Every generation thinks that knowledge will perish with it, so sometimes it is good to remember that the theory of phlogiston was once just as firmly entrenched in a past scientific generation as the theory of evolution is entrenched in our generation.

Modern-day science compared to past. When I was studying zoology we were taught that the *coelacanthid* type of fish had died out millions of years ago. The fossil remains of this fish had been found in a well-preserved state, so that its struc-

[35]Teilhard de Chardin, *op. cit., The Future* . . . , p. 85.

ture was well known.[36] The excitement in the scientific world was great when one fine day some years ago a perfect living specimen of *coelacanthus* was caught off the East African Coast. A number of these fish have now been caught and examined. Their structure resembles that of their fossil forebears in a remarkable manner. This is all the more surprising when it is remembered that it is postulated that millions of years separate the modern from the fossil fish. If the find proves anything, it must surely be that, in this case at any rate, almost perfect constancy of species has been maintained by the genetic-replicating processes of the organism over huge spans of time.

It is generally known that bees and other insects have been found preserved in resins which are supposed to be millions of years old.[37] The structure of the preserved insects resembles often in minutest detail that of their modern counterparts. Have we not here a further proof of the constancy of at least these species? And if these species, why not of other species too? *Thus, it is scientifically sound today to maintain that some species at least can apparently remain absolutely constant over very long periods of time.* One would expect this if the replicative processes of the organism were exact and efficient. Genetic work in the last twenty years definitely has shown this to be the case in very many species besides the ones mentioned above.

A few years ago our family went to Denmark for the summer and in Aarhus visited the Grauballemanden (see Fig. 1). This man was found in a well-preserved state in a Jutland peat bog. His finders are reported to have notified the police because they thought they had found the victim of a recent murder. The large gaping wound in the neck showed the man to have been executed and then thrown into the bog where the peat acids preserved him so well that one can still recognize the expression on his face. Even his fingerprints

---

[36]Cf. *Nature* (Jan. 3, 1953), CLXXI, 17, 99; (Sept. 4, 1954), CLXXIV, 426; (Nov. 5, 1954), CLXXIV, 745.
[37]See Appendix IV.

(see Fig. 2) are well preserved. He is a representative of the Iron Age.

There are a number of other similar finds which have been made in northern Europe. The Borremosemanden is an example (see Fig. 3). He was executed by hanging, and the noose round his neck and his clothes are well preserved. The expression on his face is recognizable, although he, too, is an Iron Age man. See also the Tollundmanden (Fig. 4) and the Grauballemanden (Fig. 5).

These examples are, of course, from a geological point of view, very recent indeed and evolution is postulated as working over hundreds of thousands of years to account for its changes. But, one thing will strike the observant person: except for the clothes sewn out of the skins of animals and turned inward, these men might have been seen on the street of any modern European city today. They have fine brows and good chins; the crow's feet round the eyes of the Tollundmanden make one think he must have been an intelligent humorist. One wonders whom this humorist annoyed to warrant death by hanging.

Although only moments of time have passed, geologically speaking, between the Iron Age and the present, one is surprised to see Iron Age men before one's very eyes, looking so modern.

In order to prove the change of one species into another in the course of evolution, many fossil examples of series of animals are quoted. The series purporting to demonstrate the evolution of the horse is the most famous. Although the members of the series of fossils existed, of course, and are therefore generally recognized as facts, yet there is no formal proof that the links in this series were in fact organic and genetic. We know that entire ranges of animals which existed once are now extinct. Both animal and plant kingdoms are much poorer in species today than formerly. Yet even today, among animals which are still extant, one could without much difficulty construct "family trees" showing the next "highest" member to have been "derived" from its next lowest neighbor. If one were to find in some future age the fossil remains of such a contemporaneous series, one might postulate that one species had been derived from the other. And yet they all lived contemporaneously.

Easier to resynthesize from scratch. If my memory serves me right, it was Sir Cyril Hinshelwood who said that it would be more difficult to convert the proteins of one species into those of another than it would be to burn them down to water, ammonia and carbon dioxide and then start to resynthesize everything from scratch. It would be difficult indeed, for instance, to modify the antigens of an ape into those of a man by straight chemical synthesis as technology stands today.

The nontechnical mind may not appreciate the extreme finesse of structure of the proteins of the body, so we will risk another example to clarify the concept. Volkswagen and Cadillacs do bear superficial resemblances to one another. The same basic principles are used to build both, their motors both function on the Otto cycle principle, both burn gasoline, both run on four wheels, being guided by the two front ones. But ask your service station mechanic which he would rather do: modify your Volkswagen into a Cadillac or scrap your Volkswagen entirely, melt the metal down, etc., and start afresh building a Cadillac? This example is a vast oversimplification compared with the problem of changing one species of protein into another. To hope that your Volkswagen would be changed by chance modification (road accidents?) into a Cadillac in the course of years would show perhaps less naïveté than to hope that one specific protein enzyme type would be changed by chance into another.

Problem of Vestigial Organs.

Ontogeny recapitulates phylogeny. An important postulate on the theory of evolution is that ontogeny recapitulates phylogeny. This means that the embryonic development of every animal or plant individually passes through the same stages through which the ancestral forms of the organism passed. According to this theory, man's ancestral past included fishlike forms, so that one would expect man's embryonic development to include a fishlike stage. Fishlike vestigial gill structures, which are therefore looked upon as supporting evolutionary theory, are in fact present in the young human and other mammal embryos.

There are many other vestigial structures in man and animals which are regarded as evidence for the same point. The *appendix vermiformis* is interpreted as being a vestige of the period when man's ancestors ate cellulose, which was supposedly digested in this then much larger organ. The presence of the *appendix vermiformis* is therefore regarded as proof positive that man's ancestors digested cellulose from their vegetarian diet. The external ear muscles are also considered vestigial by evolutionists. The slender red crescent at the inner corner of the human eye known as the semilunar fold resembles the third eyelid found in birds and some modern reptiles. Many consider this fold vestigial. The hind legs of whales are so reduced in some species that they cannot be seen from the surface of the body at all. They are considered to be vestigial and to represent the four-footed ancestry of whales which supposedly possessed four functional legs.

The splint bones at the sides of horses' feet are also supposed to be vestigial and to represent proof of an ancestral stage.[38]

Can postulate explain all types of vestigial organs? If now the above interpretation of vestigial organs is of general validity it ought to supply an absolutely general explanation of all types of vestigial organs. The question is, does evolutionary theory do just this? To investigate this point, let us take one or two instances of such vestigial organs in our own body and rigorously apply evolutionary theory on vestigial organs to them. If we get a sensible answer, we confirm evolutionary theory; and if we get a nonsensical answer, we do not confirm.

[38]For further references see Mixter, *op. cit.*, p. 11., where some of the foregoing material has been mentioned.

Take, for example, the rudimentary breasts and nipples which every male mammal possesses. If mammals were derived ancestrally via reptiles, as the theory of evolution demands, we are forced to the following conclusions:

Reptiles do not suckle their young and do not possess, of course, any mammae or nipples. In consequence mammae must be, according to theory, organs which are in process of evolutionary development *since* the "reptile stage." Thus mammae in general cannot be considered to be organs in process of disappearing, for they have developed in relatively recent geological time. Thus mammae must be developing, evolving, organs even in male mammals. If these evolving male organs were useless they could not have developed at all, for they would then have given their owners no advantage in natural selection. So we conclude that their usefulness must either lie in the past or just possibly in the future. If the latter is the case then male mammals will, at some future date, happily suckle the young! Or if the function of the male mammae lies in the past then we must assume that the male suckled the young in the past and that this function was only recently taken over by the female.

It should not be thought that this is just an isolated case we are reducing to the ridiculous by application of evolutionary theory. The female has a number of male "vestigial" organs, all of which could be reduced to the ridiculous in the same way by treating them according to the standard Darwinian interpretation of vestigial organs. By it women must have had male functions in their ancestry—or in the future will have such functions.

Postulate as applied to biochemistry. This line of thought could be applied not only to the vestigial organs but also to biochemistry. Why do females synthesize male hormones and males female hormones? Must it mean, if current evolutionary theory is applied, that in past ancestry the females were males? All men and male mammals likewise synthesize female hormones. Were they then in the past females? For after all,

apes do synthesize blood groups, antibodies, etc., which resemble the human counterparts, which fact is used as evidence
by the Darwinists that men have developed in their ancestry
through common apelike forebears![39] But what is good for
the goose should be good for the gander! Surely, if women
possess not only male vestigial organs (and they possess several) as well as synthesize male sex hormones, then this is
compelling evidence that they exercised male functions in the
past. And, of course, exactly the same holds true for men, who
possess plenty of female vestigial organs and synthesize female
sex hormones. They must have exercised female functions in
past ancestry!

Thus the use of currently accepted theories of vestigial organs to prove that ontogeny recapitulates phylogeny is by no
means on such firm ground as is commonly thought and insisted. In these cases insistence on evolutionary theory leads
to nonsense.

Vestigial organs in plants and animals. The presence of
vestigial organs in plants and animals is susceptible to other
interpretations than those advanced by Darwinists. It has
been frequently pointed out that there is an extraordinary
biochemical similarity of all living matter. It is a fact that all
mammalian, reptilian and amphibian types show a tendency
to possess four legs, or limbs, either in the functional or vestigial form. The common type of biochemistry in all life is
equally challenging of explanation. One finds the same complex cofactors and prosthetic groups, essentially the same enzymes and similar hormones in the most diverse organisms.
As Dixon and Webb[40] point out, the essential unity of all life
extends even to stereochemistry. The same optical isomers
are used metabolically almost throughout the living kingdoms. There is never any question of one species metaboliz-
ing D-glucose and another L-glucose. Indeed, the stereospecificity of the enzyme systems would make this impossible.

[39]Malcom Dixon and E. C. Webb, *Enzymes*, 2d ed. (New York: Academic
Press, Inc., 1964), p. 665.
[40]*Ibid.*, p. 665.

Laboratory chemical synthesis usually results (unless previously existing stereospecificity is used in forms of optical resolution techniques) in equal mixtures of the D and L forms, that is, of racemates. This simply means that if molecules can be made up of exactly the same substituent atoms around a central atom of four valency bonds, but so constructed that the arrangement of the substituent atoms round the central one varies in space, then there arises the possibility of two stereoisomers having exactly the same chemical constitution. The only difference between these molecules lies in their arrangement of substituents in space. Put simply, the two isomers differ from one another as a right-handed glove differs from a left-handed one. Such isomers are known as stereoisomers.

Stereoisomers having a left-handed structure are known as the L-isomers and those with a right-handed configuration are known as the D-isomers. Now if the left-handed molecule is dissolved in a solvent and polarized light is passed through, then the plane of the polarized light will be deflected to the left. Similarly the right-handed molecule will deflect the plane in the opposite direction. This deflection of the plane of polarized light by an asymmetric molecule is known as optical activity. A mixture of 50 percent L-isomer and 50 percent D-isomer will produce no deflection of the plane of polarized light and is known as a racemate. Special chemical methods allow the chemist to pick out and separate the right-handed molecules from the left-handed ones. Such processes are known as optical resolutions.

During ordinary chemical synthesis in the laboratory, equal proportions of both right-handed and left-handed molecules are formed if asymmetry is possible in the molecular structure, so that no optical activity is present in the product. *But living proteins, enzymes, etc., are always optically active*, that is, asymmetric, and for this very reason cannot have *originated* by ordinary chance chemical synthesis. Asymmetry and mirror images, left-handed and right-handed molecules, are regularly produced by life processes, so that many products showing optically active forms are found in the living cell. Chance chemical processes produce, on the other hand, racemates. Again, a new problem is introduced into explaining arche-biopoiesis as a chance process over long periods. Leaving optically active products for long time periods is often sufficient to destroy their optical activity. This loss of optical activity is known as racemization and presents a further problem in explaining life's origin as a chance process. All this constitutes one more reason why spontaneous chance formation of the first protein enzyme systems lies beyond the realms of statistical possibility. If chance, ordinary chemical reactions, were at the base of the origin of life, one would have expected no optical activity but rather racemate formation. Circularly polarized light produced by passage through quartz crystals has been invoked[41] to account for the formation of optically active isomers where racemates would ordinarily be expected. But in view of the improbability of such a set of circumstances all occurring simultaneously this solution would appear to be very far-fetched.

As Webb and Dixon point out, the singleness of pattern of asymmetry in life and living processes does strongly suggest a common origin of all existing living matters: "If life had originated otherwise than on one single and unique occasion, one would have expected that sometimes one asymmetric form and sometimes the other would have been produced."[42]

This once-and-for-all idea of the production of all life, whether by chance or plan, would lead one to expect the similarities in construction of the physiology, biochemistry and anatomy of life as we see it now, regardless of whether one type of life has actually *evolved* from another or not. But, as we have pointed out, chance and ordinary chemical reactions would lead one to expect racemates rather than optically active isomers. On the other hand, if thought (creative synthesis) is at the back of life, as the creationist holds, the prob-

---

[41]J. D. Bernal, "The Problem of Stages in Biopoeisis," *The Origin of Life on the Earth,* I, 38, 46.
[42]Dixon and Webb, *op. cit.,* p. 664.

lem is easier to solve. The Creator used one basic plan of construction for anatomy, physiology, biochemistry and stereochemistry in all the organisms he planned and then varied his plan like a Bach fugue. Some organisms then had reduced legs, for example, some long legs and some vestigial legs. Thus variety was obtained on the basis of a common plan of construction.

Some scientists believe that the solution of the problem of vestigial organs lies in the basic physiological construction of the whole body. Obviously man and other mammals must have the chance of becoming either male or female during their development, so that the basis of both sexes must be present in all organisms. Further, the physical base, for example, for the *appendix vermiformis* in one species could form the physiological basis of a secretory organ or digestive sac in another. On this basis the presence of both types of sex organs in either sex becomes a physiological necessity, so that by change in hormone function and concentration the male or female structure may be developed at will.

Finally, it is, of course, a mistake to imagine that a vestigial organ is always useless. The vermiform appendix, for example, has probably a secretory function.

Thus the ancient slogan that ontogeny recapitulates phylogeny is not so scientifically well based as is often held. It certainly does not present perfect evidence for the "fact" of evolution as is often maintained, since it is susceptible of other nonevolutionary interpretations.

3

THE PROBLEMS OF THE AGE OF
MAN AND THE MISSING LINKS

The biblical account of the creation of heaven and earth, of man, plants and animals, the deluge, etc., is not considered worthy of serious discussion in scientific circles today. Particular exception is often taken to the idea of a worldwide flood and to Eve's being taken from Adam's side. The rejection of the biblical account often includes what passes for biblical chronology. There are, of course, good reasons for rejecting some kinds of "biblical" chronology, which every Christian ought to consider carefully. Years ago Bishop Ussher calculated from the biblical genealogies that the date of creation was 4004 B.C., which figures in some of the older King James Versions of the English Bible.

Bishop Ussher used as a main basis of his calculations the tables of Genesis 11. On the basis of the Masoretic text and this table, one arrives at the conclusion that the worldwide deluge must have taken place during the third millennium before Christ, while the Septuagint text would be interpreted as teaching that the flood occurred during the fourth millennium B.C.

It would seem, however, according to recent archaeological findings, that the civilizations of the ancient Near Orient were relatively undisturbed for at least 5,000 years B.C., so that a large catastrophe such as Noah's deluge during this time ought to be questioned.

BIBLICAL CHRONOLOGY

DATA IN GENESIS

It will be necessary here to briefly examine the questions of the chronology of Genesis in particular. The chief biblical chronological evidence is usually based on Genesis 11. This table, however, does not pretend to give us the total span of time between the flood and Abraham, a fact which is often overlooked today as it was in Ussher's time. In this table of Genesis 11 the years of the individuals mentioned are never totaled so as to give a complete span of years.

In contrast to this incompleteness of data in Genesis 11, other genealogies do profess to give complete spans of time in years as, for example, in Genesis 5:3-5 (RSV): "When Adam had lived a hundred and thirty years, he became the father of a son in his own likeness, after his image, and named him Seth. The days of Adam after he became the father of Seth were eight hundred years; and he had other sons and daughters. Thus, all the days that Adam lived were nine hundred and thirty years; and he died."

Moses also gives us the complete time span of the captivity in Egypt in Exodus 12:40 (RSV): "The time that the people of Israel dwelt in Egypt was four hundred and thirty years. And at the end of four hundred and thirty years, on that very day, all the hosts of the LORD went out from the land of Egypt." Moses is careful in these cases to do the computing work for us in adding up and setting down exact totals.

In view of the fact, therefore, that some genealogies and time charts are specifically very complete, it is remarkable that the important genealogy of Genesis 11 does not profess to be complete and does not sum up the total number of years elapsed from the start to finish. It looks as if Moses knew that his table was incomplete and that he therefore deliberately avoided his usual custom of totaling the years. Thus, for this reason, it is probably not possible to fix the exact time of the Genesis flood from the biblical family trees. This entails the consequence that the creation in seven days, and the flood, could have been very much older than Ussher and his friends imagined. An excellent exposé of this question of the incompleteness of the genealogies in the Old Testament was published nearly eighty years ago by the Rev. Professor William Henry Green of Princeton Theological Seminary.[1]

GENEALOGIES

The older editions of some Bibles (e.g., the Elberfelder German Bible) carry notes and tables based on the assumption that Genesis 11 is complete. This would make Noah to have been still alive when Abram was fifty years old. And Peleg's father Heber would still have had two years to live after Jacob arrived in Mesopotamia to work for Laban. But Joshua 24:2, 14-15 would, on general grounds, seem to exclude this contemporaneousness with its reference to Abram's ancestors, including Terah, the father of Abraham and Nahor, as having served other gods while they lived *"of old"* beyond the Euphrates. If some of these ancestors had still been living in Abraham's days, this expression "of old" would appear to be rather remarkable. Morris and Whitcomb, to whom the reader is referred for further detail,[2] discuss this problem at length.

It is sufficient for our purposes here to point out that the Bible does not teach from its genealogies that the creation took place in the year 4004 B.C. Much longer time spans are legitimately allowable on the basis of the biblical world view and genealogies.

TOWER OF BABEL

Although gaps are almost certainly present in the genealogies mentioned and although the creation certainly is very much older than the 4004 B.C. calculated by Ussher, yet is is still not possible to put the creation of man back into a period of time which would harmonize with current uniformitarianism.

[1]W. H. Green, *Bibliotheca Sacra* (April, 1890), pp. 285-303.
[2]Henry Morris and John C. Whitcomb, *The Genesis Flood* (Philadelphia: Presbyterian & Reformed Publishing Co., 1961).

The building of the Tower of Babel may have taken place about two to four millennia before Abraham but not some tens of millennia before him. The gaps in the genealogies are probably to be found in the period *before* the Tower of Babel and not afterward. So that after Babel it is not possible to greatly lengthen the periods of time covered by the genealogies. It would seem, therefore, that there cannot be question of hundreds of millennia lying between Adam and Abraham.

The real solution to the problem would seem to lie between the two extremes. Indeed, the mythologies of the flood, which many people possess, tend to confirm this intermediate view. It is well known today that the Babylonian Gilgamesh Epic presents many details of the flood also given by Moses, with the exception, of course, of the polytheism which separates the two reports. But the fact remains that many details in the two stories are so close that some archaeologists believe that Moses used the Gilgamesh Epic as the source and basis of his account of Noah and the deluge. Christian archaeologists maintain the opposite view, that the Gilgamesh Epic is a corruption of the true facts, and that God has given through Moses the original and true account.[3]

A good report on the traditions of the flood among many peoples is found in a book by Alfred M. Rehwinkel, Professor of Theology, Concordia Seminary.[4] Dr. Rehwinkel reports on flood traditions from Alaska, Sudan, Mexico, Hawaii, Lithuania, Australia, etc.

The important question we must consider now is: "How could all the exact details of the Gilgamesh Epic have been handed down so perfectly via an oral tradition over hundreds of millennia of a stone-age culture, if the enormous spans of time required by evolutionary doctrine are true?" A detailed oral tradition might possibly have been passed down fairly

---

[3]For a discussion of the similarities and differences between the Genesis story and the Gilgamesh Epic see Alexander Heidel, *The Gilgamesh Epic and Old Testament Parallels* (Chicago: University of Chicago Press, 1946).
[4]Alfred M. Rehwinkel, *The Flood in the Light of the Bible, Geology and Archaeology* (2d ed., St. Louis: Concordia Publishing House, 1957).

GEOLOGICAL TIME TABLE

Eras	Periods	Types of Organisms	Years Ago
Cenozoic	Quaternary: Recent	Rise of modern plants, animals and man	25,000
	Pleistocene		975,000
	Tertiary: Pliocene	Rise of mammals and highest plants	12,000,000
	Miocene		25,000,000
	Oligocene		35,000,000
	Eocene		60,000,000
	Paleocene		70,000,000
Mesozoic	Cretaceous	Angiosperms and insect abundant Foraminifers, Dinosaurs extinct First reptilian birds	70,000,000
	Jurassic	First primitive Angiosperms	to
	Triassic	Earliest dinosaurs Earliest ammonites	200,000,000
Paleozoic	Permian	Primitive reptiles Extinction of trilobites, first modern corals	200,000,000
	Pennsylvanian	Earliest known insects	
	Mississippian	Rise of amphibians	to
	Devonian	First seed plants Cartilage fish types	
	Silurian	Rise of fishes, earliest known land animals	500,000,000
	Ordovician	Earliest vertebrates	
	Cambrian	Brachiopods and trilobites	
Proterozoic		Primitive water-dwelling plants and animals	500,000,000 to 1,000,000,000
Archeozoic		Oldest known life (mostly indirect evidence)	1,000,000,000 to 1,800,000,000

exactly for, say, five thousand years. But the requirement of, for example, one hundred thousand years in an entirely different proposition. That the Gilgamesh Epic is extant in its relatively perfect form renders the long time spans required for early history and prehistory by uniformitarianism highly unlikely, unless writing had been developed for tens of hundreds of millennia, which is again unlikely.

So we will assume that the flood took place some three to five millennia before Abraham and that the Tower of Babel was built not much later than a millennium after the flood. After the flood our dating systems become historically more exact.

GEOLOGICAL AGES

Geological ages are usually divided up today into the type of scheme shown on the chart on page 114.

The sequence of the ice ages is usually presented as follows though there is still a good deal of discussion on this subject. One usually reckons with the following scheme:

Age	Millennia B.C.	Culture
Postglacial	11-19	La Madalène
Bul	19-24	
Interglacial	24-64	
Würm II	64-72	
Interglacial	72-108	Le Moustier
Würm I	108-16	
Interglacial	116-39	
Pre-Würm	139-44	
Interglacial	144-83	
Riss II	183-93	
Interglacial	193-225	
Riss I	225-36	Acheuil
Interglacial	236-302	
Pre-Riss	302-6	
Interglacial	306-429	
Mindel II	429-34	
Interglacial	434-470	
Mindel I	470-78	Chelles
Interglacial	478-543	
Günz II	543-62	
Interglacial	562-85	
Günz I	585-92	
Pre-Glacial	592-800	

The age of the older formations is determined by their content of radium, thorium, uranium, lead, etc. The rate of formation of certain isomers of lead from radioactive precursors is known, so that the age of an ore is given by its content of lead. The age of younger formations is not susceptible of determination by this method. For them Milankowich's method is sometimes used which depends upon the amount of radiation reaching the earth from the sun.

The accompanying tables are given to furnish an indication of the huge time spans with which modern historical geology deals.

THE C^{14} DATING METHOD

A different method of dating is now used for periods ranging from between 3,000 to 14,000 years back. It was worked out by Professor Libby of California, who received the Nobel Prize for the development. The method is dependent upon the rate of decay of C^{14} which, in contrast to C^{12}, is radioactive.

We shall briefly examine the C^{14} dating method, since it is so widely used to date historic and prehistoric objects, which are important for placing an estimate on the age of man.

PRINCIPLES OF METHOD

The method depends upon the following facts. In the stratosphere the air is bombarded by cosmic rays which react with the atmospheric nitrogen (N^{14}) to form radioactive carbon (C^{14}). All living things contain, of course, carbon, which is the basis of organic matter. But normal carbon (C^{12}) is not radioactive, whereas C^{14}, which is also present in living matter, disintegrates slowly, liberating radioactivity which can be measured by suitable instruments. This radioactive decay prevents the concentration of C^{14} in the atmosphere from rising above certain limits, although it is continually being formed from N^{14} by cosmic ray bombardment. An equilibrium concentration of C^{14} is reached at which it is formed at the same rate as it decays. The result of there being an equilibrium concentration of C^{14} in C^{12} is that all organic substances in equilibrium with the atmosphere emit a weak but constant radiation.

Since all living organisms take in C^{12} and C^{14} in the constant proportion found in the atmosphere, all living tissue in equilibrium with the atmosphere will contain the same proportions of C^{12} and C^{14} that are found in the atmosphere.

As long as there is free exchange between living tissue and the air these relative proportions will remain identical in air and in tissue. But if the tissue dies and the equilibrium exchange between it and the air ceases—as when wood is charred and carbon or charcoal is formed, or a body is mummified— then the C^{14} concentration in the carbon or mummy will begin to fall below the equilibrium concentration level, since it decays by radioactivity and the radioactive C^{14} is no longer replaced from stocks in the atmosphere. Thus, if a piece of wood was charred, for example, 5,000 years ago, or a body mummified at the same date, their concentration of C^{14} will have steadily decreased during these 5,000 years and this decrease rate, being constant, will reflect the time during which the carbon or mummy has been cut off from equilibrium with the supply of C^{14} from the air. If any sample of C^{14} loses, for example, half its radioactivity in 6,000 years (for the purpose of argument) this time is known as the half life of C^{14}. Thus, if half the expected amount of radioactivity is found in any sample of C^{14} cut off from exchange with the supply of C^{14} in the atmosphere or food supply, then that sample may be reckoned to be 6,000 years old.

Because the radioactivity of C^{14} is very weak the method is not applicable to samples much more than 10,000 to 15,000 years old. The radiation from such old samples would be too weak to measure accurately. The carbon in mineral oil and coal is so old that it shows no activity.

POTENTIAL ERRORS OF METHOD

This elegant dating method has some built-in potential errors that we must look at briefly.

Constant Synthesis of C^{14} from N^{14}. The method is obviously dependent on the synthesis of C^{14} from N^{14} by cosmic radiation at a rate which remains constant over long periods of time. An example will suffice to make this clear. If the state of the stratosphere 5,000 years ago was such that cosmic bombardment was reduced, compared with the present intensity, then 5,000 years ago there would have been less C^{14} synthesis than now. This would mean that living organisms 5,000 years ago would have borne less C^{14} in them than now, which means that such organisms if charred or mummified and tested by our method today would appear to be older than they in fact are. Let us take an extreme case and assume that 5,000 years ago there was no C^{14} in the atmosphere. Any wood being charred or bodies being mummified at this time would under these circumstances be radioactively dead already at the time of their physical death. Their age by our method would therefore appear to be at the limit of the method, that is, 10,000 to 15,000 years old at the least. But actually they are only 5,000 years old.

Cosmic Radiation. There are many reasons for believing that cosmic radiation in space has remained constant for long periods of time. But we have no guarantee that the upper atmosphere did not at one time protect the lower atmosphere and the earth better against cosmic radiation than at present. If this, in effect, has been the case, then all samples laid down at such time of diminished stratospheric cosmic radiation will appear older, when dated by our method, than they really are.

Changes in Water Economy. From evidence in the Bible and from evidence of climatic changes in the earth there is a possibility that fundamental changes in the water economy of the planet have occurred. As Morris and Whitcomb[5] point

---

[5]Morris and Whitcomb, *op. cit.*, pp. 254-57, 303-11.

out in their chapter on this subject, there will scarcely have
been enough water vapor in the atmosphere, as we know it,
to have accounted for a worldwide deluge as reported in Genesis. If, however, there had been a belt of water vapor above
the stratosphere before the flood, which then for some unknown reason (maybe seeding by cosmic dust) was suddenly
precipitated, the consequences would have been far-reaching.
First, there might have been a shielding effect from cosmic
radiation, which would have protected the earth from the undesirable consequences of radioactivity, and lengthened life.
And second, the climate of the planet would have been much
hotter owing to the "greenhouse" effect of such a layer. A
colossal flood could have resulted from sudden condensation.

Genesis 2:5 notes one remarkable observation to the effect
that, before the flood in Eden, no condensation of water vapor
to produce rain took place. The earth is reported to have
been watered by a *rising* mist and not by falling rain at that
time. Thus, the water economy must have been very different
then from what it is now.

Difference in Ionizing Radiation. A changed water economy of the above type would have produced an effect on climate as well as on life in general. All forms of life would
have been more long lived and viable than today if radioactivity from cosmic radiation had been materially cut down by
screening. Radioactive exposure is well known to shorten life
in many organisms and to accelerate aging processes. Pure-
strain mice exposed to ionizing radiation do not live as long
as nonexposed litter mates. The exposed animals age more
quickly and are often more susceptible to cancer and other
degenerative diseases.[6]

Today it is a well-founded scientific fact that *all* unnecessary exposure to ionizing radiation should be avoided. Grave
doubts have been expressed as to the wisdom of the use of
mass X-ray techniques in the campaign against tuberculosis.

[6]*Science* (May 17, 1957), CXXV, 965.

And for the same reason there has been an outcry in some countries against the use of the Pedoscope in shoe stores to aid shoe fitting by X-raying the feet, even though the dose of ionizing radiation received from these machines is very much less than that received from a chest X ray. It must be remembered that the heart, liver, spleen and lung are a good deal more vulnerable than the bones of the feet.

In the absence or reduction of ionizing radiation, man, animals and plants would be much more viable and would live longer than they do in the presence of radiation. This fact might possibly have some connection with the longevity of antediluvian organisms, including man, and the tendency to gigantism observed in man, plants and animals, both before and soon after the flood.

Warmer Climate on Earth. The climate of the earth would have been much warmer right up to the poles if a layer of water vapor had been present above the stratosphere producing the "greenhouse" effect.

During the recent geophysical year we took a trip up to Spitsbergen in the far North and visited, among other things, a Polish scientific expedition camp which was established on Bellsund. There we saw many proofs of the fact that at one time the climate in this now arctic region was once subtropical. Now there are no trees, except the minute trailing arctic birch, a few inches long, and very little other vegetation except that of the high alpine type. Scarcely a blade of grass grows there. There are only bare rocks covered in some places by lichens and at rare intervals by a very few brilliant alpine-like flowers. But, as the coal measures just beneath this poor vegetation in present-day Spitsbergen show, the vegetation there formerly was subtropical and luxurious. The fossilized tropical ferns just below the surface in the coal show this.

The fact that Spitsbergen was formerly able to support a subtropical vegetation might be explained in the following ways: Spitsbergen formerly did not have six months of darkness followed by six months of light as is now the case. It would seem highly unlikely that tropical vegetation could ever have flourished in a climate involving nearly six months of darkness followed by six months of light. Even tropical temperatures would not be able to compensate for the necessary sunlight that plants need. We must therefore assume that either Spitsbergen was not always at its present latitude but lay much farther south than at present, so that it would get light for its vegetation all the year round (this theory might stretch the continental drift theory more than a little). Or we might assume that the axis of the earth was formerly not inclined at 23.5°, so that even at its present latitude Spitsbergen would have received twelve hours of light and twelve hours of darkness daily. If this were the case a higher temperature, together with the light it would receive even at this latitude, would be sufficient to support a subtropical vegetation.

Dr. Wallace S. Broecker of Columbia University[7] thinks that alterations in the angle of the axis of the earth may account for the changes in the climate of the earth, thus precipitating the various glaciations. It would seem that this second possibility of explaining the tropical vegetation on Spitsbergen and in other arctic areas would be preferable to the first (continental drift). If this is true, the changing of the axis of the earth with respect to the sun would, if it took place suddenly, cause huge floods, storms and other catastrophes of the large scale required for Noah's deluge. For the Bible says that the water of the flood originated not only in the heavens but also from the oceans. Over and above this, the loss of water vapor from the upper atmosphere would cause a general reduction of temperature by loss of the "greenhouse" effect. The reduction of temperature and the loss of light during the six-month arctic night would rapidly put an end to the luxurious vegetation of Spitsbergen together with its fauna. Moreover, an increase in ionizing radiation would

[7]Cf. *Science* (1966), CLI, 299, and *Science News Letter* (Feb. 5, 1966), p. 83.

have occurred, bringing with it the shorter life span reported by the Bible to have occurred after the flood.

With regard to the possibility of changes in the axis of rotation of the earth and corresponding shifting in the location of the arctic and antarctic polar areas, Immanuel Velikovsky, in his *Worlds in Collision*[8] points out that, although modern astronomy does not admit the possibility of such shifts, yet there is a mass of evidence from historical times pointing to such changes, accompanied by historical climatic and seasonal alterations. Changes in glaciation areas figure prominently in Velikovsky's evidence.

In support of his thesis, Velikovsky mentions the charts of the sky found in the tomb of Senmut, the Egyptian vizier.[9] This tomb dates from a time following the exodus but before the days of Amos and Isaiah and shows two charts of the Egyptian sky, one from before and one from the time during which Senmut lived. "The first chart startled the investigators because in it east and west are reversed." The second chart shows east and west as they are now.[10] Velikovsky produces much evidence of an historical nature to show that in very ancient times the sun was, in fact, represented as not rising in the east but in the west. Velikovsky then mentions further evidence of changed sunrise and sunset positions as has been found in archaeological excavations: "Besides temples and their gates, the obelisks served the purpose of fixing the direction of east and west or of sunrise and sunset on equinoctial days."[11] As older temples were destroyed, newer ones were built on the older foundations, but the direction of these, with respect to east and west, was corrected to agree with changed positions of sunrise and sunset. These corrections in the succeeding foundations, which lie on top of one another, are still visible today in some excavations. The cor-

---

[8]Immanuel Velikovsky, *Worlds in Collision* (New York: Macmillan Co., 1950).
[9]*Ibid.*, p. 312.
[10]*Ibid.*, p. 113.
[11]*Ibid.*, p. 319.

rections in direction of ruined foundation are silent witness today to the changes in the position of sunrise in ages past.

Velikovsky also adduces the evidence of the calendar changes which have become necessary in the course of time in order to account for changes in the solar system. Both the solar and the lunar calendars have had to be modified within historical times and Velikovsky discusses the ancient 360-day year, the ten-day week and the ten-month year,[12] putting forward the view that these changes can be accounted for on the assumption that the geographical poles of the earth have been repeatedly displaced (if not reversed) by encounters with celestial bodies. The fact that certain rocks show a reversed magnetism to that expected on the basis of the present magnetic poles, bears this out.[13] As candidates for the celestial bodies causing the changes, Mars and Venus are cited, and historical evidence is produced which validates this.

The water clock of Amenhotep III has long been an archaeological enigma. Velikovsky shows how its figures fit in with the theory of a changed earth's axis accompanied by altered climatic and seasonal conditions.[14]

The sudden extermination of the mammoth in Siberia has long been enigmatical and the subject of scientific discussion. Velikovsky explains this phenomenon on the same basis as above. Northeastern Siberia, the former home of the mammoth whose frozen remains have been found in such large numbers, was in historical times an area possessing a warm, temperate climate. By a near encounter with a celestial body, which resulted in the tilting of the earth's axis, the warm temperate climate of the land of the mammoth was suddenly and catastrophically changed to that of an arctic region, killing its animal population instantly by the sudden drop in temperature. For the tilt of the axis made this formerly temperate land an arctic area instantly. The sudden change in climatic conditions will probably have produced arctic

[12]*Ibid.*, pp. 321, 344-45.
[13]*Ibid.*, p. 307. See also *Science News Letter* (Feb. 5, 1966), p. 83, and *Science Journal* (Sept. 1967), Vol. III, No. 9, p. 56.
[14]Velikovsky, *ibid.*, p. 324.

storms and drops in temperature unknown today. As is well known, the mammoths must have been frozen catastrophically to have been preserved as fresh as they are today. If such a large body as that of a mammoth is killed and kept at, for example, —10° C., it would putrify inwardly, due to the insulating properties of the flesh and the large bulk, so that temperature drops of about one hundred degrees must have occurred to produce effective preservation such as is seen in the bodies today.[15] Some of the mammoths contain in their stomachs the undigested remains of flowers and herbs, showing how catastrophic the freezing must have been.

There is, according to Velikovsky, further evidence from the Arctic to this sudden and catastrophic change of climate. At Ipiutak, on Point Hope on the Bering Strait in Alaska, an ancient city has been excavated showing an advanced Japanese-type culture without any traces of civilization typical of the Arctic. Its tombs and houses show no signs of life characteristic of Eskimo or Arctic culture.[16] The climate at the time the town flourished (at least some twenty centuries ago) was apparently temperate. Velikovsky reasons that glaciation in this region, too, came suddenly and was due to changes in the axis of rotation of the earth following a near encounter with Mars or Venus. Thus the changes in areas of glaciation producing differing areas of Arctic and Antarctic icecap coverage, are, according to Velikovsky, due to sudden changes in the earth's axis of rotation. Areas possessing mild or warm climates were changed overnight into frigid arctic areas.

The axis changes are thought by Velikovsky to have been accompanied by perturbations in the moon's orbit as well as in the orbits of Mars and Venus. The surface of the moon bears today the marks of these catastrophes, unmitigated by weathering such as an atmosphere would produce. Axis and orbit perturbations of this type would, in the case of the earth, also account for the ancient nine-day week and 360-day year. The change from one axis and orbit to another would

[15]*Ibid.*, pp. 326-27. See also *Science* (Aug. 10, 1962), p. 449; (1961), CXXXIII, 729.
[16]Velikovsky, *ibid.*, p. 327.

be accompanied by the portents in the sky of which the ancients report so much and of which we in our generation see so little.

One other interesting point emerges from Velikovsky's researches into ancient history. The Chaldeans apparently knew that "the moon's light is reflected and her eclipses are due to the shadow of the earth. . . ." This implies that they knew the earth is a sphere in space, a fact also known to a number of Greek philosophers.[17] Even the Romans knew this. Pliny, for example, wrote: "Human beings are distributed all around the earth and stand with their feet pointing towards each other. . . . Another marvel, that the earth herself hangs suspended and does not fall and carry us with it."[18] The chaos among the planets, with its consequences for the earth, may explain the preoccupation of the ancients with the portents of heaven and astrology.[19]

In summary, Velikovsky believes that he has good evidence for two series of cosmic catastrophes involving the earth and explaining much which took place in historical times thirty-four and twenty-six centuries ago. The long day of Joshua[20] and the retrograde movement by ten degrees of Ahaz' sundial[21] in the time of King Hezekiah are therefore regarded not

---

[17]*Ibid.*, p. 271. Cf. Aristarchus of Samos, who knew that the earth revolves with other planets round the sun.

[18]*Ibid.*, p. 272. Cf. Pliny, *Natural History*, ii, 45.

[19]C. S. Lewis comments on the modern myth that the ancients thought that the earth was flat in the following terms: "It would be an error to reply that our ancestors were ignorant and therefore entertained pleasing illusions about nature which the progress of science has since dispelled. For centuries, during which all men believed, the nightmare size and emptiness of the universe was already known. You will read in some books that the men of the Middle Ages thought the earth was flat and the stars near, *but that is a lie.* Ptolemy has told them that the earth was a mathematical point without size in relation to the distance of the fixed stars—a distance which one mediaeval popular text estimates as a hundred and seventeen million miles. And in times yet earlier, even from the beginnings, men must have got the same sense of hostile immensity from a more obvious source." C. S. Lewis, *The Problem of Pain*, (New York: Macmillan Co., 1948), pp. 3-4. There may be thus little reason to suppose that Moses' and the prophets' ideas on the universe were so very "pre-scientific"—as many scientists, not brought up in the classics, fondly imagine.

[20] Joshua 10.

[21]II Kings 20:9-11.

as tales for the credulous but as statements of fact which would account for much not accounted for by today's fashionable uniformitarianism. Velikovsky cites evidence from peoples all over the world, from the South Sea islanders to the American Indians, from the Incas to the Maoris showing that these celestial catastrophes did actually occur within historical times, were recorded by many widely separated races and were accompanied by terrestrial consequences involving changes in climate (glaciation), calendar and season.

Thus it is possible, with all these changes (which have obviously been of a pretty catastrophic nature), that C^{14} synthesis may not have always remained constant through the ages. It may have been carried on at a much lower rate than at present, which, in turn, would lead to life residues containing carbon appearing to be much older than they really are. So that C^{14} dating is, in a way, dependent upon the validity of uniformitarianism, which has by no means been proved.

Changes in Earth's Cosmic Irradiation. There is a further possibility by which the cosmic irradiation of the earth may have been drastically altered in the course of history, thus modifying C^{14} synthesis and changing C^{14} apparent dates. This possibility is perhaps best set forth in the words of a recent article appearing in *The New Scientist:*

> Most geophysicists now accept that the earth's magnetism has switched itself round approximately every million years. . . . Presumably during these periods the earth's Van Allen belts of trapped energetic particles ceased to exist and the intensity of cosmic rays reaching the earth was stepped up. . . . It is nevertheless conceivable that the faunal extinction [in some geologic formations] and the magnetic reversal are only indirectly related.[22]

The article describes an effort to relate the extinction of certain species in fossil history with increased ionizing radiation. What interests us here is, of course, the fact that if radiation and therefore C^{14} synthesis can be stepped up by varia-

[22]Cf. N. D. Opdyke, article in *The New Scientist* (June 8, 1967), p. 601.

tions or reduction in the earth's magnetism, presumably reductions in cosmic radiation could be effected by the same mechanism. This would render C^{14} dating a good deal more relative than is thought at present.

INDEX FOSSILS

The last important method used for determining the age of geological formations, which we will consider briefly, is very important indeed. It is known as the index-fossil method and is dependent on the following principles:

OLDEST FORMATIONS CONTAIN SIMPLEST FORMS OF LIFE

According to evolutionary doctrine the oldest geological formations contain *only* the simplest forms of life. The more complex forms of life were, according to theory, not yet developed at the time the older formations were laid down. If, therefore, a formation contains trilobites, for example, from this one fact alone it is deduced that the formation belongs to the Paleozoic age. Certain types of fossils are thus indicative of certain ages, so that wherever these fossils appear, according to theory, the age of the formation may be diagnosed with certainty. Thus the trilobites *prove* the formation to be Paleozoic.

EVOLUTION USED TO PROVE VALIDITY OF EVOLUTION

The question we must ask is: Is this type of logic allowable? For, looked at very closely, by using this logic one is applying the theory of evolution to prove the correctness of evolution. For we are *assuming that the oldest formations contain only the most primitive and least complex organisms, which is the basic assumption of Darwinism.* This means that Darwinists assume that at biogenesis only primitive simplicity will have obtained, which is then reflected in the simplicity of formations or the fossils contained in them, which were laid down at the time of biogenesis. The later blossoming out of simplicity into complexity will have been shown by the increasing complexity of the fossil content of increasingly later formations. If now we assume that only simple organisms will occur in old formations, we are assuming the basic premise of Darwinism to be correct. To use, therefore, for dating purposes, the assumption that only simple organisms will be present in old formations is to thoroughly beg the whole question. It is arguing in a circle. If one remembers that the creationist believes that at biogenesis the whole range of organisms from the simplest to the most complex was formed at once, one can see more clearly the whole basic assumption of Darwinism as it differs from the older views. For Darwinism assumes only simplicity at biogenesis and therefore simplicity in the older formations, whereas creationism would lead us to expect the whole spectrum of simplicity to complexity from the very start. Thus the index-fossil method of dating is absolutely and squarely based on the Darwinistic concept of simple biogenesis.

Yet this index-fossil method of dating is perhaps one of the most important of modern geology. So firmly does the modern geologist believe in evolution up from simple organisms to complex ones over huge time spans, that he is perfectly willing to use the theory of evolution to prove the theory of evolution, and so effectively to beg the whole question.

Other scientists have, of course, recognized this rather hair-raising logic, which is at the base of geological and biological thinking today. R. S. Rastall of the Department of Economic Geology at Cambridge University, writes that one cannot deny that from the strictly philosophical standpoint the geologists are arguing in the circle pointed out above. For, by studying a series of fossil contents within a formation one has determined their succession in time. Whereupon one then calmly determines the succession in time of the formations by means of their fossil contents.[23]

The geological formations in which the fossils are found are nearly always those which have been laid down by water (sedimentary). These sedimentary rocks lie on crystalline

[23]R. H. Rastall, "Geology," *Encyclopaedia Britannica* (1956), X, 168.

rocks which were probably formed much earlier than the sedimentary ones. According to evolutionary theory, one would therefore expect that the sedimentary formations lying directly on the crystalline ones would be the oldest. If this is so those sedimentary rocks lying directly on the crystalline base should contain only the most primitive forms of life, if evolutionary theory is correct. To be more specific: the Cambrian and Precambrian formations should always lie nearest the crystalline formations in areas which, as far as one can see, have not been greatly disturbed.

PRACTICE DOES NOT PROVE THEORY

But, in practice, this is not found to be the case, for formations of all "ages" are found to lie directly on the crystalline rocks. E. M. Spieker wonders how many geologists have considered the fact that not only Cambrian formations but formations of all ages are found lying directly on the crystalline complex.[24]

In practice, it is difficult to find a formation sequence which actually fits evolutionary theory, that is, a sequence in which formations containing the remains of the most primitive forms of life lie directly on the crystalline base while the uppermost layers contain the highest organisms. W. E. Lammerts reminds us that the percentage of cases which correspond to the required sequence from simplest to most complex organisms is surprisingly small. In actual fact, formations containing highly developed forms of life often lie directly on the foundation granite. Lammerts points out that he has in his dossier over five hundred cases which show the reversed sequence, that is, simpler forms lying on top of complex forms.[25]

[24]E. M. Spieker, *Mountain Building Chronology and Nature of Geologic Time Scale*, p. 1805, as cited by Henry M. Morris, *The Twilight of Evolution* (Nutley, N.J.: Presbyterian & Reformed Publishing Co., 1964), p. 53.
[25]W. E. Lammerts, *Growing Doubts: Is Evolutionary Theory Valid?* p. 4 as cited by Morris, *ibid.*, p. 54.

IMPOSSIBLE TO DISPROVE

One of the strongest aspects of the index-fossil theory lies in the impossibility of disproving it. Even in the cases where the sequence of formations does not correspond to evolutionary theory, there is in the method a built-in possibility which allows corrections of any kind deemed necessary. The fossils present in any formation (no matter what its position with respect to the crystalline base or anything else) alone determine the geological age of formation. This means then, that according to present theory, a formation lying undisturbed as far as we can see on the basic crystalline rocks does not need to be geologically old. If it contains trilobites it is old and if it contains mammals it is young. Neither the physical form of the formation nor its sequential position with respect to other formations is reckoned as being important. Evolutionary doctrine demands that primitive organisms be found in early sedimentary rocks, so that rocks containing primitive organisms must be old. It is as simple as that.

But what if the biogenesis of complex organisms took place before the simple ones, what if simplicity happened to be secondary and degenerative? Or what if, as the creationists maintain, simple and complex organisms were generated contemporaneously? Such possibilities would throw modern theoretical geology into complete chaos, for the simple reason that it is founded on evolutionary doctrine. Almost anything is to be preferred to a reversion to creationism, and thus evolutionary theory is used to prove the truth and infallibility of evolutionary theory! For example, O. D. von Engeln and Kenneth E. Kaster point out that the geologist uses his evolutionary knowledge, as paleontology discloses it, in order to identify formations arising in former ages and to classify them.[26]

We may sum up by saying that evolutionary doctrine determines the age of many geological formations.

[26]O. D. von Engeln and Kenneth E. Kaster, *Geology* (New York: McGraw-Hill, 1952), p. 417. Cf. Morris, *ibid.*, p. 51.

This will conclude our short survey of dating methods. Other methods are used which we cannot go into here. But no survey would be complete without citing a few practical results issuing from these theories and techniques.

Coelacanthus fossils found before 1953 would have "proved" a formation to have been very old—this kind of organism was "known" to have died out in the quite distant past. However, since the recent finds of living *coelacanthus,* the "age" of any *coelacanthus* remains might vary anything from "ancient" to very "modern" indeed. Who could determine whether the remains came from a really ancient individual or a modern one?

The same applies to the problem of the Piltdown man. One could have dated the formation in which this find was made as very old—based on the true fossil human skull. But the modern ape's jawbone found with the skull could have been used to determine the date as very recent. And here we will review the whole question of the Piltdown hoax with reference to the difficulties of dating ancient finds.

THE PILTDOWN MAN

Some fifty years ago two well-known British geologists were working in a quarry in Southern England. One of them, Dr. Charles Dawson, discovered at Piltdown a human skull in association with a jawbone which showed apelike properties. One incisor, which belonged to the jaw, was worn flat and resembled a human tooth.

A little later Professor Sir Arthur Smith-Woodward made a second find of a human skull and a tooth in the same area. The skull was remarkably thick but otherwise definitely human. After the second find Professor Sir Arthur was convinced that the skull and the jawbone belonged together and that he had found an important missing link in the evolution of man from lower ancestors. One must admit that after the first find many anthropologists were still skeptical. But the second find evaporated the doubt from most of their minds.

The new discovery received the name of *Eoanthropus daw-soni* and there have been many publications on this find. It has been estimated that some five hundred publications have appeared on this subject.

Professor von Huene estimated the importance of this find very conservatively:

> I do not wish to discuss here a *relatively ancient* much talked of find at Piltdown in Southern England. Its parts are rather puzzling and its nature therefore not yet clear. But recently Oakley and Hoskins (1950) have determined its age to be that of *recent quaternary* (Riss-Würm Interglacial). Until then (1950) the age had been given as *old quaternary*—i.e., about 0.8 million years.[27]

Drs. J. S. Steiner, K. P. Oakley and Professor Le Gros Clark published a joint paper on *Eoanthropus* in 1953 from the laboratories of the Department of Anatomy of the University of Oxford and the British Museum, London.

The upshot of this important paper is as follows: Either someone had knowingly falsified the Piltdown findings or played a practical joke. Who played the joke or did the falsifying has never been discovered, but today it is absolutely certain that either one or the other account for the Piltdown find. The skull of the first find is a fossil of modern man from the Upper Pleistocene. The proof of this lies in the fluorine content of the skull. The nitrogen content is low, which also shows the skull to be truly fossilized. But the jawbone shows the nitrogen and fluorine contents of a modern ape jawbone. The iron and chromium contents prove that the jawbone had been stained with potassium bichromate and iron salts in order to make it look old.

The teeth had been filed down with carborundum so as to make the ape's teeth about as flat as human teeth. X-ray photos show the small scratches made by the carborundum

[27]von. Huene, *Die Erschaffung des Menschen* ("The Creation of Man") (Frankfurt/Main: Anker Verlag, n.d.), p. 23.

quite clearly. Even the flint "tools" discovered associated with the skull are a hoax. In order to make them look old they too had been treated with iron salts and bichromate. When the surface was scratched off, these "tools" looked just like the other flints lying around the site. The scientific reports on the Piltdown hoax may be read in *Nature*.[28] They were the scientific sensation of the year and are very sobering.

Though the instigator of the hoax has never been discovered, it does strike one as remarkable that Professor Smith-Woodward allowed very few other scientists to study the original skull or even to handle it. Plaster casts were always made and the studies carried out with their aid. Plaster casts, however, do not give the very fine details needed for study, nor can one determine with their help whether a find really is a fossil or not. Even more important, no one can analyze a skull chemically with only a plaster cast to work with!

Under no circumstances do we wish to create the impression that all the human fossil discoveries have been of the caliber of the Piltdown hoax. They have not. The point we wish to emphasize here is that it is easy, even today, to make huge errors where datings of ancient specimens are concerned, especially if one works too much on a theoretical background.

DR. S. B. LEAKEY

No description of fossil man would be complete today without mentioning Dr. S. B. Leakey's work in East Africa on this subject.[29] Dr. Leakey has carried out extensive excavations in the Olduvai Gorge in Tanzania. He gave a report on his work at a symposium in Chicago at the beginning of 1965. He maintains that he has discovered various species of man (*Zinjanthropus, Homo habilis,* LLK-skull, etc.) which all lived contemporaneously and in competition with one another. Dr. Leakey thinks that the evolution of man from

---

[28]*Nature* (Nov. 28, 1953) p. 981; (Dec. 12, 1953), p. 1110; (July 10, 1954), p. 60; (April 2, 1955), p. 569.
[29]Cf. *Science News Letter* (April 17, 1965), p. 243.

animal ancestors was not "orderly" as is generally thought to be the case in animal evolution. He places the age of the LLK skull at some 600,000 years and is of the opinion that it represents one of man's "cousins."

Heavy fire was directed against Dr. Leakey's theories by his colleagues while he was in Chicago, which goes to show how difficult it is to interpret fossil finds of this type. The existence of the LLK skull is one matter but its interpretation entirely another.

Recently Leakey's work has been followed up by the Peabody Museum of Yale University. Professor Simon has recovered a small skull from the Fayum desert region of Egypt, which is thought to be some eight to ten million years older than any previously uncovered specimen. It is well preserved and has been named Aegyptopithecus. The animal was about the size of a small monkey and reminiscent of the early lemurs. The brain case, relative to face size, is smaller than that in any subsequent ape or hominid. Professor Simons maintains that it is a "major connecting link" in the evolution of primates. It is thought to be the only Old World primate skull known from the millions of years separating the Eocene and Miocene epochs.[30]

While we are considering ancient races of man it should be pointed out that the Cro-Magnon race is represented by complete skeletons which have been found in Aurignacian layers.[31] The people of this race averaged six feet in height and their cranial capacity was greater than that of modern man. Yet their skeletons have been found in caves on Mount Carmel along with the bones of Neanderthal man, which has been considered primitive. Some of the Mount Carmel skeletons were intermediate, suggesting intermarriage between the two types and, of course, if true, establishing the unity of species of the two groups.

[30]Elwyn L. Simons, review in *Science News* (Nov. 25, 1967) XCII, 514.
[31]D. de Sonneville-Bordes, "Upper Paleolithic Cultures," *Science* (Oct. 18, 1963), CXLII, 355.

It is also interesting to know that Dr. Dubois, the discover-
er of Pithecanthropus erectus at Wadjak in Java, discovered
two other human skulls at the same level as Pithecanthropus.[32] But he kept these two other skulls, which resemble
those of the modern Australian black aboriginal, securely
locked up for twenty years and wrote nothing about them.
Knowledge of the existence of these two modern skulls found
at the same level as Pithecanthropus erectus, would certainly
have modified a number of theories about the evolutionary
significance of Pithecanthropus.

DINOSAUR AND MAN TRACKS IN A RIVERBED

At the end of the Mesozoic era in the Cretaceous (i.e.,
about 140 million years ago according to geological dating
today) we would scarcely expect to find modern human
traces. And yet there is convincing evidence of modern man
in Cretaceous formations.

Fine clear tracks of dinosaurs, brontosaurs and also probably of tyrannosaurs have been found in the Paluxy Riverbed near Glen Rose, Texas,[33] which identify the formation
there as Cretaceous. It is difficult to believe that such beautifully preserved tracks (I have seen them myself) could be so
old, but the dating stands firm in geologists' eyes. In the
same riverbed, at the same depth, only a few yards from the
dinosaur tracks, unmistakable human tracks have also been
discovered[34] (see Fig. 6) by Dr. Roland T. Bird of the Department of Vertebrate Paleontology, The American Museum of Natural History.

On the subject of the dinosaur and man tracks in this
Cretaceous formation, the author carried on a lengthy correspondence with Dr. Clifford L. Burdick before taking a
journey to Glen Rose with Dr. Burdick to see the tracks *in
situ.* Dr. Burdick is a qualified and experienced geologist

[32]William Howells, *Mankind in the Making* (Garden City, N.Y.: Doubleday & Co., Inc., 1959), pp. 220 f., as cited by William J. Tinkle, *Heredity:
A Study in Science and the Bible* (Houston, Tex.: St. Thomas Press, 1967).
[33]Cf. Morris and Whitcomb, *op. cit.*, pp. 167, 174-75.
[34]Cf. Roland T. Bird, *Natural History* (May, 1939), pp. 225, 261, 302.
(See Appendix III).

who knows the Paluxy River site well. He wrote the author on July 21, 1965, as follows:

> Last March I was at the Paluxy River site of the tracks and Mr. McFall, who lives beside the river, showed me a large circular hole in the river bed where *he dug up both dinosaur and human tracks in a circular block of limestone about four feet in circumference and the thickness of the stratum about 10 inches.* . . . Upstream about 300 yards, appears a three-toed dinosaur track in the same formation. Then downstream about half a mile are many dinosaur tracks, some of them four-toed belonging to the brontosaurus. In fact, come to think of it, there are good three-toed dinosaur tracks on the ground or in the stream bed.[35]

How may we interpret such facts? It would seem to be clear that a human being made the tracks at about the same time as the dinosaur. Even Dr. Roland T. Bird admits that the tracks are perfect human ones.[36] At least we might interpret the tracks in this way, if theories did not stand in the way, producing mental blocks.

Let us consider the situation. If the dinosaur is in reality 140 million or so years old (the formation in which the footprints are found is doubtless Cretaceous) then the human who made the footprints in the same formation must be some 140 million years old too. Which is, according to evolutionary doctrine, frankly absurd. If this one observation were true, the whole structure of Darwinism, and a good deal of modern geological theory too, would fall to pieces. For Darwinistic theory could not possibly admit a human to have lived contemporaneously with a dinosaur! Man could never be 140 million years old. Even his supposed primate ancestors had scarcely started to evolve then! But if man appeared only in recent geological times, then the dinosaur must have

---

[35]Figures 6 to 10 were photographed by Dr. Burdick, whom the author thanks for permission to reproduce them herewith, and also for permission to quote from his letter. Cf. also Appendix III.

[36]Bird, *op. cit.*, p. 255.

lived in recent geological times too, which Darwinism again cannot permit.

It is quite interesting to see what is done in scientific circles with such awkward observations as contemporaneous dinosaur and man tracks. First of all *both kinds of tracks were duly reported,* but it was suggested by Dr. Bird, who first found them, that either the man tracks or the dinosaur tracks must have been falsified, because according to theory, the two could not exist together! It became clear that if the man tracks were falsifications, then there was no reason at all why the dinosaur tracks should not be falsifications too. Then one begins to doubt all evidence.

Dr. Bird reports as follows:

> For a moment I had them [the stones] to myself,—the strangest things of their kind I had ever seen. On the surface of each was splayed the near-likeness of a human foot, *perfect in every detail.* But each imprint was 15 inches long. . . . *When I heard there were dinosaur tracks in exactly the same type of stone from apparently an identical stratographic level, my thoroughly revived curiosity could scarcely be contained. Even the possibility of such an association seemed incredible.* . . . Both types came from Glen Rose.[37]

Dr. Bird reproduces a photograph of the man tracks in his article mentioned. But except for saying that they were probably falsified, for which assumption there is not the slightest evidence, the matter is left unsolved. The main interest is concentrated on the brontosaur tracks and in later articles on these tracks, the man tracks are not mentioned again. They are relegated to the scientific limbo reserved for facts which fit no current theories. So what could one do with them? Forget them! Almost everyone is inclined to do the same under similar circumstances. We repress unpleasant thoughts or problems, and even scientists are only human in this respect.

[37]*Ibid.*, pp. 255-56.

Forty years ago, when Dr. Fleming discovered penicillin, he was quite unable to interest scientists in his find or show them the possibilities of the subject. The administrations of learned societies who decide where and how much grant money should be given, certainly gave him, the unknown Dr. Fleming, no money for such harebrained ideas. The chemotherapy of those days taught that systemic treatment with chemical agents could not influence infectious diseases. That was the doctrine taught in all the medical schools at that time and no one had ever proved it to be wrong. So why did Dr. Fleming have the temerity to fly in the face of the established opinion of the great men? Therefore penicillin was not developed and the substance not isolated, though the principle of it had already been proved. The idea of penicillin just did not catch on, for an innovation of this type was not ripe for the scientific atmosphere. As a result, the whole idea of penicillin was laid to rest for ten years until Professor Domagk turned all established opinion on its head by showing that systemic infections could be treated by systemic chemotherapy by means of sulphonamides. But Domagk had a progressive and extremely wealthy firm behind him, which was prepared to believe results and experiments rather than opinions. Thus the old ideas of the medical schools of the pre-Domagk era were thrown overboard with the advent of the sulphonamides, which showed that systemic treatment of infectious diseases had become a reality.

But if sulphonamides worked systemically then why not penicillin? In this way the atmosphere was cleared for penicillin, which, under the pressure of war needs, was revived and soon became available for general use.

It is a fact, of course, that a good percentage of really new ideas are received in the same way. The real hindrance to a great deal of progress is prejudice based on old theory, which produces a kind of mental block. Once the superseded theories are removed, the green light to progress is given. A very famous man of science was once discussing with the author the sad passing of another famous man of science. He made a shocking remark to the effect that it was a good thing that old _____ had gone, for his ideas had hindered any progress in his area of science for long enough!

In just this same way present Darwinistic dogma may be hindering the finding of correct interpretations of the giant human tracks at Glen Rose.[35]

HUMAN TRACKS IN THE CARBONIFEROUS AND CRETACEOUS

According to theory, we would scarcely expect to find traces of man in the Carboniferous formations (310 million years old). We may be sure that the textbooks do not mention such finds either. For theory says that man is, at a maximum, a few million years old. But the fact remains that tracks, in all probability human, have been repeatedly found in Carboniferous formations.[38] We quote Albert C. Ingalls:

> On sites reaching from Virginia and Pennsylvania through Kentucky, Illinois, Missouri and westward toward the Rocky Mountains, prints similar to those above [referring to several accompanying photos] and from five to ten inches long have been found on the surface of exposed rock, and more keep turning up as the years go by.[39]

This type of find of human traces, existing in what are thought to be formations of the very earliest ages, is continually turning up. The recognition of the genuineness of a single one of these finds would, of course, put the whole theory of evolution into confusion. Recognition is, according to evolutionary theory today, simply inconceivable. But it seems just as inconceivable to ordinary human thought that tracks could have been so perfectly preserved during over 300 million years. The tracks are so beautifully preserved that we can scarcely conceive of their being as old as the geologists maintain they are. So one is just silent about the whole matter, or denies the genuineness of these prints.

[35]Appendix III.
[38]See Appendix III.
[39]Cf. Appendix V.

We will cite Ingalls[40] again, since these facts are obviously so important:

> If man, or even his ape ancestor, or even the ape an-
> cestor's early mammal ancestor, existed as far back as in
> the carboniferous period in any shape, then the whole
> science of geology is so completely wrong that all geol-
> ogists will resign their jobs and take up truck driving.
> Hence, for the present at least, science rejects the attrac-
> tive explanation that man made these mysterious prints
> in the mud of the carboniferous period with his feet.[41]

We must take these words of Ingalls very seriously. As he says, the consequences of accepting one of these finds as gen-uine would turn modern geology, biology and anthropology upside down. And with the disappearance of Darwinian and evolutionary doctrine, one of the main weapons of the athe-ists in the East and the West against Christians and other theists would disappear. But the scientific "atmosphere" today prevents and will prevent the disappearance of such weapons.

Although the dinosaur and human tracks were found in the same riverbed at Glen Rose and quite near to one another in the same formation, Dr. Bird declares that the dinosaur tracks are genuine but that the human tracks are not be-cause "no man had ever existed in the age of reptiles."[42] Thus for the sake of the fact that evolutionary theory does not allow man tracks to have been made contemporaneously with the dinosaur tracks, the perfect man tracks found with the dinosaur tracks (equally perfect) are suppressed. In fact, Dr. Bird does not mention the man tracks again, although he often described the brontosaur tracks.[43]

The human tracks of Glen Rose, in the cretaceous forma-tions there exposed, are those of a giant human (see Fig. 9)

[40]Albert C. Ingalls, "The Carboniferous Mystery," *Scientific American* (Jan., 1940), CLXII, 14.
[41]*Ibid.*, cf. Appendix IV.
[42]Bird, *op. cit.*, p. 257.
[43]Cf. Bird, *National Geographic* (May, 1954), CV, 707-22.

In Arizona, California and New Mexico similar giant tracks have been found. These giants possessed five toes per foot, in contradistinction to the giants mentioned in II Samuel 21:20, who possessed six toes per foot and six fingers per hand. Morris and Whitcomb[44] reproduce some fine photographs of the Glen Rose footprints taken by Dr. Burdick (see Fig. 10). The finds remind us of the text in Genesis 6:4, telling us that "there were giants in the earth in those days."

The formations in which these finds occur are without doubt Cretaceous. The author visited this area with Dr. Burdick and convinced himself of the above facts. The remains of the excavations which Dr. Bird made are still to be seen, together with the holes he left behind after removing his track finds. The facts speak for the contemporaneous existence of giant humans, who went barefooted, and of dinosaurs, whereas theory demands that the dinosaurs lived up to 139 million years before the first man appeared about a million years ago. The existence of the giant human tracks gives signal confirmation of the scriptural report that giant humans did exist in early times.

One further fact deserves mention here. A number of modern languages possess words for huge and terrible animals called dragons which do not exist today. Why should various peoples possess vocabularies for an animal which never existed? For this class of being surely falls into a different category than that of hobgoblins and gnomes! Might it be that the dinosaur represents the dragon of our fairy tales and myths of old? It looks as if their often horrible appearance might qualify them somewhat for the descriptions given. And what if early man did hunt dragons as the stories tell us? Of course, this is all absolute nonsense in the eyes of modern geological theory. But surely other and perhaps better ideas have been rejected as consummate pipe dreaming by scientific leaders before now (e.g., antibiotics). And the

[44]Morris and Whitcomb, *op. cit.*, pp. 167, 174-75.

experts certainly thought they knew what they were talking about at the time; they represented the most advanced knowledge of their era. It is perhaps safer to keep an open mind for any "nonsense" of this sort. It is often quite productive, at least more productive than a hermetically sealed mind. It is better to keep an unsolved fact squarely in view all the time than to bury or repress it. Did not C. S. Lewis say the following with respect to the very human habit of being silent about and hiding unpleasant facts which fit into none of our theories: "There is always hope if we keep an unsolved problem fairly in view; there's none if we pretend it's not there."[45]

THE PROBLEM OF INTERMEDIATE STAGES

This brings us to a further vital matter connected with geology and fossils. It is that of missing links and intermediate stages in plant and animal organisms.

The geological formations are full of plants and animals which are no longer extant today. Many animals and plants were larger in their fossil forms than those we know today. Even today's polar and arctic regions showed luxuriant subtropical growth at the time the fossil forms were laid down and this luxuriant plant life supported a correspondingly heavy animal population. Today the same areas are practically bare of vegetation and support a sparse animal life. Darwinistic theory demands that the present forms of life developed via the ancient forms, and that among these fossilized forms of life missing links joining the various evolutionary stages should be found.

One thing is clear. A huge variety of life, both animal and plant, has become extinct today. Evolutionary doctrine interprets this fact by saying that the lower varieties of living forms have given place to a higher development of life.

Could not this state of affairs be interpreted quite differently? The creation of each variety of life represents, so to say, a lowering of entropy (cf. chap. 2). The dying out of various

[45]C. S. Lewis, *Letters to Malcolm* (London: Geoffrey Bles, 1964), p. 83.

kinds of life could be interpreted as a reduction of improbability or an "increase of entropy." The perishing of each variety could then be thought of as an "increase of entropy." Plants and animals could have been produced at original biogenesis in a profusion of varieties and forms, in other words, entropy was sharply and maximally reduced at the creation of life. C. S. Lewis in his Narnia series of books intended for children (but equally useful and interesting to grown-up children) brings out exquisitely the thought of the exuberance of the pristine creative period during which Aslan the Great Lion sang Narnia into existence. This exuberance of created forms was then followed by a drought in creativity.[46] Thus immediately after biogenesis, there is a beginning of disorganization, and increase in entropy, and one species after another commences to die out.

Would it not be possible to interpret the finds which are regarded as representing missing links rather as species which have died out in the general increase in entropy? At the beginning the "spectrum" of varieties and species was much larger than today, so that there was a more complete "assortment" of organisms from amoeba to man. The dying out of some of these species would cause "gaps" in this "assortment" or "spectrum" of organisms. Perhaps the gap between *homo sapiens* and the great apes was bridged originally by many species forming a graded series between them. These intermediate species, if found as fossils, would be interpreted by Darwinists today as "missing links" through which man's ancestry would be supposed to have passed. Creationists would, on the other hand, interpret these same fossils as the perishing of some "bridges" in a once much fuller spectrum of living organisms which had arisen from an exuberance of creative activity. And in view of the known fuller spectrum of organisms, both plant and animal, in the past compared to the present, the creationist would be well within the extant evidence.

[46]Lewis, *The Magician's Nephew, The Bodley Head* (London: Geoffrey Bles, 1963), pp. 102-14.

This process of weeding out species is still going on today. The whooping cranes are almost at the point of extinction. Elephants and some other forms of big game, certain types of whales, the dodo, the kiwi, the wombat and many others are either extinct or are on the list of organisms threatened with extinction. Their actual extinction will leave still wider gaps between living genera. It is obvious that this same process has occurred in the past, especially if the present is the key to the understanding of the past! Might not the same process account for *Notharctus, Proconsul* (Leakey), *Australopithicus, Giganthropus, Plesianthropus, Meganthropus, Pithecanthropus, Aegyptopithecus* and even *Homo neandertalensis?* They do not need to be derived genetically one from the other. The more complex spectrum of living species at biogenesis, and the gradual increase of entropy resulting in their gradual but regular dying out, would account for these series perfectly well without invoking evolutionary doctrine, as is commonly done. All these finds would then merely confirm well-known natural laws.

There are also grave difficulties in the more general application of the idea of intermediate forms. It is often impossible to account for a complex organ and its derivation. It is only understandable in its fully developed form. The halfway stages in its evolution would serve no purpose, being completely useless. As an example take the complex structure possessed by the female whale for suckling its young under the water without drowning the suckling. No halfway stage of development from an ordinary nipple to that of the fully developed whale nipple, adapted for underwater feeding, is conceivable. Either it was completely developed and functional, or it was not. To expect such a system to arise gradually by chance mutations upward is to condemn all suckling whales during the development period of thousands of years to a watery grave by certain drowning. *To deny planning when studying such a system is to strain credulity more than to ask one to believe in an intelligent nipple de-*

signer, who incidentally must have understood hydraulics rather well (see pp. 207-208) .

The same applies, of course, to many other intermediate organs and states. But lack of space forbids us to go into further details here. The principle remains the same: in a highly developed complex organ intermediate stages must of necessity have often been less than functional and therefore probably a hindrance rather than a help in natural selection.

DATING METHODS AND AGE, THEIR RELATIONSHIP TO CREATION

To close the section we propose to discuss one or two problems having a fundamental relationship to time measurement, dating methods and age.

All science, as it stands today, teaches us that the world and the cosmos are millions of years old. This conclusion is based upon time measurements made mostly during the last few hundred years, a relatively short span, geologically speaking. By means of these observations, one is willing to extrapolate back millions of years. There is sense in this, though we must remember that the slightest mistake in the short time we have had at our disposal to make our observations will be vastly magnified by the time our back extrapolation reaches millions of years. If one takes aim with a rifle at a target which is fifty yards away, the error, if one misses, is going to be smaller than if the target is two miles away. Obviously, the farther away the target, the greater the margin of error. Which means that if one makes observations and calculations over ten years and extrapolates back for millions of years, the margin of error may be considerable.

Added to these margins of error are the difficulties about the nature of time itself. We are carefully measuring something (time) which is by no means fully understood. What is time? Without the aid of matter one could not measure it at all. It is relatively well known today that, theoretically, if I enter a rocket and travel for ten years in space at the speed of light and then return to the earth I shall be ten years older. But my wife, who remained behind on earth during my absence, will be twenty-four years older. If I undertake the same journey into space at the speed of light but lengthen my stay in space to twenty years and then return, the world back home on earth has become 270 years older, whereas I am only twenty years older. If I prolong my space travel at the speed of light for forty years and return to earth, I find that my wife had died some 36,000 years ago. And if I finally succeeded in traveling sixty years in space at the speed of light, on my return the earth would be scarcely recognizable, for it would have become some five million years older while I was aging to the extent of sixty years.[47]

Discussion of these findings is continuing and there are some scientists who do not agree with Dr. von Hoerner's results. But those who propose these views have very good grounds for doing so, before risking their reputation as scientists. The calculation shows how new knowledge gained in the last few decades can change ideas involving millions of years, so that sixty years can be stretched into millions of years, and millennia compressed into decades, just by traveling relatively to the earth at the speed of light. This represents new knowledge gained from Einstein's relativity theory. What additional new knowledge might do with respect to the millions of years which science reckons as the ages through which this earth and cosmos have passed! Perhaps the evolutionary tree of millions of years (as one reckons today) has been actually passed through in a few days or seconds. *This would mean, in the last analysis, that the whole process of evolution, today thought to be slow, might have been passed through under creative conditions in a flash of time, and would, if we could view the process from outside, look like a lightning act of creation. Perhaps evolution and creation mechanisms could at some future date, when more is understood about the nature of time, be reconciled on this basis of changing time values, so that we could forget for the time being all about dating methods valid today.* The knowl-

[47]Cf. Sebastian von Hoerner, *Science* (July 6, 1962), p. 18.

edge we need concerns the essential nature of our fourth dimension, which we call time.

However, even if time scales were flexible (there is apparently no theoretical reason why they should not be so), this would still not affect the basic thermodynamic energy considerations we have discussed and which must have been observed for archebiopoiesis to have occurred. It would still be necessary to supply energy to a system to reduce entropy so as to attain molecules of a given degree of complexity. So that from the point of view of energy relationships pure and simple, it would have been no "harder" for the agency (whatever it was) behind archebiopoiesis (or creation, whichever way we prefer to look at the problem) to have "created" in a flash of time or over a period of millions of years. The total creative "energy" required in both cases would be identical. So that the postulation of huge time spans by Darwinists to allow for the "creative" activity of chance and natural selection to get to work, does not really help to solve the problem in the least. The postulation of the "compression" in time of all upward organization of matter to aggregates capable of bearing life likewise does not introduce in principle any new difficulties from an energetic point of view. For it is not time itself which is our problem in connection with origins, but rather the infinitely more important matter of the source of the "planning energy" behind archebiopoiesis and order in our universe. This means that the mechanism of evolution postulated by Darwinians cannot really be influenced by the allowing of huge time spans, which they regard as the *conditio sine qua non* for their ideas.

It may be objected that if the energy for archebiopoiesis was supplied by the sun, longer time spans would allow more energy per unit time to be available from this source. This might be the case if any metabolic motor could be postulated to make available the sun's energy required, but which motor itself was not dependent for its origin on life. There being no such metabolic motor in sight, which is not dependent on previous life, we come to the conclusion that time increases would not place more sun energy at the disposal of archebiopoiesis. This means, then, that Darwinian evolutionary postulates are untenable whether it is supposed that they took place over millions of years or whether they occurred in a flash of creative activity during a time scale different from the present one to which we are accustomed. The postulated Darwinian schemes all founder on the available energy problem. The Christian, on the other hand, believes that the Creator supplied this creative energy working from a multidimensional system.

THE NATURE OF MATTER

Recent researches have shown the existence of a new type of matter, which is in a sense a "mirror image" of the matter we know in our cosmos. This "mirror image" matter would compare with our matter somewhat as a right-handed glove compares to a left-handed one. It is known as anti-matter. Some scientists are of the opinion that the huge explosion which took place in Siberia in 1908 was caused by anti-matter colliding with this planet. For when matter and anti-matter meet they annihilate one another with the liberation of energy. One of the scientists who has supported the view that the Siberian explosion was caused by anti-matter reaching the earth is Dr. Williard E. Libby, the Nobel Laureate, who developed the C^{14} dating method.[48]

If other worlds exist which consist of anti-matter rather than matter, then one or two important consequences arise. Some scientists believe that anti-matter and matter are formed together in equal quantities, both in the laboratory and in nature. Dr. Leon M. Lederman, Professor of Physics at Columbia University, writes: ". . . the Antiworld, which is supposed to be precisely identical to our world, not only has anti-particles instead of particles but is a mirror image of our world and *one in which the flow of time is also reversed.*"[49]

[48]Cf. *Nature* (1965), CCVI, 861; and *Science News Letter* (June 12, 1965), p. 382.
[49]*Science News Letter* (June 26, 1965), p. 402.

Presumably, therefore, in the antiworld the decrease of entropy with time would belong to the normal laws of thermodynamics there rather than the increase of the same which occurs here. There, with the passage of "time," molecules would presumably order themselves, and synthesis rather than decomposition would be the rule. And again, presumably, everything would get younger every day instead of older.[50] Such presumptive conditions in the world of anti-matter are, of course, not comprehensible in our world of matter. But this does not mean that they are impossible.

Where such a world of anti-matter could exist is not known. The search has been carried on so far in vain. But Dr. Lederman believes that originally just as much anti-matter as matter is likely to have been made. For in the laboratory, collisions between high energy particles always yield equal numbers of particles and anti-particles. Which all goes to show how careful one must be before becoming dogmatic about problems of time (and eternity)! There is still so much to learn that may reverse even the most up-to-date fundamental knowledge. And if matter and anti-matter are complex subjects, so are the problems of life and its genesis!

CREATION

At this point we must look briefly into another aspect of the problem of time. When the world as we know it came into being, laws other than those which govern it now, must have been in effect. Our present experience teaches us that entropy is always increasing under the present order of things.

[50]But see Fred Hoyle, *Galaxies, Nuclei and Quasars* (New York: Harper & Row, 1965), pp. 68-69, with regard to anti-matter and time: "There should be no difference between an anti-observer who reads the universe from future to past, and our ordinary procedure of reading it from past to future. This is because particles and antiparticles can be switched by switching the sense of time. . . . Yet, because electromagnetic processes do not switch, this cannot be the case. To our anti-observer there would still be an asymmetry of time—the asymmetry that allows us to break an egg very easily, but which does not permit even Humpty Dumpty or the king's men to put it together again. Anti-eggs would still be broken and would refuse to reassemble themselves, and they would do so in the same time sense as do the eggs of our familiar world."

But at creation even this fundamental law governing the increase of entropy must have been reversed. We measure the passage of time by making use of the running down of the clock or by applying the rate of radioactive decay to measurement. Both methods are coupled to entropy increase. But our ideas of entropy must be completely invalid during an act of creation. Let us take an example to visualize this state of affairs:

In the beginning God is reported as having taken the "dust of the earth" and as having formed Adam from it.[51] He then breathed the breath of life into him and Adam became a living soul. The Bible does not report Adam as having arisen as a newborn babe. According to the scriptural record, no parents were there to take care of him. So he must have been adult at his creation and have possessed immediately his five senses in full state of development so as to have been able to fend for himself from the start.

Let us now consider some consequences of the creative act. Adam is standing there in·all the beauty of new creation, straight from the Creator's hand. Shall we say, for the sake of argument, that he is just two breaths, or some five seconds old? His lungs have just filled themselves with the pure air of Eden. But how old does Adam look, judging his age by our time-measuring experience? He is adult, perhaps handsome, mature. It takes, according to our way of reckoning time, some twenty to thirty years to allow a man to come to maturity, and Adam is obviously a mature man. Accordingly, we would guess Adam's age to be some twenty to thirty years. But in reality, we know he is just two breaths, or about five seconds, old.

This example makes it clear that where creation is concerned the laws of thermodynamics, as we know them, are turned upside down. Here the laws governing time do not function either. Adam is just five seconds old and yet looks as though he were twenty to thirty years old. What is more,

[51]Gen. 2:7.

at every act of creation there must be the same illusion of age. Dr. Karl Barth, the famous Swiss theologian and founder of neo-orthodoxy, maintains a similar idea of creation in his well-known saying that when God created, he created with a past.[52] There must be this built-in illusion of the passage of time. This must be the case, for our concept of entropy—and thus of the passage of time—cannot be valid during any creative act. In a primitive sort of way, the same applies to any true synthetic act, even today. If, for instance, we measure time by the natural half life of a biologically active compound, then any synthetic act involving cancellation of the natural decay of biological activity would be in a way a reversal of "time" and decrease in entropy as far as that system is concerned.

This must also be the case with respect to the creation of the cosmos and the earth. Here too, an act of creation must bring with it an illusion of age and this illusion lies in the very nature of creation *ex nihilo*. That this illusion is a built-in one may be seen from the following example:

If a mixture of lead and uranium in an ore was created at the beginning, it would automatically give an illusion of age. For we know that certain isomers of lead arise as the end stage during the radioactive decay of uranium. By measuring the amount of lead in an uranium ore we can determine the ore's age. Since it takes X years to form so many milligrams of lead from a given amount of uranium, by measuring the amount of lead in the ore we can determine the ore's age, for this decay rate remains constant. But after an act of creation in which an ore is made containing, for example, five grams of lead and five grams of uranium, later calculations must go awry for the following reasons: the five grams of lead will automatically produce the illusion of having been *derived* from the uranium over millions of years. But it was actually not derived, but created *de novo*. In reality the mixture of lead and uranium has been created as such, but after

[52]Karl Barth, as cited by Richard Overman, *Evolution and the Christian Doctrine of Creation* (Philadelphia: Westminster Press, 1967), p. 281.

creation it cannot avoid producing the illusion that it is millions of years old.

Bernard Ramm in maintaining that God's creative act must have involved "time" and therefore "process" does not take sufficiently into consideration the relationship of time to matter as demanded by Einsteinian relativity. For creative acts involve reversal of entropy laws so interfering with our entire time concept. Indeed it is often difficult to follow Ramm's reasoning even on less abstruse matters, as, for example, when he stoutly defends the theory of organic evolution only to call it a "fallacy" later on in the same book.[53]

An act of creation lies so much outside our present-day knowledge that we do not really know how to calculate to take it truly into account, even though all physics demands an active creation to explain the very being and order of life, atoms and of the subatomic world of particles, waves and orbits. For this basic reason of an act of creation at the back of the cosmos, it is on principle impossible to arrive at an absolutely definitive and meaningful date for creation. Science demands an act of creation as an explanation of being, but this act of creation must produce an illusion of age and time. We must remember too, in addition to all this, that before matter and space existed, no time existed either. So, to be scientifically sound, we must be very cautious in matters concerning time in general and dating in particular.

The true situation is, in fact, the one which Sir James Jeans describes:

> As I see it, we are unlikely to reach any definite conclusions on these questions [determinism and causation] *until we have a better understanding of the true nature of time. The fundamental laws of nature, in so far as we are at present acquainted with them, give no reason why time should flow steadily on: they are equally prepared to consider the possibility of time standing still or flowing backwards. The steady onward flow of time, which*

[53]Bernard Ramm, *The Christian View of Science and the Scripture* (Grand Rapids: Wm. B. Eerdmans Publishing Co., 1954), pp. 219, 301, 344.

is the essence of the cause-effect relation, is something which we superimpose on to the ascertained laws of nature out of our own experience; whether or not it is inherent in the nature of time, we simply do not know, although, as we shall see shortly, the theory of relativity goes at any rate some distance towards stigmatising this steady onward flow of time and the cause-effect relation as illusions; it regards time merely as a fourth dimension to be added to the three dimensions of space, so that *post hoc ergo propter hoc* may be no more true of a sequence of happenings in time than it is of the sequence of telegraph poles along the Great North Road. It is always the puzzle of the nature of time that brings our thoughts to a standstill. And if time is so fundamental that an understanding of its true nature is for ever beyond our reach, then so also in all probability is a decision in the age-long controversy between determinism and free-will.[54]

If there are, in fact, no fundamental reasons why time should not stop or even run backward, it is obviously going to be very difficult for us to fix a date for creation, or indeed for any other event in the very distant past. So that dogmatism on dating and dating methods can usually be attributed to an ignorance of fundamental issues at stake in this area of thought. This also applies to statements on the historicity, or lack of it, in biblical chronology.

Sir James Jeans writes: "It is the general recognition that we are not yet in contact with ultimate reality."[55] Sir James comes to this conclusion in a discussion of the practical significance of mathematical findings on the nature of the universe.

Philip Henry Gosse in 1857 postulated that "[creation] is *the sudden bursting into a circle.* Since there is no one state in the course of existence, which more than any other affords a natural commencing point, whatever stage selected by the

[54]Sir James Jeans, *The Mysterious Universe* (New York: Macmillan Co., 1930), p. 32.
[55]*Ibid.*, p. 135.

arbitrary will of God must be an unnatural, or rather a preter-
natural, commencing point."[56] Thus, if God created a tree,
it would have rings in it the moment it was created. That is,
creation of the tree would bring with it the built-in illusion
of age, where no age, in fact, existed.

---

[56]Philip Henry Gosse, *Omphalos, An Attempt to Untie the Geological Knot*
(1857), p. 123, cited by Bernard Ramm, *op. cit.*, p. 192.

4

PLANNED EVOLUTION

IMPROVEMENT OF A RACE OR STRAIN BY SELECTIVE BREEDING

GOOD RESULTS FROM ANIMALS

The possibility of improving the human race, biologically as well as psychically, by planned breeding has interested scientists and others for a long time. Animal breeding projects have shown wonderful results. Cows yield more milk, produce better meat and give a better percentage exploitation of the food they eat, both with respect to milk yield and meat quantity and quality. All sorts of strange and wonderful types of dogs, cats, pigeons, etc., have been produced by selective breeding. Could we not apply the same principles to our own race and build a better one? Could one not arrive at a superman from the genetic materials we have now on hand?

MAN COULD BE IMPROVED BIOLOGICALLY

Let us be clear about one point. Viewed from a purely biological standpoint, there can be little doubt that present-day man could be improved upon fairly quickly and easily. It might be possible to breed from our race a man with almost the physical properties of Adam who lived over nine hundred years. We would have to breed out some recessives and their accompanying degenerative properties, but this would not be insuperable, using proper selective breeding.

155

All the physical characteristics of man are determined by the genes distributed on the chromosomes in a chemical code. In certain species the exact position of the various genes on the chromosomes is known. Today great progress is being made in efforts to "break" the genetic code of life, and its "alphabet" of amino acids.

PROPERTIES MUST BE PRESENT ON GENES

Although knowledge is daily increasing with respect to the code units or codons, one matter is often overlooked, especially among nonspecialists in this field. That is that by selective breeding one can "breed up" only the properties which are already present on the genetic mass and only "breed out" or eliminate undesirable recessives and other genes. All the properties of a frog are present in the genetic material of a frog and by selective breeding, one could theoretically breed all the types of frogs present on the original genetic material —green frogs, yellow frogs, long-legged frogs or short-legged frogs. But no geneticist would have practical hopes of producing a race of crocodiles from a pair of frogs by selective breeding, however long the experiment continued. And this would be for the simple reason that no crocodile properties were present originally on the frog's genetic code. From the mixed genetic properties of a wolf and a hyena it would, perhaps, be possible to breed a poodle or an alsatian, simply because poodle and alsatian properties are present (in a mixed form) on the genetic code of the wolf and hyena. But from the wolf and hyena one would never arrive at a great ape even by the most careful and prolonged selective breeding experiment. Great ape genetic code properties are not present on wolf or hyena genes.

The genes on the chromosomes carry specific chemical information, just as the magnetic tape of a tape recorder carries information. But tape information can also contain garbled information or extraneous noise. With the aid of suitable filters which separate off undesirable noise, the information can be clarified. Some filters will separate music from the human voice, for example. But if no magnetic information is on the tape, but only noise, the best filter in the world is not going to filter out music which is not there. Or if one has a mixture of large and small sugar lumps, a suitable sieve will separate the small from the large lumps. But no sieve will separate a mixture of such sugar lumps into sand and sugar no matter how good it is. This may sound naïve, but it is paralleled in matters genetic.

The fact which we must keep firmly in view in thinking about evolution by selective breeding is that only properties which are already present in the genetic material as information can be brought out by selective breeding. Only what is in the bottles can be poured out. In other words, there are definite limits to selective breeding. We might be able to breed out of the human race today an Adam who would live nine hundred years, that is, we could breed out the recessive and damaging genes which seem to have arisen over the centuries, probably by exposure to toxic substances and maybe ionizing radiation. But it would not be possible to breed up from man more than is already contained in him as chemical genetical information. That is, a *new* type of superman of a different race cannot be bred out of man, nor could a human be bred out of a chimpanzee, or presumably a chimpanzee out of a human.

CAPABILITIES OF IONIZING RADIATION

However, it must be remembered that ionizing radiation is capable of producing *new* properties on genetic material. Nevertheless, these new properties are nearly always of a degenerative nature and not more highly developed, so that it is not likely, as we have already pointed out, that ionizing radiation will produce true synthesis on the gene. The effect of ionizing radiation on protoplasm can be shown by the following illustration. For automobile spark plug cleaning one uses a so-called sandblaster, which sends a stream of high-speed sand particles into the plug electrodes. The abrasive action of the sand cleans the plug. If we were to direct a stream of these high-speed sand particles into a more complex mechanism like a nice new Swiss watch to "clean" and "improve" it, we would certainly cause changes in the watch. However, they would be of a degenerative type and not of a synthetic quality improving the watch movement! The "mutations" thus produced in the watch could be compared to mutations in the genetic mass of a cell produced by ionizing radiation. Super watches will scarcely arise by the use of this technique. It would be not less naïve to expect new and better organisms to develop by using ionizing radiation technique to produce new mutations, for a watch is a crude piece of machinery compared to a living cell.

By selective breeding it is possible to sieve out and filter off undesirable genes in an organism, so that by this technique one can remove certain degenerate or undesirable characteristics and improve a race. By combination with other genes (using crossing techniques) we can produce new strains. But strictly speaking, with only genes themselves in mind and not various combinations of genes, selective breeding is not a *creative* process. It does allow *new combinations* to be formed but they are new combinations of old chemical information on previously existing genes, even though the proximity of one gene to another does influence the properties of both (see pp. 205-8). One cannot combine genes with genes that are not present in the genetic material, so that the chances of producing a crocodile from a frog by breeding must be practically nil. And if this is the case it would seem that the chances of producing a man out of chemical information coded on the frog are also nil.

MUTATION OFFERS THEORETICAL POSSIBILITY

The weight of the foregoing lies in the fact that selective breeding is only a sieve or a filter and produces its results by recombination and separation of material already present on the genes. But the situation is quite different when one considers selective breeding coupled with mutation. Here, by mutation, *new* chemical information becomes available which can then be recombined in selective breeding. Could we attain a superrace by this method? Could mutation followed by selective breeding produce a superman?

Obviously, if it were possible to so steer mutation that true synthesis occurred, with the result that more highly developed chemical coding was developed on the gene, then this, followed by selective breeding, should do the trick. But the "sandblast technique" for producing upward synthesis on the gene does not offer much hope of arriving at our goal.

If, however, the whole chemical structure of a human gene were known, if it could be discovered just what chemical groups are responsible for blue eyes or large brain structures, for example, then suitable synthetic biochemical technique applied to the gene should be able *to modify it constructively* and develop the coded information of genes so as to result in a more highly developed organism. It is already possible to impose certain parts of the genetic material of one bacterium or virus onto another, so that the second bacterium takes on some of the genetic properties of the first. It is also possible that certain viruses enter the nucleus of cells and bring into that nucleus some of their own genetic properties with them. Thus the directive influence of the genetic material of the nucleus over the metabolism of the whole cell is altered. There is some suspicion that the altered metabolism of the malignant (cancer) cell may arise in this way, though cancer cells seem to have lost rather than gained properties and chemical information. But by altering the metabolism of a cell by the mechanisms of changing the directive influence proceeding from the nucleus, chemical synthesis at the nucleus may be changed and true evolutionary synthesis thus becomes theoretically possible. More complex foreign molecules or chemical groups combining with the nucleus directing the mechanisms of metabolism have already been shown to produce this type of change.

From this we conclude that planned evolution, resulting in a species changing to a more complex one, is possible if one supplies the necessary planning for the synthesis of the chemical groups monitoring gene structure controlling upward development. But pure recombination of existing genes and chromosomes by selective breeding within a species, together with chance mutations, will not offer much possibility of success in really synthetic evolutionary processes.

THE SYNTHETIC PRODUCTION OF LIFE AND THE DENIAL OF THE POSTULATE OF GOD

CONFIRMATION OF DARWINISM?

We concluded in the last section that by synthesis in the genetic material there is the theoretical possibility of true upward evolution. True creation of new order would have occurred in this case. But, we may well ask ourselves, where do we differ then from the usual Darwinian concepts? To which we may simply reply that the Darwinist conceives of such an upward synthesis as having originated by chance and having been directed by natural selection through vast periods of time. We are denying that the origin of such complex upward syntheses and increased order on the monitoring and directing genetic material can be sought in chance but must be sought in planned energy expenditure and biochemical technique. Of course, the moment we allow a plan and reject chance, we automatically postulate a planner who orders matter exogenously. And therein lies the grand difficulty. Science today, on the whole, denies the synthesizer for the syntheses. It regards any postulate of a planner behind everything as unnecessary, rejecting at the same time sound mathematical evidence that chance will not suffice. Science itself has given no answer to precisely this question of plan, and yet we see evidence of plan everywhere, from the structure of matter itself, of the electrons in their orbits, of the nucleus in physics, and of genes and chromosomes in living matter. However, we really ought not to expect science, which deals with the properties of matter, to give us any answer on the planner either—if the planner is extramaterial. But it is an entirely different matter when science *denies* a planner, who is a mathematical necessity, just because that science knows nothing about supramaterial matters. To deny the existence of anything simply because one does not know about it, is an entirely different matter, and a serious one too. Suffice it to say here, that modern science, from Newton on, regards the universe as consisting of entirely purposeless particles.

SCIENCE HAS NOT EXPLAINED PLAN IN UNIVERSE

Though we cannot prove the existence of God, we are entitled to point out all the indirect but overwhelming evidence for his planning, and that *science has by no means accounted for plan by crying "chance."* From the scorn which is brought to bear on those who hold that the postulate of a God is necessary to account for the ordered cosmos, we suspect that the scorners are propagandists and are not acting as objective and reasonable thinkers.

For example, on the occasion of a lecture before the American Association for the Advancement of Science entitled "The World into Which Darwin Led Us," Dr. George Gaylord Simpson is reported as saying that the modern advances in biological sciences had made the religious superstitions, so rampant in North America, untenable, intellectually speaking.[1] If the whole world of life, such as we know it, has arisen *spontaneously* from nonliving material, it is highly unlikely that anything in this world exists which was created for the well-being of mankind. Dr. Simpson points out that a poll of a number of international experts in Chicago showed them to be of the opinion that life will soon be synthesized in the laboratory. One expert was convinced that the synthesis of life had already been achieved. Dr. Simpson used the occasion to state that it was high time for Americans to throw overboard their naïve theism and divine services. The fact that so many still partake in these exercises is, according to Simpson, proof of the sad lack of scientific education and the rampant nature of superstition among Americans.

[1]George Gaylord Simpson, *Science* (April 1, 1960).

But all frills aside, how does modern biology help or hinder us in these questions? Does it really force us to throw overboard the idea of a supreme Creator or Planner, as Dr. George Gaylord Simpson of Harvard and other learned doctors from the East and West would lead us to believe? They insist *ad nauseam* that it does just this. We could understand a scientist saying that he does not know how to evaluate these questions, that he is an agnostic. But *denial* of all belief in a Supreme Being in face of the fact that nature obeys laws and thereby reveals plan, is something quite different.

IF SCIENCE PRODUCES LIFE, WHAT WOULD THIS PROVE?

It is possibly true that scientists are on the way to synthesizing living units from nonliving matter. But will the success of this project really be the last nail in God's coffin, as we have already asked ourselves and as some apparently hope? What exactly would such an experiment prove, if successful? Surely, just that if nonliving molecules are exposed to certain exogenous technical and chemical influences at planned time intervals, life may arise. When nonliving molecules are experimentally manipulated under certain exactly controlled conditions, viable units may arise. But we must remember that the exogenously controlled experimental conditions are critical for the success of the project—the pH and temperature must be just right at the right time and may have to be changed during the course of the experiment. The correct amount of reagents and catalysts must be present and perhaps changed too during the exercise.

But perhaps most important, as we have already pointed out, is the cooperation of a good biochemist to program the whole synthesis, if success is to be assured. If an oratorio singer, prima donna or gardener were to undertake this critical experiment, without having learned some fundamental biochemistry, it is hardly likely that life would result (without wishing to cast any aspersions at all on gardeners or oratorio singers!). It would be the purest nihilism to expect a "stew technique," where everything is thrown into a pot and boiled together one hour with the lid on before serving, to yield any useful results, biologically speaking. The degree of complexity is far too high. Equally nihilistic would be the idea that, if we let such a mixture just stand long enough in a sterile condition for millions of years, the chance of spontaneous life production would become greater with the years. As we have already pointed out, equilibrium would be more nearly reached, not the improbability known as life.

Every scientist knows instinctively that nothing can replace the carefully planned intelligent experiment, if success is to be achieved. If uniformitarianism is true and if matter reacts now, as it did in ages past, then we know that a planner must be behind such an experiment. This assumption forces itself on us—we must assume it, if the laws of thermodynamics are correct. And if the idea of a material God up in the sky is primitive, as most modern theologians and scientists seem to think (and as it may well be), why *deny* an *extra*material planner whom we cannot "prove"?

LAYMEN, NOT SCIENTISTS, ARE DECEIVED

Let us return for a moment to the writings of Dr. Harlow Shapley of Harvard. In an article in *Science News Letter* Dr. Shapley is quoted as having stated: *"There is no need of explaining the origin of life in terms of the miraculous or the supernatural. Life occurs automatically when ever the conditions are right. It will not only emerge but persist and evolve."*[2]

Now this is a typical example of the kind of statement made by some eminent scientists the world over. Such statements can only mislead the lay, but not the scientific public. Let us quote Dixon and Webb to investigate the other side of statements of the above type: "To say airily, as some do, that whenever conditions are suitable for life to exist, life will inevitably emerge, *is to betray a complete ignorance of the problems involved.*"[3] Webb and Dixon then treat some of these

[2]Harlow Shapley, *Science News Letter* (July 3, 1965), p. 10.
[3]Malcom Dixon and E. C. Webb, *Enzymes* (2d ed., New York: Academic Press, Inc., 1964), p. 665.

until now insuperable problems. Teilhard also has a similar habit of airily making statements of the same kind as that attributed to Dr. Shapley. *These statements are a wonderful basis for building up high-sounding theories and earning for their proponents the title of a great thinker, but a little laboratory biochemical synthetical experience would blow a lot of them away. Experiment is a great clarifier of thought and theory.*

What does it actually mean to state that life will occur automatically whenever the conditions are right? Surely the purpose of the *planned* experiment is *simply to get conditions right and not to leave them to chance, which will certainly get them wrong.* Can any scientist refer to even one experimental observation that would back up Dr. Shapley's statement, that life will occur, persist and evolve from nonliving material whenever conditions are right? Our *experiments* have shown us *that to get conditions right, one needs intensive planning and not chance.* So Dr. Shapley's statement really is a begging of the question. For by insisting on "right conditions" he is insisting on exceedingly complex conditions, which are just those which chance will be unlikely to provide. Where did Dr. Shapley, or anyone else, observe such a complicated experiment, necessitating concentrated adjustment of conditions (which chance cannot do), taking place?

If the best evolutionary mathematicians cannot yet account even theoretically for the synthesis of the first enzymatic proteins by chance and pure chemical evolution, using as their basis the known laws of physics and chemistry, *then why do some materialistic scientists pour scorn on those who suggest something outside matter in an effort to explain? The position is that we cannot yet explain the riddle of life ourselves, on the basis of material physics and chemistry alone, yet we are forbidden, on pain of excommunication, to suggest the only other possible explanation left us, namely, that there is an extramaterial cause. What some scientists fear is the necessity (humiliation, according to Shapley) of being driven to admit that there is something apart from matter with which we must reckon.* Yet the accumulated wisdom of ages of mankind has believed in just this necessity.

RIGHT CONDITIONS DO NOT HAPPEN BY CHANCE

No true scientist is taken in by such statements as Dr. Shapley's but the layman is. And it is at him, the layman, that this kind of statement is aimed, so that he will be afraid to stick to his beliefs for fear of not being intellectually acceptable. To deny the existence of everything and anything we do not yet know about, is less than scientific, and yet this is what is commonly practiced today, especially when eminent men are questioned as to faith by reporters. Personally, I am for allowing for the existence of extra or supranatural phenomena, if there is no natural material explanation in sight. I know that many events, formerly thought to be of supernatural or extra-material origin, have turned out to be, with growing knowledge, susceptible of a natural explanation. The process of weeding out explanations is quite reasonable and any reasonable person will allow it. But this does not guarantee that *all* phenomena can and will be explained on the same purely material basis. It is agreed today in some circles that extra-sensory perception (ESP), such as telepathy, for example, exists, but there is no material explanation for it in sight yet. If we cannot find a purely material explanation for life (we should try hard first) why scoff at an extramaterial one?

SCIENTIFIC PROGRESS COINCIDES WITH BIBLE

Of course, no thinking Christian or theist believes that God is really a planner who *experimented* with matter in order to produce life and the cosmos. Even though we think he has controlled experimental conditions obtaining in matter to produce life, we do not think of him as going about his experiment as we would. God, being omniscient and omnipotent by definition, does not need to carry out experiments, as we do, in order to gain knowledge, or to see if and how things can be done. He knows the answers from the beginning and never needs to extend his knowledge by experiments as we do! Over and above this, he has infinite energy at his elbow, as it were, to supply the energy for synthesis!

The Bible would lead us to expect just the present situation with respect to the development of science and maybe the synthesis of life and matter by man. Since we have been made in the image of God, we would expect man to be capable, with the passage of time, of thinking more and more of God's thoughts after him—even respecting the creation of life and matter. If God has *creative* thoughts, we would expect man also to be capable of similar thoughts, even though they are infinitely less magnificent. For man is called a "god" a number of times by the Holy Writ,[4] so it is not very remarkable if he can, in his own little way, occasionally think like one. Man has already created matter—and new matter too—like plutonium. Why should he not follow up with life? Test-tube life should therefore not surprise the believer in Scripture or undermine his faith in God in the least.

The marvelous thing about the dangerous age in which we live is perhaps that man *is* beginning to think the creative thoughts of God, in a small way at least, after him. Man *is* learning the Creator's biochemistry, both synthetic and analytical. And the Creator's enzymology is also getting better known. If this process is allowed to continue and wars and other catastrophes do not halt its progress, there is, as far as we can see, no reason why man should not synthesize some sort of self-reproducing biological living system, that is, if life itself is not some sort of combination of matter with a supramaterial force about which we at present know nothing. This should be taken into consideration by scientists. But there we may ask ourselves how far thought itself is supranatural.

The span of progress from nonliving material to primitive life is scarcely as great as the span dividing primitive life from man. Thus there is room for a lot of progress, for primitive life has scarcely yet been reached in the test tube. Man is almost infinitely complex compared with the amoeba.

[4]E.g., John 10:34-35.

But while the secrets of "simple" life are gradually being unraveled in the hope of finding the way to more complex life, there is one other development which seems incongruous in all this intellectual and logical progress.

It is truly a strange conviction among scientists that man's synthesis of life and matter by carefully and intricately planned experiment proves that nobody planned life and matter originally and that therefore God either does not exist or is dead! We have already commented on the "logic" of this astounding development in thought right in the middle of unheard of technical development (see p. 93).

Evolution with the Postulate of God

BELIEFS OF THEISTIC EVOLUTIONISTS

We have already mentioned that in many countries there are Christians and theistic scientists who would classify themselves as theistic evolutionists. Such are Father Teilhard de Chardin, Professor von Huene and many others. They see the whole development of life from the amoeba type of cell to *homo sapiens,* which from the outside looks as if it were spontaneous, as a development which has taken place under the hidden guiding hand of God. Mutations and natural selection are, in their way of thought, God's method for producing his creation. This means that viewing the whole realm of nature developing upward by mutation followed by natural selection to man and beyond (maybe to Point Omega with Teilhard) is simply to watch the Creator at work.

Apart from the thermodynamic principles we have already looked into and which forbid a *spontaneous* upsurge of organization, there is theoretically no reason why a Creator should not use this slow method of producing his creation, and this is what the theistic evolutionist envisages. Such an evolution could be accounted for simply on the basis of the "work" done by the Creator. No theoretical difficulties would be involved—if one allows the existence of God. God would play the role of the great experimenter (with the limitations already noted). The dinosaurs and other extinct animals and plants would then be looked upon as stages in the grand experiment.

How ought a Christian or a theist to react to this sort of view of God's experimental methods? For a majority of scientists who are Christians or theists are inclined to believe this way. The mechanism of such a process could easily be that developed by Teilhard, who so extended evolutionary doctrine as to include the view that matter possesses a built-in force which causes it to automatically surge upward, slowly and irresistibly (to use Teilhard's expressions), to more and higher complexity, ending in psychic pressure build-ups (Teilhard), cephalization and Point Omega. That is, God so constructed matter that it had to evolve. Many academically trained persons are willing to believe this type of theory and apply it to their religious beliefs.

What can we reply to such views? First, examining the problem from a purely philosophical standpoint, there is nothing to say against the idea that slow or rapid synthesis on the genes could lead to "upward" mutations, so long as we do not invoke pure chance to account for it, and as long as we supply the energy required. Of course, the thoroughgoing Darwinist insists on chance as the primary principle governing evolution, followed then by natural selection. This follows from the materialistic beliefs of many Darwinists. But what about the Christian and the sincere theist faced with *natural selection* working on chance variation as main principles of evolutionary doctrine? What about their attitudes toward the struggle for existence acting on chance mutation as the mechanism of creative evolution?

NATURAL SELECTION AS A PRINCIPLE

We must therefore examine the principle of natural selection itself in the struggle for existence. It demands that the weak, ill or otherwise unfitted (physically or psychically) organism be denied an existence in favor of the stronger and

maybe more brutal forms which can "elbow" their way to
the fore through life or otherwise match their environment
better. The "less vigorous," the shy, the retiring, the sickly,
etc., are simply trampled underfoot in this struggle, whereas
the vigorous, vital individuals force their way to the top,
survive and reproduce. It seems a true observation of reality
to represent life thus. Life is in all realms just like this. It is
a real jungle, where the strongest wins and the weakest loses
even the weakness he had, by perishing in his weakness.

WOULD GOD USE SUCH METHODS?

But the question we must ask ourselves is whether a Christian (or a theist) could ever defend the idea of his God
populating his earth by the use of such "creative" methods.
The methods of work we use in life reveal our inmost character. Chance mutation acted upon by natural selection
would, in this view, be God's method of creation and as such
would reveal his inmost character. We must ask ourselves
what sort of God we would have, what would be his character,
if he used such a method of creation? And would his character, thus revealed by his work methods, be the same as that
revealed in the Bible? Can the Darwinistic hypothesis be
lined up with Christianity's revelation of God's attributes?

THE CHARACTER OF GOD

In order to answer this question we first must call to mind
the Christian view of the real character of God. Then we
must see if we can harmonize this Christian picture with the
view that emerges from evolutionary theory.

First, only a *person* (ego or individual endowed with intelligence of some sort) can possess a character. A character
sums up the total attributes of this individual in such terms
as patience, faithfulness, intelligence and quick wittedness.
And Holy Writ teaches us that God has just such a character,
and its attributes are described in detail. In fact, the character picture of God drawn for us by the Bible is extraordi-
narily well developed and sharp. This picture teaches us that

God *loves* the sinner but hates the sin. Because he is the Person behind the universe, he is the Planner of it all, with a plan for every individual. That is, he is omniscient.

But over and above this, the Bible teaches us that whoever has seen Jesus Christ has at the same time seen the Father God.[5] Jesus insisted that he and the Father are one, which means, among other things, that they are one in character. So we conclude that if we have seen or studied the character of Jesus we have at the same time studied and seen the character of God, the Father.

It is important to emphasize the above points because by definition God must be infinite, omniscient, omnipresent and omnipotent, which for us is beyond all comprehension. To try to paint the picture of this infinite character for us who are finite characters would be like trying to describe the ocean to a person who has never seen it by showing him a drop of sea water in a glass and telling him to multiply that by a few billion billions to get an idea of the immenseness, the appearance, the behavior, and the character of the ocean. It is just that the figures represented by a few billion billions make no mark on our comprehension. They are too great. So it is with the infinite characteristics of God. We call him love, meaning love as we know it, and by multiplying it by a few billion billions we hope to arrive at an idea of his love. So it is with the other infinite attributes of God. If we really wish to get an idea of what he is like, he must be described and, as it were, reduced to properties and measurements which are meaningful to us. There is only one way to do this and that is the way God himself did it. He reduced himself to the level of a man, the divine Man. Only as such, in human measurements which we understand, can we know anything of the infinite nature of God's character.

CHRIST REVEALED GOD'S CHARACTER

Jesus Christ set about showing us as man these characteristics of God. He was eager for us to know them so that we

[5]John 14:9.

can practice them ourselves. A person who even in a small way exercises the characteristic of love is exercising one of the attributes of God. He can go on following God's example in other ways such as patience, faithfulness, stability, verity, etc. For us human beings, human characteristics stand out very clearly. Because we are human and other humans are very like us, we can compare notes with one another. The differences between us and him stand out too, of course. He is the divine Human and we mere earthly humans. So Jesus Christ shows us the character of God "programmed" in a form that our mutual "computers" can handle. He shows us the Infinite programmed in finite terms suitable for our level of comprehension.

We return now to our earlier question on theistic evolutionary theory and ask ourselves whether a God with the character of Jesus, the divine Man, could synthesize his creation by the methods Darwin and his friends propose. We are really asking ourselves if his own character, that is, attributes, allow the use of Darwin's methods. We have the right to ask ourselves whether Jesus Christ could use certain creative methods, for the Bible teaches us not only that Christ was the character image of God but that he, Jesus Christ, *made* all things. All things were created by him—he is the Creator. They were also created for him.[6] We are therefore on safe ground if we ask ourselves (on the basis of the character of Christ) by what method Christ's creation could have been carried out.

If we know a person's character we can make a fairly accurate guess as to how he is likely to react or how he is likely to go to work in solving specific problems. So if we know Christ's character we can make fair deductions as to how he would have gone about creative work, as far as our finite minds can grasp creation at all.

One of the most exhaustive unveilings of the character of Christ is to be found in chapter 5 of Matthew's gospel. The

[6]Col. 1:16; John 1:3; Heb. 1:2.

following verses highlight these instructive declarations:

> Blessed are the poor in spirit: for their's is the kingdom of heaven. . . . Blessed are the meek: for they shall inherit the earth. . . . Blessed are the merciful: for they shall obtain mercy. . . . Blessed are the peacemakers: for they shall be called the children of God.
>
> But I say unto you, Love your enemies, bless them that curse you, do good to them that hate you, and pray for them which despitefully use you, and persecute you; that ye may be the children of your Father which is in heaven: for he maketh his sun to rise on the evil and on the good, and sendeth rain on the just and on the unjust. . . . Be ye therefore perfect, even as your Father which is in heaven is perfect.[7]

In these verses the Lord Jesus shows various aspects of his own perfect character, so that his disciples can use it as a mirror by which to model their own characters. Let us look at some of these perfections a little more closely.

"Blessed are the poor in spirit." This is surely not the expression of one who believes in the strongest elbowing his way to the top of the ladder or swimming ahead by treading others underwater. Nor is it the description of one who simply hides safely in his environmental niche. Rather, it is a description of One who allowed himself to be tried and disciplined by the trials of life. It is the description of One who knowingly allowed *himself* to be trodden down. He is the One who learned obedience by the things he suffered.[8] The person who does not and will not learn to be meek and patient, who rejects the whole spirit behind this verse, can very easily become brutal and impatient of all but himself. But the poor in spirit are going to inherit the earth simply because their characters, molded and disciplined by suffering for what they believe, will fit them for positions of authority on earth when the King takes up the rule of his kingdom there. This is the highest honor God can give, the kingdom itself.

[7]Matt. 5:3, 5, 7, 9, 44, 45, 48.
[8]See Heb. 5:8.

"Blessed are the meek: for they shall inherit the earth."
Humanly speaking, it is not exactly the meek who inherit
the earth today! The meek soon learn that they live in a
jungle in life today, no matter what their profession or walk
of life. It certainly is dangerous to be meek today just as it
was in the Lord's day. It led to his crucifixion. In us today
it will be mistaken for weakness and hypocrisy, with all the
attending complications. *Does it seem at all likely that One
who thus prized and lived out meekness would build his very
creation using a tool which may completely deny this characteristic? Natural selection, involving the merciless extinction of the weak and the meek or unfitted at the expense of
the strong, fit and selfish, does not seem to point to a merciful
and meek Creator. How could he violate all his personal
principles of meekness and poverty of spirit in making use
of a ruthless struggle for existence as his own creative method?*
Even Ghandi's India, which made the policy of meekness
and nonviolence the official one of the country, did not use
nonviolence and meekness in its fight against Red China.
Nor did the "meek" Indians take Goa from the Portuguese
by means of meekness and nonviolence. And yet, in this day
and age, the Indians do possess the Goan earth, but not because of meekness!

"Blessed are the merciful: for they shall obtain mercy." Is
the struggle for existence ever motivated by mercy? If it
were, it would cease to be a *struggle for existence.*

*"Blessed are the peacemakers: for they shall be called the
children of God."* It is these peacemakers who do not insist
on victory over others in the struggle for existence. We
should love our enemies. But how do we show love to them
in war and combat? Many today would, I suppose, try to
rationalize here and think this means killing your enemy as
quickly and painlessly as possible, but they certainly do not
mean letting the enemy kill them first.

IS PERFECTION POSSIBLE TODAY?

Let us be quite clear about the fact that the above precepts of perfection are unthinkable in the present world. Anyone who seriously and earnestly tries to practice them, and therefore to become perfect as the Father in heaven is perfect, that person is going to get into trouble with his country's military authorities if he is of military age! Here, in our world of brutal struggle, ruthlessness, pitilessness, suffering, and fighting to the death are the order of the day, not only in Viet Nam but, with perhaps other weapons, in most walks of business and academic life. Darwin observed pretty exactly when he described the state of the world as one of struggle for existence. As the Scriptures say, the whole creation groans with suffering which often far outweighs the joys of life. Even the joy of love and marriage is tinged with darker colors by the thought that it is "until death us do part"—brought to mind just when we would not have such thoughts called to mind.

CHRIST VALUES VIRTUES IN BELIEVERS

Of course, it is a different question to ask oneself whether, or how far, the serious Christian should or should not take part in this embittered fight. Some of it he is thankful to avoid if he can. Some cannot be avoided. But through all life the precepts of Christ must go above all others for the Christian; they are absolutely binding on him. Indeed, he is told that in keeping these precepts he can become perfect, as his Father in heaven is perfect, and this is possible by no other method. There are no two ways about it; the serious Christian must aim at being like the revealed character of Christ *all the time*. And the Sermon on the Mount shows us just what Christ is like, morally speaking.

What is important for us is the unveiling of the perfect character of God in the passages we have quoted. Because he is perfected himself, he values in us just such virtues as poverty of spirit, meekness and mercy and prefers the peacemaker to the warmonger and ruthless person. It is in just such revelations of God's holy character that we see to what extent mankind's character in general has slipped. Of course, this does not by any stretch of imagination mean that God's meekness is weakness or that his mercy will let any injustice slide by. In him there is a complete blending of all facets of perfect human character which add up to the perfect Person, infinite and yet human in the form of Jesus Christ. Being such a perfect Person whose perfect character displays infinite wisdom, power and knowledge, we should expect his methods of creation to match the perfection of his character. He has the marks of infiniteness and eternity (which is more than mere timelessness) in the character the Scripture attributes to him, so that one would expect these properties to show through in all his creational work too. Thus we should look for the marks of eternity and infinity in studying the creation. In point of fact, we do discern these properties in nature if we are observant. Take, for example, the apparently infinite motion of the electrons in their orbits around the nucleus. It is well known that the deeper we dig into the secrets of nature, the more profound and complex they get, so that knowledge itself seems to bear the mark of infinity too. Indeed, it would be a naïve scientist who thought that he could learn everything about his subject, let alone about the totality of the universe. *So, we have already admitted to the marks of eternity and infiniteness in creation and time.*

In view of what Jesus himself said about the fall of man and of its results, we would also expect to see the marks of time, decay and destruction in this once-perfect area and these marks would be expected to stand out among the marks of eternity and perfection in nature. The second law of thermodynamics shows this aspect well enough.

CREATION AND HUMANS REFLECT CHRIST

Thus, in view of Christ's perfect, infinite and yet human character, we would expect the creation which Christ made to unmistakably reflect him in spite of the fall. And it certainly does this. As we have already seen, *it looks as if the creative act itself was timeless* or that creation was accomplished not *in* time but *with* time.[9] *For before creation there could be no time at all.* Also, it looks as if the universe bears, as we have already pointed out, the depths of infinity, *for the deeper we search into atomic and subatomic matter, and even into life itself, the more we remark that its secrets go on and on forever. It looks as if there will be problems to solve forever, which is infinity.* And the higher we search in heaven among the stars, quasars and interstellar space, the more we find to explain. *Even though the universe may have a definite size and apparent limits, knowledge and problems bear the marks of limitlessness. Thus the creation certainly does bear the indelible marks of an infinite Author.*

We humans also bear the same marks of an infinite Maker. The deeper we dig into the secrets of our own cells, nerve fibers, muscle fibers—indeed, the ego itself—the deeper we find we can dig. Here the marks nature reveals on investigation of nature's problems differ greatly from the marks we leave on our own works. We can so easily reach the bottom of our own creations, showing thereby our own finiteness.

It would seem, therefore, that God's creative methods would fit his own infinite standard and thus match his own character. There is no explaining characteristics of nature which reveal infinity on any other basis. The question then arises: How could we attribute to our Maker any methods in creation which do not reflect his perfection? Could such a Maker produce life here on earth by the methods the Darwinists postulate?

GOD DOES NOT USE CHANCE

First, take the basic Darwinian concept of chance as the prime mover in life. *Chance does not and cannot exist in any divine omniscience.* We do not know in a million radi-

[9]*"Non in tempore, sed cum tempore, finxit Deus mundum,"* Sir James Jeans, *The Mysterious Universe* (New York: Macmillan Co., 1930), p. 155.

um atoms which atom will be the next one to decompose. So we treat the matter statistically to help us around our ignorance. But God, if he is omniscient, must know which atom is next on the list for explosion, so that chance cannot exist in his divine omniscience. Chance is therefore a very finite concept belonging to finite beings. How then can we imagine God using a method as finite and uncertain as chance as an expression of his infinite omniscience and omnipotence in biogenesis? Would the use of chance express God's character? The whole concept is utterly incongruous. The use of what we in our ignorance may call chance, *could,* of course, be used by God, but it would not be chance for him, but absolute certainty. Thus *true* chance could never be used by God.

GOD CANNOT BE BOUND BY TIME

Second, and equally incongruous, is the matter of the huge time spans which are the *conditio sine qua non* for Darwinian evolution. If God is eternal and absolutely independent of time, how can we bind him, the timeless One, to absolute dependence on time for the creation by evolution of life? Yet millions of years and chance are the keystones of Darwinian thought, even though, as we have shown, both these concepts are impotent before the demands of creative synthesis. He could, of course, have used long time spans for creation, but to maintain that he could not have created without the use of long time spans is a different matter.

How then could we imagine God having to use either one or both of the above concepts for his creative purposes? Neither of them gives expression to the divine character of God, either as he is revealed in Holy Scripture or as he is conceived by secular minds.

GOD IS THE PEACEMAKER

God is known to the Christian as the Peacemaker, among many other roles. How then could he use the ruthless destruction of the weak and sickly as an integral part of his creative method? If his creative work is accomplished on principle by destroyers—by those organisms which use ruses, biological "war" or deception in order to win their struggle for existence—would not this also be a contradiction of the Creator's character? If God's technique for the creation of higher life involves struggle for existence *with no holds barred* (as does take place in our biological jungle) then what of the character of God who planned on the use of *this* creative technique to achieve his ends?

We might well ask ourselves why God could use destructive methods involving war, death and often unspeakable cruelty in achieving his redemptive and elective purposes for Israel in the Old Testament and yet not use similar methods in achieving his general creative purposes with life in the creation of evolution of species? It is suggested that God uses purely destructive methods either as a judgment in answer to sin against his commandments or as a disciplinary method for specific purposes, as in the case of his servant Job. But in the creation of life and development of species *at the beginning,* surely there was neither sin to punish nor reason to discipline or test his servants. Moreover, the Genesis account does not suggest he made the various kinds of life by any other method than by fiat pure and simple.

The situation now, in respect to God's techniques of work, must be different from those at the creation. *For now, sin being present, God has a perfect right to use even it to glorify his own perfect person.* If he, the Creator, were in any way sullied by the sin and his making use of it, there would be no honor to him in so doing. But, now that sin has filled the world, God will use even it to achieve his own ends. No sin being present at the beginning, and God not being the author of sin, it is impossible that he could have used it for his creative purposes then. This argument does not apply after the fall of man.

HE IS THE GOD OF JUDGMENT

God has shown conclusively in Matthew 5 and other passages that he does not approve of any "no holds barred" technique, even in the jungle of life in which we live. How could he then approve of it in his own creative technique? After reading the Sermon on the Mount as an exposé of God's character, it seems almost like blasphemy to attribute no-holds-barred methods to him.

Somebody will object that in the New Testament this might apply to the revelation of God's character, but certainly not in the Old Testament. For in Old Testament times wars and destruction were carried through in God's name, as part of his program. To be sure, there is a great deal of judgment in the Old Testament but there is also the same in the New Testament. We must not forget Christ's many references to the judgment of hell, and to the judgment seat on which he himself will sit at the end of time. Nor may we forget the whipcords with which he drove the moneychangers out of the temple. Christ spoke repeatedly of the terrors of the judgment of hellfire. The judgment foretold at the end of the New Testament is far more severe than anything we find in the whole Old Testament from Genesis to Malachi. And we dare not forget that all this judgment at the end of this dispensation, terrible as it is described, is committed to Christ's hands personally. All judgment is committed to him. Thus we ought never dare to state that there is a different God in the Old Testament to the One revealed in the New, on the basis that the Old Testament reveals a God of judgment and the New Testament a God of love. Love and judgment are present in both Testaments. Of course, the *consequences* of Adam's fall reach throughout Adam's kingdom. These consequences of the fall of Adam cannot mean that God is *punishing* the animal and plant kingdoms any more than catching a cold can be a consequence of theft of other people's property.

The important point to realize is that God is a God of

judgment in both the Old and New Testaments where sin is present and where justice and punishment must be meted out. Judgment is his *answer* both in the New Testament and the Old Testament to sin and disobedience to his good laws. He does not act that way if there is no reason for him to act that way. This being the case, why should he *create* his universe by the method he otherwise only uses to justly punish sin? Destruction is meted out for certain sin but is never used in the whole account of Scripture as a *creative* method. By contrast, we must realize that discord and strife between individuals and nations today are largely the result of man's sinful selfish nature, also a result of the fall. The miseries of the world today, the sickness, the pain, the sorrow, death and decay, are all results of a fall in creation which is already present and already existing. *The struggle for existence among living organisms today is a result of sin entering a perfect creation and is not the method of bringing that creation into existence.*

It is perhaps not exactly true to state that the struggle for existence is directly a judgment of God. For how could judgment be merited by being sick, underdeveloped or weak? But so-called creative natural selection, with all its destruction by no-holds-barred techniques would make God's creative method dependent on God's destroying the weak or sickly or unlucky for no fault whatsoever of their own, just in order to arrive at creating higher forms of life. Surely no God of perfect character could be so immeasurably and calculatedly unjust in arriving at his ends at the expense of the weaker individuals to "benefit" the race of posterity? Injustice would be the basis of God's technique of creation, to say nothing of "chance," the "antipole" of God's foresight. *Injustice and chance would thus be the foundation pillars of God's creation, if Darwinian theory is correct.*

STORIES OF CHIVALRY IN BIBLE

Furthermore, we must remember that even in the Old Testament, which reports a great deal about judgment, we

do find such stories of chivalry as those attributed to David
in the case of Saul. David could have liquidated Saul twice
when Saul was in a weak position, with no danger to himself.[10] And David was a man after God's own heart. Like
God, judgment was abhorrent to him even when it meant
sparing Saul, who was seeking every opportunity of killing
David. Once, in the cave at Engedi, David could easily have
gotten rid of Saul. Even David's own servants told him that
this was the day the Lord had spoken of, in which he would
deliver David's enemies over to him, so that he could do
what he liked with them. David proved, by cutting off the
hem of Saul's garment when he could have cut off his head,
that he really loved his enemy.[11]

And this case was not just an exception. For the same thing
happened again in the desert of Ziph. Saul and his men were
asleep and David came with Abishai and stole Saul's spear and
water cup, which lay at his side. When Abishai saw this situation, he told David that God had delivered his enemy into
his hands and asked for permission to run his spear through
Saul and pierce him to the ground once and for all.[12] But
David hated vengeance, even against the guilty, and would
not lift his hand against Saul, the Lord's anointed, when he
was in a weak position, even though Saul would have liquidated David at the first opportunity. So strong was David's
dislike of even just judgment that he risked his own safety in
not dealing with Saul. If the victory in the struggle for existence had been all-important for David, David ought to
have acted decisively on these two occasions, for it was David's
very existence which was at stake. And David was a man after
God's heart.

After Saul's death David showed the same chivalry toward
Saul's progeny. He sought out those who had escaped who
were of the house of Jonathan (Saul's son) *in order to show
them kindness*.[13] He found the cripple boy Mephibosheth,

[10]I Sam. 24 and 26.
[11]I Sam. 24:4.
[12]I Sam. 26:8.
[13]II Sam. 9.

invited the boy to come and take a place among his own royal
sons, making at the same time arrangements that Mephibosheth should have a place at David's table all the days of
his life. Then Mephibosheth received back all the property
and land which had belonged to his grandfather Saul, David's
archenemy, so that the little cripple would not have to sit in
the royal household at the royal table as a pauper among the
wealthy king's sons. Boys can be very tactless, so David took
no risks when making Mephibosheth really welcome and at
ease. How chivalrous and thoughtful David was! It encour-
ages me in depressing days to think that it was *David who was
the man after God's own heart. This is how God acts with
me and his other enemies.*

GOD'S CHARACTER IS BALANCED

When it came to a direct command of God to exercise judgment, then David, of course, obeyed, but only if he was quite
sure of the justice of this case. This was the case when he in-
structed Solomon how to exercise justice after he became
king.[14] Thus we find that God's character is balanced. "Normally" God is merciful, chivalrous, kind and loving. But imposed upon this basic character may be severity and judgment in the face of sin. God's love balances his severity and
God's judgment balances his love of mercy. The character of
love is called for where love is fitting, and severity where
judgment is due. *But the question we must ask ourselves is
whether God would employ that side of his character which
he used in exercising judgment, for creating a universe which,
at its creation, was obviously innocent.*

In the beginning God commented on his creation that it
was very good. In case we are not clear what "good" might
mean, God has defined the situation for us in no uncertain
terms. The Bible teaches us that at the end of the dispensation in which we now are, God will *restore* the conditions
described at the beginning as "good" or "very good."[15] *So, if*

[14]I Kings 2.
[15]Gen. 7:39.

we can get an idea of the conditions as God has promised them to us at the end of this dispensation, we are also getting at the same time an idea of the conditions as they were at the beginning of the creation. Both the conditions at the end and at the beginning are described by the Bible as "good." Revelation 21:4-5 shows what they will be at the end: "And God shall wipe away all tears from their eyes; and there shall be no more death, neither sorrow, nor crying, neither shall there be any more pain: for the former things are passed away. . . . Behold, I make all things new." Acts 3:21 calls this condition of things at the end of time "the times of *restitution* of all things."

We therefore conclude that God has promised to restore everything which has been destroyed by the fall and then, after restoration of things as they were at the beginning, there will be no struggle, no tears, no pain, no suffering and no death. All these will be put away as something *foreign* to God's creative plan, and *the original conditions at creation will return. Now if these conditions of perfect harmony in creation are to be returned to us and the condition of struggle and death removed as something foreign to God's plan, how can one who believes in God's Word believe that God made, created or synthesized the cosmos of life by methods foreign to his perfect plan and character? If chance, on which Darwinism is partly founded, is foreign to him, the omniscient One, how much more is strife, pain, tears, struggle and death foreign to the character and creative plan of the One who is called the God of love, of peace and of life?*

The struggle, according to Darwinism, is creative, for in the passage of millions of years it is supposed to have *produced* the world of living organisms as we know it. The Bible teaches us, however, that this same struggle started only after the entire creation had already appeared as such in perfection. Imperfections and disharmony were introduced by the fall into sin. *Therefore, the struggle, in the eyes of the Bible, is a proof and symptom of the degeneration of a creation which was once perfect.* The struggle is an expression of in-

creasing entropy (and probability) and a proof of degeneration from perfection. Struggle does not produce a reduction
of entropy but is rather an expression of its increase (de-
creation or decay).

SUMMARY

To summarize: According to Darwinian evolution the *consequences of the fall of creation* (struggle, suffering, pain,
death, decay, etc.) have aided in the creation of the world of
living organisms. Therefore what confusion of thought and
logic must exist among Christians to ever countenance any
possibility of harmonizing the one method of thought with
the other! For the creation of life took place, of course, before the fall. According to Darwin, and those theistic evolutionists and Christians who go along with him, the effect pre-
cedes the cause, or produces it. According to the Bible, in the
beginning of the creation everything was harmonious and
perfect. There was no death, suffering or pain. After this
complete creation the fall came and, with it, struggle and
death. How can these consequences of the fall of a complete
and perfect creation have been the cause and creative method
behind it? The creation produced, after sin, the fall, but not
the fall the creation!

Some Consequences of Darwin's Doctrine in the World of Politics

CHIVALRY REPLACED BY WAR'S GLORIFICATION

The history of the world of politics is largely the history of
wars, tyranny, the conquering of peoples and their liberation.
It is a history of killing and ruling, or ruling by killing, so
much that the saying goes: "Blessed is the people with no history." And yet those who fought most of the battles of old
recognized certain forms of chivalry and good sportsmanship.
Individual bravery in combat was recognized. Sometimes,
perhaps, the best did win in combat between individuals. But
the net result of all these wars and fights was recognized to be

generally weakening and detrimental to all involved. It was conceded that often the best (not necessarily the strongest) perished.

Struggle Seen as Beneficial. However, since the publication of Darwin's *Origin of Species* the doctrine of the virtue of struggle for its own sake has become widespread. Struggle has been represented as a beneficial means of purifying the blood of a nation; it is supposed to be beneficial. War has been glorified by many nations suffering under dictatorships. Huxley maintains that the *whole of reality*—the present state of cosmic life and development—has been brought about by the bitterest struggle for existence involving ruthlessness to death through millions of years. He says that evolution, in the sense in which we have described it, is the whole of reality.

Now if struggle to the death—ruthlessness to the wiping out of species less well endowed with genetic factors than the victors—*if this struggle is God's technique and method of creation, what can we say against ruthlessness and the no-holds-barred technique which God is supposed to have used in evolution, on moral and Christian grounds?* The struggle for existence, and its consequences (terror, pain, suffering, agony and death) must on this basis be "good," especially if it has been crowned with such extraordinary success in building our human, animal and plant organisms. In fact Dr. H. C. Waddington comes to this precise conclusion[16] when he writes: "An existence which is essentially evolutionary is itself the justification for an evolution towards a more comprehensive existence."[17] That is, evolution's struggle for existence, must, in principle, be good, for its consequences are good, even though it does involve the ruthless killing and parasitizing of the weak. For the end result of all the horror is a fuller existence for those who survive. That is, if the death of the individual serves the well-being of the survivors, then the

[16]Cf. C. S. Lewis, *The Abolition of Man* (London: Geoffrey Bles, 1962), p. 29.
[17]C. H. Waddington, *Science and Ethics* (London: Allen & Unwin, 1942), p. 14.

death and suffering of the weaker individual must be classified as "good" or at least necessary. That is, upward evolution of the race justifies any methods to attain it, even at the
expense of the weaker individual. No wonder that ignorant
and unscrupulous dictators like Hitler and Mussolini, together with their modern counterparts, find evolutionary
doctrine a real windfall, in fact a godsend. It gives them the
excuse to enslave whole peoples, or wipe them out, if they
consider them less highly evolved than their own people. The
whole concept invites and *justifies* the terrors of fascism, communism and other types of tyranny.

*Temptation to Accelerate "Good." It is difficult for men
who have come to this conclusion (that upward development
according to the general theory of organic evolution must be
"good" simply because its "fruits" [a better race] are good) to
reject the thought that they have the right to accelerate the
achievement of this "good" by applying a little private "natural selection." Surely "theory" justifies the weeding out
of the "weaklings" of the human race by the application of a
whiff of gas or the bullet of a firing squad. It must, according
to this principle, be a good thing to encourage the dying out
of degenerate races. Nature (God, to some) uses the same
method! Why should not man come to nature's (God's) aid
in reaching a good objective a little more quickly and maybe
scientifically?* If God (or nature) uses the same method, can
it be "godless" (or against nature) for us to employ the same
technique ourselves in producing a better human race or
society? *Thus, if one once allows these evolutionary principles to be the true representation of God's (or nature's) methods, the door to the concentration camp, the ghetto, the
planned breeding or the planned destruction experiment
(using humanity as its guinea pig) is wide open.* The ruling
by the *Herrenvolk* ("master race") of the slave races must follow as a consequence of this logic, and indeed it has followed
this logic in practice, in spite of violent intellectual dis-
claimers on the part of some Darwinists.

Hot denial by Intellectuals. Thus, the first conclusion we draw on the effect of Darwinian doctrine in the political world is that it favors glorification of war and struggle in general. Anything which leads to struggle, and therefore to selection in struggle, is to be welcomed, since it opens the way to progress and the upward evolution of living organisms. The intellectuals among the Darwinists hotly deny this conclusion, although their theory leads patently and logically directly to it. And if the intellectual Darwinists themselves do not draw this conclusion from their own teachings, men like Hitler, Mussolini, Karl Marx, Lenin, Stalin and Castro have drawn their conclusions for them, and acted. We must keep steadily in mind the fact that Darwinism is the official state doctrine of all Communist countries. And the evolutionary doctrine is applied by the Communists, not only to biological mechanisms, but to political ones too. The weak, the enemy, or the unwary is fair game to be liquidated in the interests of the strong party and of Communist world victory. Communistic literature is saturated with crude Darwinistic thought of this type.

EFFECT ON HITLER

It is noteworthy that many of our Western intellectuals have socialistic as well as Darwinistic views. Perhaps the two positions may be related. But it is more remarkable that Darwinism is not only the state doctrine of the Communists but was also that of the National Socialists and Fascists.

Basis of Racial Policies. Of course, the National Socialists developed their ideas on *Blut und Boden* ("Blood and Homeland") somewhat differently than the Communists, but a few quotations from Hitler's *Mein Kampf* ("My Struggle") will be sufficient to show how full Hitler was of Darwinistic thought and how he based his racial policies upon distortions of it.

Hitler wrote:

> In the popular state the education of the mind and the body will play an important role, but human selection is just as important.

... The state has the responsibility of declaring as unfit for reproductive purposes anyone who is obviously ill or genetically unsound ... and must carry through with this responsibility ruthlessly without respect to understanding or lack of understanding on the part of anyone.

... Stopping reproduction of the bodily degenerate or psychically ill for a period of only 600 years would lead ... to an improvement in human health which can hardly be envisaged today. If the fertility of the healthiest members of the race were realized and planned the result would be a race which ... would have lost the seeds of bodily and spiritual decay which we now carry.[18]

We can only ask ourselves if spiritual and bodily decay do *really* always accompany one another as they seem to in Hitler's mind.

Hitler's words may have the appearance of containing much common sense. What interests us most here is the practical outworking of his beliefs. For although they may appear to be reasonable on the surface, they become unreasonable when one tries to determine who is going to decide on what is a desirable biological or psychic property in man. One matter is at once clear: A dictator is the last person who should have absolute power in deciding the future of any of his subjects. As soon as Hitler had accumulated enough power, it turned out that, in practice, the "genetically tainted" were often in Hitler's practical opinion, the "politically tainted," and as such were liquidated. Hitler's enemies together with their friends, wives and children were liquidated, just as has happened before throughout the history of mankind. The doctrines as such may sound quite sensible and even reasonable, but their application by men of bad faith often brings appalling results. This difference between doctrine and application is often overlooked simply because we do not recognize that our human race is a fallen one, in which hatred and

[18]Adolf Hitler, *Mein Kampf* (München: Verlag Franz Eher Nachfolger, 1933), pp. 44, 447-48.

jealousy still play an important (even leading?) role, even in our so-called educated circles.

Thus the theory of organic evolution on the basis of struggle for existence and natural selection became, in Hitler's mind, the excuse to wipe out whole races to "improve" the rest of the human stock. We need not think that Hitler wished to be a pure intellectual Darwinist. What he wanted, no doubt, was to get his own way and let off steam against races he hated and despised. No doubt he used Darwinism as a hedge to hide behind and to cover up his crooked mind in his efforts to gain political supremacy. Darwinism provided him with just the excuse he needed to wipe out whole races in order to "improve" human stock and at the same time to destroy those whom he hated and despised. The moral to be drawn from all this is to agree to no system, political or otherwise, which gives absolute power to anyone on any excuse or pretext! "Power corrupts, and absolute power corrupts absolutely," said the wise Lord Acton, and he was right. Our race of fallen man is morally too crooked to bear safely the dangers of absolute power. The moment Hitler obtained absolute power he did what all his kind have done ever since history began—he murdered his enemies and opponents. But he justified this murder and his policy by saying he was helping along natural selection and improving human biology. He attempted to cover up his depravity by saying that his purpose was good. Other dictators before him had not had the advantage of such a ready-made excuse for their wickedness as Darwinism offered.

Of course, it must be clear that if mankind's characteristics were noble there would be less danger of the misapplication of Darwin's theories. But, our race being what it is, Darwinistic principles have been used to justify the world's most horrible crimes in the twentieth century.

Human-Breeding Experiment. A perusal of *Mein Kampf* will reveal to the reader that Hitler was ready to carry out (and indeed actually started in a small way in some SS organizations) the most gigantic human-breeding experiment the world has ever seen. He encouraged his soldiers to have any "Nordic" girl and beget children by her, with or without marriage. He promised that the German State would bring up the children resulting from this process of "upgrading" the German race, and would arrange camps where "genetically suitable" young men could breed with similarly "suitable" young girls. Hitler said such experiments were far more important than wasting time on breeding dogs, cats or pigeons.[19]

He further maintained that the first effort in all education should lie in the direction of purely physical, bodily training. Training of the mind was a secondary matter. Scientific training was the least important training aspect of all, for Hitler said: "In the decisive struggle for existence it is seldom the man who knows least that gets beaten, but the man who poorly draws conclusions from the knowledge he has."[20]

Hitler "Helped" Nature. Darwin's concepts of struggle for existence dominated Hitler's whole thinking and, by guiding selection in this struggle, *Hitler intended to help nature a little.* If nature, in its struggle, was not quick enough in the elimination of the inferior races, then he, Hitler, was going to speed matters up. *If nature worked this way, it could not be immoral for him, Hitler, to accelerate matters and wipe out all the Jews, Czechs, etc., who were "obviously" inferior to his race.* The irony of the whole situation lies in the fact that it was a number of Jewish scientists of superior scientific stature who supplied the Western powers with the scientific know-how to beat Hitler at his own game. So the scientifically trained mind was victorious over Hitler's healthy physical training.

A hundred years ago Professor Adam Sedgwick of Cambridge remarked, after reading and digesting the *Origin of Species* by Darwin, that if this book were to find general public acceptance, it would bring with it a brutalization of the

[19]*Ibid.*, p. 449.
[20]*Ibid.*, pp. 452-53.

human race such as it had never seen before.[21] Dr. R. E. D.
Clark remarks that in our generation we have seen the fulfillment to the hilt of Sedgwick's prophecy. Hitler and Mussolini glorified struggle and war on the basis that the fittest
would survive and the race would be thus cleansed. Stalin
used any force at his disposal to trick his enemies or rob banks
to supply money for "the party." Like the Fascists and National Socialists, his power policy was one of "no holds
barred."

Called Negroes and Jews "Missing Links." To round off
our appraisal of the effect of Darwinism on Hitler's thought
we draw attention to some comparatively small matters. His
reason for promoting boxing was on the grounds that it pro-
moted pugnacity.[22] We recall his derision of "peaceable aes-
thetics" and his classifying such with "physical degenerates."
Hitler did not see any purpose in life for the "virtuous old
maid." His ideal of manly vigor was to be found in men of
defiance and in women who could bring defiant men into the
world. He wrote with anger about the colored "half apes,"
whom the Western world had drilled until they could go
through the external motions of the lawyer or the singer.[23]
Hitler made no bones about his belief that Negroes and Jews
were "missing links" between anthropoid apes and human
beings. If any reader has doubts about the full consequences
of these beliefs on Hitler's policy, he is advised to read Professor Eugen Kogon's *Der SS-Staat*.[24]

Views on Birth Control. Any remaining doubts about the
true fountainhead of Hitler's thoughts should be dispersed
by his views on birth control. He said that he despised the
practice of birth control not on the basis that there would not
be enough food to go round, or enough educational facilities to
train more, or jobs to employ a burgeoning population. Hit-

---

[21]Cf. R. E. D. Clark, *Darwin, Before and After* (Chicago: Moody Press,
1967).
[22]*Ibid.*, p. 454.
[23]*Ibid.*, pp. 455, 479.
[24]Eugen Kogon, *Der SS-Staat* (Frankfurt/Main: Europäische Verlagsanstalt, 1964).

ler's grounds for rejection of birth control were quite different. He said that by reducing the number of babies born,
one reduces the competition of struggle (natural selection)
between them. As a consequence of this reduction in natural
selection every weakling would have to survive and be reared
to the detriment of the race. He was convinced that the weaklings should be put to the wall by the strong ones, that there
should be no effort at birth control. He wanted them all to be
born and all to fight it out among themselves afterward.[25] The
sufferings of the weak at the hands of the strong meant nothing to him as long as natural selection took place and the race
profited. How different is Christ's mind! He takes note of
every sparrow falling from the roof; he even counts the hairs
of our heads.[26]

EFFECT ON COMMUNISM

Marx Used Darwin's Concepts. The above citations con-
cern Hitler and the National Socialists. Remarkably enough,
we find just such a development of thought among the Communists. It is well known that Karl Marx wished to dedicate
his book *Das Kapital* to Charles Darwin because he had taken
a number of Darwin's biological concepts into his political
thought.[27] For reasons of expediency Darwin refused Marx's
request. But the political and antireligious propaganda put
out by the Communists since Marx's time writhes with the
most primitive Darwinism. We continually find the same sort
of Darwinistic reasoning as we found among the National
Socialists, and the same brutalizing effect on the humans in-
doctrinated with it soon makes itself apparent.

Teaching to Oppose Religion. J. C. Pollock in his book
The Christians from Siberia describes the development of
atheistic propaganda in modern Soviet Russia. In 1964 a
university chair in "Scientific Atheism" was endowed by the

[25]*Ibid.,* p. 275.
[26]Matt. 10:29-30.
[27]Sir Gavin de Beer, *Charles Darwin* (Garden City, N.Y.: Doubleday &
Co., Inc., 1964), p. 266.

party.[28] If the state is honestly convinced that atheism represents the truth and can be scientifically backed up, then no
one has any right to object to the chair. But the purpose of
the endowment of the chair was not to serve this end but the
end of propaganda: "We do not want our boys and girls to
grow up merely ignorant of religious questions. We want
them to become convinced, militant atheists."[29] The Communists believe all religion to be false, to be opium for the
people. Religion of any sort is supposed to make "moral
cripples" of men and women (this expression is used a great
deal). Which all adds up to the fact that new university chairs
of this kind are intended to serve propaganda ends in order to
remove the "evil" of any religion.

The active fight against all religion in the Soviet Union
is being carried on ruthlessly. The theater of this war is, of
course, the school. Communist opinion holds that no children can possibly develop normally or fully if religion of any
sort is allowed to influence their lives. They will become
moral cripples if they allow themselves to be influenced by
"traces of the past," which refers to religion. "It is incumbent
on the school to fight so that the children of religious parents
shall not grow up into moral cripples but into real builders of
communism and fully developed people."[30]

The crusading atheistic schoolmistress in *The Miraculous
Icon*[31] calls religious parents "social criminals."

> My pupil learns one thing at school and the opposite at
> home. Either the school will educate him to deny God
> or his family will bring him up as a two faced hypocrite.
> There can be no compromise. Let the parents believe
> whatever they like. But the future of the children does
> not belong only to them. Parents like that are social
> criminals.[32]

[28]J. C. Pollock, *The Christians from Siberia* (London: Hodder & Stoughton, Ltd., 1964), p. 129.
[29]*Ibid.*
[30]*Ibid.*, p. 130.
[31]No references are given by Pollock as to publication.
[32]Pollock, *loc. cit.*

. . . Communists . . . maintain that a child is a moral cripple unless he is growing up to be "a new Communist man," self-sufficient, proud, scornful of meekness head held high in the manner of W. E. Henley's "I am the master of my fate, I am the captain of my soul" and of Swinburne's "Glory to Man in the highest! For man is the master of things!" Because the Christian kneels he must be a miserable creature; because he owns a Master, he must be a cringing slave: "A pickpocket takes a man's money or his watch, a bandit inflicts a mortal wound, a burglar steals all the valuables in a house. But the "brothers and sisters in Christ" distort a man's very mind, steal everything from him, deflect him from happiness in life to dreams of bliss after death and kill his pride and his confidence in his own powers."[33]

Parent-Child Relationship. If Christian couples resist this propaganda and raise their children to love their Creator above all, they risk the loss of all their parental rights over their children's upbringing. They are regarded as immoral enemies of the good Communist state. The children are forcibly taken away from them and placed in a state-operated boarding school, where they are educated on entirely atheistic principles. Today more and more Christian parents are losing their rights over their children in this way in the Soviet Union. And the reason is that Communism today is in a hurry. By 1980 all "traces of the past" (religion) must be removed, so that today's socialist state in Russia can be transformed into the purely communist one. By 1980 the "third plan" must have been activated in which pure Communism alone will exist and no religion at all may coexist in the Soviet Union.

Pollock describes many individual cases in which boys and girls as well and men and women students are unable to keep good jobs or obtain scholarships for study if they conform to any religion. In fact, no holds are barred to the Soviet state in its fight for atheism against a good proportion of the Russian people. The brutalizing, dehumanizing effects of athe-

[33]*Ibid.*, p. 131.

ism, coupled with the Darwinism that has accompanied it, are shown by Pollock to be actively at work. It must be kept firmly in mind that the "scientific" basis of Soviet atheism has always been Darwinism, so that the latter must bear at least some of the guilt for the dehumanizing effect of Communism on peoples saddled with it.

EFFECT ON WESTERN WORLD

Though Communists and National Socialists certainly show some of the drastic fruits of Darwinism, we must not forget, in our efforts to analyze others, that we in the Western world are not exempt from some of the same fruits. It is true that the symptoms of the disease appear to be milder here than in the East in the enslaved world.

Rebellion Among Youth. In our schools and universities Darwinism is taught to the effect that man is nothing more than an intelligent animal which has worked its way up the evolutionary ladder by succeeding victories in natural selection and the struggle for existence. Our schools and universities teach almost unanimously the gospel of the fight to further raise the race by natural selection. We can understand that young people who are taught this doctrine rapidly draw their own conclusions and being young, and often honest, tend to act quickly on their new-found "knowledge." They declare war on all authority of their elders; the younger generation is a step further away from our animal forebears, therefore the young must be at least very slightly more highly evolved! Why should the more "progressive" young people be subject to the shackles of the senile and obsolete? So the struggle against all tradition of the older and more experienced is taken up.

Riots in Cities. Riots like those in Watts in 1965 and Detroit in 1967 could be easily provoked on this basis of unrest. Over and above this, they argue that young animals possess strong sexual instincts, which they are free to use as they wish, without the inhibitions of the traditions of older animals. If man is only an intelligent animal, why should he not be free to do the same? So free love is proclaimed and practiced. The consequences are unwanted babies, broken lives, syphilis and gonorrhea, to say nothing of guilt complexes, but not the satisfaction and promised delight which animals seem to reap. Because man is *not* a mere intelligent animal!

Reflection in Fine Arts. But the brutalizing effect of our beliefs today are perhaps reflected in the fine arts as much as anywhere. We note, with C. S. Lewis, that the sweet melodies and silences of heaven have been shouted down. "Noise— noise, the grand dynamism!"[34] Melodies are replaced by the incessant drumming and hammering of the same infantile passage on electronically amplified instruments. Literature is little read unless it has plenty of "action," which means plenty of violence of some sort or another, of blatant animal sex, or revenge. To get anywhere today with the critics, art has to be practically surrealistic or pornographic. Whatsoever is beautiful or of good report today is laughed out of court; it is classified as insipid or Victorian. But to return to modern music, the combo gets louder and louder, the players become more and more frenzied, the instruments more and more metallic and the rhythm more like that of the primitive jungle as the conclusion is neared. The teen-age audience stands up and shrieks its delight or falls to the floor, writhing and bellowing approval at the last outbursts on the stage. The brutalization of our Western youth is already taking place, even though it has taken a different path from the political one we have seen in the East. But it is no less real.

Brutality in Viet Nam. But it does not improve matters to ask these same youngsters, who are already endangered by the brutalizing effects of the doctrines taught in our biology classes, to burn other humans with napalm; to take revenge on Viet Cong soldiers who have cut out the vocal cords of living GI captives (without anaesthetic) just as a "warning." It does not help our teen-agers to see their fellow soldiers

---

[34]Lewis, *The Screwtape Letters and Screwtape Proposes a Toast* (London: Geoffrey Bles, 1961), p. 101.

come back from patrol duty with their eyes gouged out and hanging on their cheeks. Brutality breeds more brutality, and so a generation is being systematically dehumanized, either by evolutionary doctrine or by seeing the effect of it in wars. The struggle that evolution glorifies may be wonderful in the eyes of armchair soldiers at home, but it is certainly not creative in the humanistic sense.

THE EFFECT OF DARWINISM ON DARWIN

Difficulties Introduced by Natural Selection. Now that we have attempted to view some of the consequences of Darwinism on the general political world, we must investigate the effect that Darwin's views had, in the course of time, on his own mind, character and religious beliefs.

Unnecessary suffering. In his earlier years Darwin can be said to have been a typical English gentleman. In his youth he was passionately fond of shooting. However, he gave up this favorite sport completely when one day he found a bird that had been maimed but not killed the previous day. He saw the unnecessary suffering caused by his sport and had strong enough character to renounce his passion for it ever afterward. Speaking of the attitude of the British gentry toward vivisection at a time when there was a great outcry of wealthy and poor against it, Darwin remarked that the English gentleman was humane enough as long as humanity did not interfere with his favorite sports.

On the other hand, Darwin supported vivisection in England on the ground that senseless, unnecessary suffering was unthinkable, but that suffering, if there was reason behind it, must be permissible. We must remember that it was the question of the huge amount of what seemed to him to be senseless suffering in the world which helped to turn Darwin against the conception of a designer behind the world of life. This problem of senseless and universal suffering bothered Darwin all his life and led him eventually into complete agnosticism. That is, with the help of natural selection and

chance variation, he ruled out the necessity of postulating
design. Because Darwin believed that it was right that physiology and general science should advance for the benefit of
all, he supported vivisection as a means of advancing knowledge.

Over and above this, when the storm of abuse on the vivisection issue broke over Darwin's head, he bore the calumny
patiently and was willing to pay this price for his convictions.
But senseless pain, even in animals, he would not tolerate.

Religious disbelief grew slowly. Although Darwin was an
agnostic[35] until his death, he remained a firm friend of his
local pastor, the Rev. J. Brodie Innes, all his life. His disbelief in matters religious grew slowly, apparently causing
him no distress except for one thing: "His wife, throughout
her life, maintained a deep conviction of orthodoxy, and Darwin's agnosticism made her sad and uneasy for his sake. . . .
For all his agnosticism, Darwin was not devoid of faith . . .
faith that the universe can be rationally interpreted."[36]

He was devoted to his friends and helped them wherever
he could. For example, he helped Hooker when he was subjected to indignities and obstruction at the hands of the First
Commissioner of Works, Acton Smee Ayrton. Darwin also
wrote to Gladstone, who was then prime minister, to ask for
a pension for Wallace to help the latter in his advancing years
and declining health. Gladstone granted a pension to Wallace.[37] At the same time, Darwin could be very harsh to his
enemies, as he was in his private correspondence about Lamarck.[38]

Suffered hypochondriac condition. Darwin in his years
on the "Beagle" was a hale and hearty young man who could
put up with the hardships of life aboard ship and endure the
long and strenuous forest, pampas and mountain expeditions
he took part in. After his marriage, however, he spent his

[35]de Beer, *op. cit.*, pp. 269-70.
[36]*Ibid.*, p. 270.
[37]*Ibid.*
[38]*Ibid.*, p. 163.

whole life as a semi-invalid. Even before the "Beagle" voyage
he showed a tendency to fits of hypochondria, as shown by his
reaction to the delays in the sailing of the "Beagle." After
his return to England this hypochondriac state became a more
or less settled condition. Some diagnosed his illness as being
of neurotic origin and linked it with his loss of faith in Christianity. They maintained he suffered oedipal remorse over
having killed the "Heavenly Father."

More recently it has been shown that Darwin's symptoms
might have been the consequence of an attack he suffered by
the great black bug of the Pampas known as Benchuca.[39] This
bug is a carrier of *Trypanosoma cruzi*, which is the causative
agent of Chagas' disease. Some 70 percent of the insects are
infested with the trypanosome, so that it is quite possible that
Darwin may have harbored the parasite since he was known
to have been bitten by the insect. Chagas' disease would certainly produce symptoms which match those from which Darwin suffered. For the trypanosome invades the heart muscle,
causing extreme exhaustion, as well as concomitant gastro-
intestinal distress.

These facts are important for our analysis of the effect of
Darwinism on Darwin's outlook on life. For he was obviously
a sick man, regardless of whether his sickness was hypochondria or Chagas' disease.

From faith to agnosticism. Darwin started life as an orthodox candidate for holy orders. Even on board the "Beagle"
we find him quoting the Bible to the ship's officers.[40] But in
later life, Darwin wrote to Niklaus, Baron Mengden, on the
compatibility of evolutionary doctrine with Christianity, stating that he did not believe there ever had been any divine
revelation.[41] I know of no real evidence that he changed his
views before his death, although statements to the contrary
have been circulated.

[39]*Ibid.*, p. 115.
[40]*Ibid.*, p. 107.
[41]*Ibid.*, p. 268.

In spite of his disbelief in any revelation, Darwin hastened to add that he was not to be considered an atheist. He did not deny the existence of God. Thus the best description of Darwin's religious convictions is that he was an agnostic.[42] Darwin wrote: "My theology is a simple muddle; I cannot look at the universe as the result of blind chance, yet I can see no evidence of beneficent design of any kind in the details."[43]

Here we find one of the signposts in Darwin's spiritual development. After the voyage of the "Beagle" he found that natural selection working on chance variation explained away for him any argument from design as to the creator of life. The "Beagle's" voyage put away forever the argument from design, as it is expounded by the Apostle Paul in Romans 1. Henceforth it was impossible for Darwin to believe in design behind life.[44]

The second signpost in Darwin's spiritual development is given in his letter to two Dutch students from Utrecht, J. C. Costerus and N. D. Doedes, in which Darwin wrote: "Nor can I overlook the difficulty from the immense amount of suffering through the world . . . the safest conclusion seems to me that the whole subject is beyond the scope of man's intellect."[45]

His disbelief grew gradually, as we have already remarked. He became more and more convinced of the validity of his theory in accounting for apparent design, so putting a designer out of court. And the immense suffering in the world could not, in his view, be attributed to a benign creator willfully causing it by the might of his power, so he attributed the universal occurrence of pain and suffering to randomness and chance too. So with one stone he killed two birds—chance accounted for design and pain without the necessity of postulating a creator of life, which would introduce so many difficulties in accounting for pain, suffering, extinction of whole races, etc. Of course, if the upward development of plant and animal life could be explained by natural selection, without

[42]*Ibid.*
[43]*Ibid.*
[44]*Ibid.*, p. 201.
[45]*Ibid.*, p. 268.

the necessity of the God postulate, why not also postulate the *origin* of life itself and even of the universe itself, without God?

Although Darwin vacillated in these matters, at least in his public statements, to his friends he made no bones about his belief that even life itself was not to be thought of as the result of divine creation: "He did not hide from himself or his friends that, if miraculous interposition was not only unnecessary but inadmissible in the evolution of plants and animals, it must be the same with their origin."[46] To verify the truth of these two signposts in deciding Darwin's agnosticism, see Sir Gavin de Beer's book *Charles Darwin,* in which he gives many citations proving this point to be of fundamental importance.[47] With no design in nature, Darwin eliminated a designer.

The result of all this was that Darwin considered the scriptural report on origins to be manifestly wrong and not better than the holy books of the Hindus and Buddhists.[48] "A contributory factor was his realization that the Scriptural account of the Creation could not be reconciled with his geological observations." Thus the consequences of his two convictions about the function of natural selection on random variation in producing the appearance of design, together with rampant destruction, pain and struggle as shown by the evidence of geology, was that he was robbed of all faith in the Bible as a divine revelation. As Sir Gavin de Beer puts it: "Paley's divine watchmaker became unemployed."[49]

Effect on today's students. The naïveté of Christian educators in hoping to be able to teach students to explain the facts of nature by the same theories which Darwin developed, but without their students undergoing the same spiritual development to agnosticism (or atheism) shown by Darwin under the same influence, is thus revealed. If Darwin drew

[46]*Ibid.,* p. 270.
[47]*Ibid.,* pp. 98, 175, 201, etc.
[48]*Ibid.,* p. 107.
[49]*Ibid.,* p. 106.

these conclusions simply because he believed in his theories, why should the modern student not draw the same conclusions? For the only difference between Darwin and the modern student is that Darwin was more mature when confronted with his evidence. Thus it took many years of thought to unhorse him and his trust in divine revelation and orthodoxy. Less mature students swallow these same theories, hook, line and sinker, vomiting their biblical faith at the same time, during their freshman year.

Today a further fact must be taken into account in reviewing the effect of Darwinism on modern students. They are constantly subject to the propaganda (perhaps unwitting propaganda) of those disciples of Darwin whose line of action is to bludgeon students and others into submission to their own views with such statements as:

> Today, no *competent* person has any doubt about the truth of the evolution of man . . . where resistance to Darwin's theories was shown by the general public it was based upon *emotional* rather than *rational* lines.
>
> . . . the unanswerable case for evolution that Darwin had built up and the impossibility of treating man differently from animals had already resulted in widespread adherence to his views by *sensible* people. . . . The opposition to the idea of transmutation of species was not negligible, for in addition to the *orthodox and uninformed majority*. . . .[50]

These and similar statements show some of the intolerable arrogance which has arisen in the Darwinistic majority today and which is quite unworthy of the spirit of Darwin himself. No student can afford to be considered by his professor as *orthodox and uninformed,* nor can he risk being thought *incompetent,* if he is to pass his examinations under the same professor. So he rapidly conforms to his superior's views. The modern Darwinists exhibit to a degree the attitude of Job's

[50]*Ibid.*, pp. 225, 134.

comforters of old who were convinced that they were the people and wisdom would perish with them.[51] The Christian should see to it that he is in a position to answer with Job: "But I have understanding as well as you."[52]

Could man's brain have evolved? Let us look for a moment at the defence that Wallace, the codiscoverer with Darwin of natural selection and variation theories, put up against Darwin's materialistic agnosticism. Wallace had become interested in spiritualism and flinched at Darwin's application of their theories to "prove" man's descent from lower animals. Wallace concluded after careful study that man's brain could not have been developed solely under the influence of natural selection and random variation, because the potential mental capacities of the lowest savage were little inferior to those of the most civilized races.[53] Thus, concluded Wallace, an instrument has been developed in advance of the needs of its possessor and therefore natural selection is ruled out. He considered that this was valid evidence that a higher intelligence had directed the development of mankind.

Darwin greatly regretted Wallace's having "deserted" science and taken refuge in mysticism, and proceeded to show why he was convinced that man's brain was never in advance of his needs, thus reinstating natural selection as responsible alone for man's development, and again denying design at the back of man's brain development. Again the argument from design put forward by the Apostle Paul in Romans 1 was considered by Darwin to be untenable. The consequences of all this is that, as long as a scientist does admit that chance variations acting in natural selection are adequate explanations of design in the Darwinian sense, that scientist is putting Paley's "divine watchmaker" out of work. And it is of no importance whether that scientist is a materialistic or theistic evolutionist. Theistic evolution and Darwinistic evolution

---

[51]See Job 12:2.
[52]See Job 12:3.
[53]de Beer, *op. cit.*, p. 215. See also the views of Lévi-Strauss discussed in Appendix VII.

are mutually exclusive if applied as Darwin applied the theories.

Can we avoid Darwin's pitfalls? Is there any way around this impasse? Darwin himself saw the whole structure which he had built up was dependent upon variation being *without limits:*

> Having satisfied himself that variation could be heritable, Darwin next showed that it must be *unlimited* in extent. . . . Opposite Lyell's assertion of "indefinite divergence [from the common type] either in the way of improvement or deterioration being prevented," which was Malthus' view, Darwin commented, "If this were true, *adios* theory," which shows not only that he recognized the fact that no limit could be ascribed to the possibilities of variation, but also that he had a theory.[54]

Malthus' view was that the "possibilities of variation were strictly limited."[55] In view of the fact that selection and variation do play an obvious role in the production of varieties and perhaps nearly related species too, that is, in microevolution but not in macroevolution, what solution can a Christian find to avoid the theological pitfalls into which Darwin and his disciples have fallen for the past hundred years?

1: Microevolution and Macroevolution. There is obviously no difficulty in believing that variation leading to microevolution in varieties and near species does occur. The facts point to the correctness of this position, which certainly does not conflict with any part of the scriptural revelation. It is the "unlimited variation" which Darwin asserted took place and which transformed one species into another, ending in man's formation from lower animals, which causes the difficulties, both of a scientific and scriptural order. And Darwin recognized that it was "good-bye" to his theory if variations were not unlimited. The evidence that microevolution among species takes place is very different from the evidence that one species changes into a higher one in the course of ages. That

[54]*Ibid.*, pp. 88, 100.
[55]*Ibid.*

is, the evidence for microevolution is much stronger than that for macroevolution. Microevolution would allow for a designer producing an organism (or pool of interbreeding genes) so complexly constructed that it could react with its environment so as to change itself in the face of the various alterations the environment undergoes. Darwin thought that characteristics acquired by an organism during its lifetime could be transmitted to its offspring. Today, this Lamarckian view is no longer accepted, but a different explanation is given, which, however, leads to a similar end result.

2. *Innate and Acquired Characteristics.* Darwin thought that some characteristics were "innate" and others "acquired." But this distinction has been shown today to be incomplete, for a large number of characteristics which most would think to be innate are, in fact, dependent on environment for their development. Thus some fish embryos, which normally develop two eyes (an "innate" characteristic of most vertebrates) develop one cyclops eye if magnesium is added to the water they live in. This means that the genes only produce two eyes in response to external stimuli. It has now been discovered that every characteristic of a plant or animal is a response, or interaction, between the genes inside and the environment outside. "No character owes its existence to heredity or environment alone, and strictly speaking, no character is either inherited *or* acquired."[56] Thus, all organisms possess a highly complex package of genes which are capable of reacting to produce characteristics which are demanded by their environment. Organisms used to be thought of as brittle systems which produced willy-nilly a single constant type of life. Now it is known that this is only partly true, for all organisms contain a package of genes which will produce certain characteristics *in response to certain environmental stimuli.* For example, we possess genes which will produce a thickening of the skin of our hands if we do certain physical work with them. Thus an organism is really the result of its genes in reaction with their environment.

[56]*Ibid.*, p. 186.

Moreover, genes affect each other's effects. A complex of genes behaves differently depending on whether it is near other complexes of genes or not. The fixity and rigidity of characteristics assigned to genes has had to be modified in the light of further research work. Thus not only does the environment affect characteristics produced by genes, but the proximity of other groups of genes affects any given group of genes. This explains the plasticity of any organism within certain limits. It can, by its chemical, genetic and metabolic mechanisms, respond within certain limits to its external and internal environment.

3. Supple Nature of Living Organisms. All these considerations bring out an important point which was not known to Darwin or his friends. Living organisms are by no means just an example of what might be called organic "predestinational Calvinism." They do have limits, decided upon by genetic make-up, but within these limits the suppleness of living organisms is astounding. Now, it is obviously easy to design, for example, a steam engine which is "rigid" to its environment. Its design does not change whether we overload it or not. Even though we run it downhill all its life it will not develop better brakes. But the living organism is so constructed that it has the built-in faculty of "developing better brakes" if we "run it downhill" for long periods. This development of "better brakes" is not a question of acquired characteristics in the Lamarckian sense, for it is genetically controlled in its gene structure. Thus living organisms turn out to be much more complex and highly organized than we had guessed. They turn out to be so designed that they can respond to their environment inwardly and outwardly, in a remarkable manner, but within genetically controlled limits.

To ask an engineer to design a steam engine for use on the prairies is one matter, and one that he can easily manage. But to ask him to design one that automatically develops better brakes if one takes it to the Rocky Mountains, or one that reduces its weight if someone needs to transport it by air, is another matter entirely and one which would obviously require much more design effort than that required for our original "straight" steam engine. In addition, the designer might be asked to include one more item in his specifications. If the mechanism controlling the brake capacity or weight-reducing faculty of the engine went wrong, then it should be capable of absorbing its own mistakes, so that the engine would not blow up!

These considerations give us a crude idea of the complexity of the living organism as capable not only of replicating itself, but also of adjusting itself, within limits, to its environment. Surely this supple nature of the mechanism controlling life processes is far harder to explain by random processes than even the old rigid idea of heredity! No novice could have designed such a self-regulating mechanism. To ask any engineer to design a template to redesign itself according to environment would be to ask for the superhuman. To ask a man, as a scientist, to believe that random variations and natural selection produce this kind of self-regulatory machine is to ask him something more difficult than believing in a designer. Personally, I might with some difficulty believe that a complex rigid piece of organization could occur by the mechanism of random variation and selection. But does not such refined self-regulation just reek of design to any unprejudiced person? Thus, the small variations within a species lead me personally to the concept of design, now that we know something of the interaction of genes with environment.

But what of the infinite variation which must have occurred if Darwin was right? First, as we have pointed out, there is no evidence that a cell could use its metabolic processes to provide the enormous amounts of "conceptual" energy required for synthesis of this sort.[57] Then also, we have no experimental evidence for macroevolution or the transmutation of species, to be compared with the evidence for microevolution, which would not involve large amounts of

[57]Cf. pp. 91, 96-100.

energy. Small changes on genetic molecules can obviously occur by chance and can be absorbed. But new synthesis of entirely new molecules, such as one finds in passing from one species to another, are of an entirely different order, both from the standpoint of energy and concept. I submit that only the postulate of design can help us here, otherwise we shall not be able to make the large transitions necessary for macroevolution to have occurred.

Darwin's Problem of Pain. We must now turn to the effect that the observation of pain, struggle for existence, and death had on the evolution of Darwin's views.

Pain made him an agnostic. Darwin was a very kind man, although hard-headed at the same time. It was the enigma of pain and struggle being the cause of the upward development of life which turned him into an agnostic:

> He was also influenced [in his attitude to orthodox Christianity] by the problem of suffering and estranged by the pious platitudes and special pleading advance by theologians, including Paley, to justify it. As he pointed out to himself, suffering may be a preparation for moral improvement in man, but the number of men in the world is as nothing compared with that of all other sentient beings, and these often suffer without any moral improvement. . . . What sort of guidance can it be that has led countless species to evolve to their doom and extinction, as the geological record proves to have been the case? There is no argument here. . . . What sort of providence is it that protects organisms, but only if they happen to be of the size, weight and general constitution nearest to the mean of the species . . . when those that show variation . . . perish miserably.
> . . . What a book the devil's chaplain might write on the clumsy, wasteful, blundering, low and horribly cruel works of nature!"[58]

Darwin concluded that the "horrors of nature and the atrocious behavior of its denizens cannot be reconciled with a

[58]*Ibid.*, pp. 266-67.

Creator of allegedly unlimited power and inexhaustible compassion any more than the extinction of a species, the shipwreck of mariners, the death of a gnat snapped up by a swallow . . . are to be ascribed to his direct volition."[59]

Torn between the problem of universal pain on the one hand and the orthodox view of a compassionate Creator on the other, Darwin finally decided against the latter. Pain, especially the idea of eternal punishment, was to Darwin not compatible with a compassionate, loving Creator. This meant that, pain being present universally, Darwin rejected the idea of the compassionate Creator and Redeemer of the Bible, although he never denied belief in some sort of a God. For him neither the Bible nor his own intellect ever solved the problem of the coexistence of a compassionate Creator-God with the chaos, pain and struggle in the creation.

Remarkable result of Darwin's work. The truly remarkable, almost ironical, result of Darwin's work was that Darwin then proceeded to make God (or nature) create his world of life by means of the very enigma of pain and struggle which he found incompatible with the idea of the God he had been taught to believe in! Thus, Darwin thought that if God was compassionate, he would not allow pain and death in his world. Because pain was present in the world, Darwin rejected the idea of a Christian God, but then he promptly used the very basis of his rejection of the God of the Christians as the supposed means of the creation of life, that is, natural selection and struggle for existence.

Many other thinking men besides Darwin have, of course, come to doubt the Christian faith and biblical account of origins on the very same grounds. But until Darwin, few dared to attribute to the cause of their stumbling at the Christian message, namely, to universal pain and suffering, the very creative force operating, in their view, to produce the evolution of life and species. Yet this was precisely what Darwin did. For he considered that the presence of universal pain

[59]*Ibid.*, p. 267.

made belief in a good God impossible and yet held at the same time that universal pain coupled with natural selection was the creative agency behind the origin of life and species. Obviously Darwin must have imagined a malign creative force behind the universe.

Need solution for pain problem. The importance of a truly intellectually satisfactory reason for pain and suffering and their coexistence with a God of compassion is thus evident. What passes popularly as the Christian gospel today, particularly in the United States, scarcely touches these real problems, with the result that Christians from the New World are often totally incapable of dealing with the genuine problems of either people from the Old World, or materialistic Darwinists from both hemispheres, who are usually well versed in these matters.

The solution to the problem of pain—and this was one of Darwin's basic theological problems—is to be found just where solutions to many other problems of life are to be found, namely, in the character and life of Christ. Let us ask ourselves first of all what Christ's attitude to pain and death was. This we can rapidly ascertain if we look at his most prominent activity in life, which was, of course, going about healing and doing good.[60] This means simply that he made it his job to reverse pain and death. He raised Lazarus[61] and Jairus' daughter[62] from the dead. But this attitude was not confined to Christ, for his apostles referred to death as the last *enemy*.[63] Christ referred to people with certain sicknesses as being bound by the devil.[64] If Jesus Christ considered himself to be God's Son (there is no doubt that he did[65]), he considered that he was doing God's works in reversing pain and death, as enemies of God. He said he was doing what he saw the Father doing.[66] Thus Christ reflected God's attitude when he went

[60]John 10:32; Matt. 4:23.
[61]John 11:43.
[62]Luke 8:54.
[63]I Cor. 15:26.
[64]Luke 13:16.
[65]John 17:5; John 10:30; 5:23.
[66]John 5:19.

about reversing pain and death and their consequences.

On reading the Bible more carefully, there is really never any question of reconciling God with pain, suffering and death as though he were the real author of them—even though he may use pain for his purposes. If Christ gives any indication at all of God's attitude to pain and death, then God is the great reverser and enemy of pain and death—infinitely more so than Darwin or any other thinking men perhaps imagine. As God of the resurrection and life, He is the great annihilator of death and suffering. We can only say, then, how mistaken Darwin was in rejecting belief in a compassionate God because of the pain in the world! Darwin ought to have been the most devoted Christian on the basis of Christ's attitude to suffering, which agreed with his own so well.

To underline the fundamental misunderstanding on the part of Darwin in these matters, a misunderstanding which developed slowly but surely over many years, we must mention the fact that Christ himself of his own free will took upon himself perhaps the worst form of suffering and death which a man can be subjected to, namely, death on a cross. His suffering was so great that even he called out at last: "My God, my God, why hast thou forsaken me?" So Christ experienced that which we all experience and that which turned Darwin away from Christianity—the terrible mystery of suffering to the death. We can ask ourselves Darwin's own question and cry: Why did a compassionate God, if there is one, allow this horror? In being forsaken to the end in nameless suffering, Christ uttered the cry of all in suffering and death. So he certainly understood Darwin's problem in a very practical way. Darwin thought too deeply here to be put off with cant, which he rightly abhorred. Many today are just as unable to find an intellectually satisfying answer to these ultimate problems and will not be put off with superficiality. Darwin foundered on the reef of the problem of pain, and it is up to Christians, if they love their fellowmen and are also enemies of pain and death, to provide a real answer to the problem.

Meanwhile, one does wonder with "His Abysmal Majesty of the Miserific Vision of the deepest Lowerarchy" (with apologies to C. S. Lewis' *Screwtape Letters*[67]) at the success and excellent reception which the scientific world has given to the idea of pain (the "enemy" of God) being the responsible agent for the upward evolution of life! For he has used the tool of suffering to dislodge faith in a compassionate God and then used the same tool as a substitute god to account for living creation!

Is God a Jealous Tyrant? The remaining problem relative to Darwin's development of mind concerns that of his conviction that the God of the Bible was a jealous tyrant. Our dealing with this question will allow us at the same time to answer the question as to why God did not simply dismiss pain and suffering from his world by fiat. How could a compassionate God take no action in face of the parlous state of suffering in which the world, his creation, finds itself? Darwin expected a God who was almighty and could therefore command pain and struggle to cease.

Assuming that an almighty and just God ought to be able to do just as Darwin thought he ought to be able to do, why does he not act? Surely, to anyone who knows Christian doctrine at all, the answer ought to be clear at once. It is just because he is by definition not only almighty but also patient, compassionate and just. If he is going to destroy the destroyers by means of an almighty act, he will have to destroy all, since *all* men have deserved destruction at some time or another. He cannot go in for any favoritism, if he is just. So he has put a moratorium on general judgment until such time as a general judgment can take place on an equal basis for all. This moratorium has, according to Christian teaching, even extended to the author of pain, suffering and death himself, in whom so many today refuse to believe, but whose works are so patent and without whom an interpretation of the moral state of man really is difficult. Darwin wanted, professedly, to believe

---

[67]Lewis, *op. cit.*, *Screwtape Letters and Screwtape Proposes* . . ., p. 100.

in a patient, compassionate God, but when God turned out
to be so compassionate and patient to *all* (sparing even the
author of pain and death in the creation until such time as
general justice could be done) to the extent of taking suffering and death upon himself, rather than insisting that his
creatures suffer the consequences of their own folly, then Darwin rejected the patient One on the basis that he did not act
like an almighty One! So Darwin rejected the patient God
and the "tyrant" too!

Of course, in the long run, Darwin will get the "impossible." For God's patience will not last so long that it could
be classed as inaction or indulgence. For God has promised to
consummate his justice in banning pain and death together
with their author. But meanwhile Darwin and his fellow
thinkers resemble the children in the marketplace to whom
Christ referred.[68] When we piped, no one would dance. And
when we lamented, they again found fault, not liking that
either. So nothing could be right for them.

Surely the basic error into which Darwin and his friends fell
was that they never really ascertained with an open mind what
Christ and the Bible do really teach on suffering. They believed that the Bible was wrong on the question of origins
(further knowledge has shown how they could have been in
error here) and they then proceeded to believe it was wrong
on all the other counts on which they experienced difficulties.
So they threw out the baby with the bath water. Of course, a
great deal of guilt lies in the lap of Christian philosophers,
who certainly did give a one-sided view of Christian teachings,
making it often a caricature and therefore amusing, maybe,
but not to be taken seriously intellectually.

Other Problems in Darwin's Development. It is often forgotten that, even if Darwin did explain to his own satisfaction
the origin of species and life, yet this gave him no excuse for
believing that there was no design in the universe. For living
matter represents only a very small fraction of total matter.

[68]Luke 7:32.

Even if life showed no designer, owing to design being arti-
ficially produced by natural selection, yet the same arguments
cannot be applied to nonliving nature. Nonliving nature, as
the physicists confess, does show design of the highest order,
and design which cannot be explained away as Darwin tried
to do in the case of life. Sir James Jeans expresses the conviction of many physicists when he maintains that the universe
looks like one sublime thought and that the designer thought
on the lines of the pure mathematician (see Foreword). So
even though Darwin has, for the majority of biologists today,
explained away the argument from design for living matter,
what are his fellow thinkers proposing to do about explaining
away the argument from design in the much larger universe
of nonliving matter surrounding us on every side?

In considering all these questions it is important to recognize the fact that Darwin was an expert at so clothing his statements on "emotional" issues in ambiguous language that it is
often difficult to arrive at what he really thought himself. He
believed in the "sap and mine"[69] technique, so that the un-
suspecting would accept his more "advanced" theories without demur until it was too late to argue. He disliked antag-
onizing the susceptible, and referred therefore in his earlier
works to "throwing light on man's origin" rather than stating
that man was derived by means of natural selection from
lower animals, which latter kind of statement would, he knew,
enrage the pious. Although he and his friends had long made
up their minds that man was so derived, he watered down his
statements until such time as he could risk clarity.

Summary. Lamarck and Darwin both thought that acquired
characters were inherited. Darwin thought that natural selection sorted out the useful random and acquired variations
from the useless or deleterious ones. The useful characters
were then assumed to be responsible for the upward evolution
to higher forms of life. This process produced as a by-product
an appearance of design.

[69]De Beer, op. cit. p. 154.

Today it is known that, although inheritable variations (mutations) do occur by chance but are mostly degenerative in nature as required by thermodynamics, yet a good proportion of variations to environmental changes are actually genetically controlled responses of the cell to exogenous factors. Thus a cyclops' eye is genetically produced in some fish embryos in response to the presence of magnesium chloride in the water. This means that at least some of the inheritable variations which were formerly thought to be due to random variation (mutation) or even to acquired characters in the Lamarckian sense, were, in fact, already indwelling genetically controlled factors produced by direct genetic response to specific environmental stimuli. This means that, with respect to this type of variation at least, a large slice of chance is ruled out of Darwin's method of thought and replaced by a goodly proportion of genetic design, or predesign. All this goes to reduce appreciably Darwin's estimate of the importance of chance in certain types of variation. We are left with a living organism which is much more thoroughly designed than we had imagined, for it turns out to be much more supple in being designed to deal with the chance and vagaries of changing environment.

What we are, in fact, saying is that chance today cannot be expected to be considered to be so important in upward evolution as it was thirty years ago. The corollary to this is that design, cell and genetic design, must take over the gaps left where chance has been deposed in today's theories.

Perhaps we may hope that one day the argument from design may be reinstated in science to the position it holds in Romans 1 and Paley's watchmaker may open shop once more!

We may ask ourselves why Darwin complained about pain as being unworthy of the postulate of an almighty God and why Darwinists write about the devil's chaplain being able and in a position to author books on the "clumsy, wasteful, blundering, low and horribly cruel works of nature" the horrors of which "cannot be reconciled with a Creator of allegedly unlimited power and inexhaustible compassion.[70] For it is the Darwinists alone who have sought to make the Creator responsible for all this horror, not the Christians, who have always uncompromisingly denied that such works are authored by their God. The whole question turns, of course, on the word "almighty." Christians have always conditioned the use of words attributing omnipotence to God with patience and justice. So let us keep steadily in view the fact that the Christian does not attribute the horrors of nature to God, but places them under his long-suffering. It was the Darwinists, particularly the theistic evolutionists, who suggested that the Creator used the clumsy, wasteful, blundering, low and horribly cruel works of nature to create life. They attribute to him such low methods, and having done that, the agnostics and atheists among them, laugh him out of court for having created thus. They attribute to him evil and then proceed to laugh him out of court for that which they attribute (wrongly) to him, which does not seem to be very fair. *The real point is this: the Darwinists are saying, in thus maligning God, that the theory of creation they, the Darwinists, have developed is clumsy, blundering, low and horribly cruel.* The Christian does not wish to believe in such admittedly clumsy theories anyway and is of the conviction that the creation was brought about by mechanisms which are thermodynamically less impotent than some of these Darwinian ones we have discussed. If the scientist does not wish to believe in an almighty God, who is at the same time compassionate, just and long-suffering, that is his personal affair. Personally, no God could be a God to me if his character were entirely transparent to my finite thoughts and conceptions. No man can conceive of a union of these characters mentioned in one person. But that is just what one would expect if one were asked to conceive of God; for the various characters are too big to fit into one picture in very finite minds. However, the Darwinist having produced a theory of life's origin which is, on his own admis-

[70]*Ibid.*, p. 267.

sion, clumsy, blundering, wasteful and horribly cruel (and which one therefore cannot accept as an expression of the whole truth behind nature), then turns on the Christian with the taunt that he is orthodox and therefore at the same time uninformed in disbelieving it! Surely the lack of information might just conceivably lie in other laps than in those of the orthodox!

Finally, one respects Darwin's strength of character for having taken a strong stand against unnecessary pain and even having given up his favorite sport because of his conviction. One understands and respects him too for having supported vivisection on the grounds that the total community would profit thereby in helping man to reduce pain by the physiological knowledge gained. If there is a good reason for causing pain it may be justifiable to cause it, as in the case of amputating a limb to save the whole body. But can one follow the logic of one who, on the ground of the horrible suffering all around him, maintains that there can be no reason for allowing it *simply because he can find no reason?* A savage, seeing an arm being sawn off, might think the surgeon a terribly cruel person, just because he, the savage, does not know all about gangrene. Therefore to assert that, with respect to the destruction and pain in the world "there is no argument possible"[71] to justify divine guidance in nature, is to assert a *non sequitur*. For the finite mind of man is still facing the infinite mind of God. Man will therefore be putting himself fairly and squarely in the position of imagining himself to know everything about the reason for pain and suffering continuing in the world, if he asserts—as Sir Gavin de Beer expressly does assert—"that there is no argument possible here."[72] I somehow feel he cannot have meant quite that. For surely the fact that we do not know of an answer by no means proves there is no answer possible, unless one believes oneself to be a colleague of God and omniscient! This really would be to imagine that wisdom was going to perish with

[71]*Ibid.*
[72]*Ibid.*

one! Darwin himself was much more humble when he concluded, "The safest conclusion seems to me that the whole subject [the immense amount of suffering through the world] is beyond the scope of man's intellect."[73] Maybe there will be reason for us all to heartily support the Creator's having left pain and suffering in the world until the general judgment, when we one day do have all the eternal facts at our disposal and all secrets will be made manifest. In view of the infinity of knowledge we still do not have at our fingertips, we may appear to some, who are in a better position than we, to still resemble the savage at the amputation operation.

REACTION OF SOME MODERN MATHEMATICIANS AND PHYSICISTS TO DARWINISM AND NEO-DARWINISM

Trend away from Darwinism. It is a mistake for Darwinists and Neo-Darwinists to insist, as they often do, that all competent and informed persons agree with them and their theories on the origin and evolution of life up to man. For the plain fact—if one wishes, the handwriting on the wall—is that more and more physicists, mathematicians and even biologists are becoming worried about the whole conceptual basis of Darwinism and Neo-Darwinism, demanding, as it does, that order arise spontaneously out of chaos, the method being that of chance mutation coupled with natural selection. In fact, it is well recognized in scientific circles today that biologists are "exquisitely sensitive"[74] to any and all suggestions to the effect that Darwinism and present evolutionary theory might lack logic or wit. Sensitivity in regard to a specific point often betrays weakness in that very point.

A discussion[75] took place in the summer of 1965 in Switzerland between four mathematicians (Murray Eden, M.I.T.; S. M. Ulam, Los Alamos; V. Weisskopf, formerly director of CERN, Geneva, Switzerland, and now of M.I.T.; and M. P.

[73]*Ibid.*, p. 268.
[74]"Heresy in the Halls of Biology," *Scientific Research* (New York: McGraw-Hill, Nov. 1967), p. 59, *Science, 160* (1968), p. 408.
[75]*Ibid.*, pp. 59-66.

Schutzenberger, University of Paris; and two biologists, one of whom was Martin Kaplan) on the above subject. The mathematicians insisted that mathematical analysis of current evolutionary theories showed that there were logical flaws and that "some of their statements were vacuous."

Use Unproved Concepts to Prove Theories. Darwin believed in the "survival of the fittest," whereas Neo-Darwinists today believe in the "survival of those who leave the most off-spring." Dr. Eden, professor of electrical engineering at M.I.T., is of the conviction that both these concepts of survival are tautologous, in other words, they state that only the properties of organisms which survive to produce off-spring do survive, which is truly tautologous or vacuous. Perhaps the worst point about such tautologous theory is that it cannot be disproved. It can, on the other hand, be used to prove almost anything, and is so used today. As an example, Dr. J. C. Fentress of the University of Rochester's Brain Research Center, studied two British voles, one species of which became motionless on sighting a moving test object, while the other species ran away under the same circumstances. One species happened to live in the woods while the other inhabited the fields. Dr. Fentress then presented his findings to some zoologists, asking for an evolutionary explanation. But he first of all reversed the species belonging to each set of data. The vole which froze was presented where the one that ran should have been in the data. Even with the reversed data the zoologists, on the basis of evolutionary theory, were able to "explain" the behavior of the voles, even though their data had, unknown to them, been coupled to the wrong vole. The answers given were perfectly convincing and authoritative, though 100 percent wrong.

Time for Complex Biochemistry to Have Developed? Dr. Eden is convinced that it is highly unlikely that life could have reached its complex biochemistry in the relatively few generations at its disposal since archebiopoiesis, unless some "restriction on random variation" had occurred somewhere. Present evolutionary theories do not explain this restriction or restraint on variation which mathematics demands. Therefore, concludes Dr. Eden, something is lacking or missing in evolutionary theory as presented us today.

In discussing the synthesis of proteins from polypeptides, the following illustrates Dr. Eden's point:

> Each of these polypeptides can be thought of as a "word" consisting of 250 letters, each letter chosen from an alphabet of 20 letters, since there are 20 known, different peptide units included in protein chains. Consequently, there are about 20^{250} or 10^{325} possible protein words which could be uttered by the genetic system. Next, instead of comparing this figure with the number of different proteins known now, an upper limit on the quantity of different proteins which actually may exist, i.e., yield workable systems, is found by estimating how many protein molecules have ever existed for a nominal span of life on earth of 10^9 years. Assuming a layer of cells 30% rich in protein extending over the surface of the earth to a depth of 1 cm., this figure is computed to be about 10^{52}, which is to say that the surface of the 10^{325} possible protein molecules has barely been scratched.[76]

What Dr. Eden is saying is that there are huge numbers of possible protein molecules, which have never been formed. But we would *expect* these molecules to have been formed if random variation were responsible for their formation in the evolution of life. Evolutionary theories make little attempt to explain the obviously powerful restriction of randomness in protein and other syntheses observed in nature. Actually, Darwinists and Neo-Darwinists generally insist on the opposite position, namely, that absolute, unrestricted randomness explains every observed fact. Randomness in variation needs, according to them, only natural selection to pluck order out of chaos. Mathematically this is, on the face of things, highly unlikely, although Darwinists will disagree here.

Planning is, of course, a method of "restricting randomness." But the assumption of "overt planning" in archebiopoiesis or evolution of life is a concept that will not yet find

[76]*Ibid.*, pp. 60-63.

approval in the mind or writing of any biological scientist
who values his scientific life and limb, for that concept would
involve a planner, whom science has banned from scientific
literature since the days of Darwin, who "destroyed" the
whole concept of an argument from design, at least in biology. For this reason phrases such as "restriction of randomness" have to serve for the concept of planning, even though
their meanings are not always congruent.

Dr. Eden inclines "toward the view that out of all the possible paths, short and long, which evolution might have taken
in establishing useful proteins, it has selectively moved along
the shortest." On the other hand, he sees the use of the pure
random system for evolutionary change leading up to man
"like the possibility of typing at random a meaningful library
of one thousand volumes using the following procedure: Begin with a meaningful phrase, retype it with a few mistakes,
make it longer by adding letters, and rearrange subsequences
in the string of letters; then examine the result to see if the
new phrase is meaningful. Repeat the process until the library is complete."[77] Perhaps one may risk commenting with
Sir Gavin de Beer that such a method certainly does appear
to be a trifle clumsy and wasteful of effort. One wonders who
could have imagined a God using this sort of method to
create life and what the concept of such a God's I.Q. (with all
due reverence) must have been!

Dr. Eden then goes on to suggest that "The principal task
of the evolutionist is to discover and examine mechanisms
which constrain the variation of phenotypes to a very small
class and to *relegate the notion of randomness to a minor and
noncrucial role.*"[78] And so two of the basic pillars of Darwinism have been removed by the mathematicians. Natural selection, survival of the fittest, survival of those leaving the
most offspring, have been shown to be vacuous, tautologous
statements. Further, mathematicians are now convinced that
randomness as a cause of evolution must be reduced in im-

[77]*Ibid.*, p. 63.
[78]*Ibid.*, p. 65.

portance and relegated to a minor, noncrucial role. Both these conclusions have been reached on purely scientific mathematical grounds and, in effect, reverse the grounds for the assumptions on which Darwinism and Neo-Darwinism reject the argument from design. This is not to maintain that the argument from design has been reinstated by the mathematicians, but *that the main grounds on which the Darwinists rejected the argument from design have evaporated.* Surely we may hope that, as the mechanism of heredity becomes more manifest in its details, the mechanism by which life has really evolved upward from nonliving matter may become clearer. That chaotic, nonliving matter has reached a high state of organization in living matter is manifest. That random processes are not sufficient to account for this process of upward organization in every living organism is also clear, at least to many mathematicians and physicists. The only question remaining open is just *how the observed restriction of randomness has occurred. Two views are open to us: Either this restriction of randomness has taken place as a result of intrinsic properties in matter, or the restriction has been imposed on matter from without, that is, supramaterially.* Most scientists who are materialists believe in the first explanation simply because they, as materialists, are not prepared to believe in phenomena ascribed to supramatter or supranature. *But there is no evidence that matter, left to itself, can effect this restriction of randomness.* It is therefore quite unscientific to scorn the scientist who admits the possibility of supranature being active in processes involving restriction of randomness.

Genetic System Not a Blueprint. It is believed today that the genetic system is not simply a template or blueprint carrying all the details of the recipe for producing an organism in response to the reaction of its genes with the environment. The genetic system is thought today to resemble rather an algorithm, that is, a minimal generative procedure giving the least set of instructions necessary to attain its ends. In order to generate, for example, a table of numbers for every piece of information given, further information is calculated from the skeleton information provided so that the missing pieces of information may be calculated from that already on hand. A blueprint, as opposed to an algorithm, gives the instructions for the complete table of numbers. This means that the genetic algorithm is intrinsically even more highly improbable as a random phenomenon than a straight blueprint or template system.

If the genetic system is built as an algorithm, then its "language" is still undiscovered even though molecular biology has elucidated its alphabet. This state of affairs can be likened to an understanding of a typewriter's alphabet but also to a nonunderstanding of the language in which the typist types on the typewriter. It will suffice here to point out that such genetic alphabets and languages run counter to all modern Neo-Darwinistic theories of randomness, for the simple reason that no language can ever tolerate random changes in the symbol sequences expressing its sentences.[79] No computer algorithmic procedures can make sense out of nonsense by random means.

Robert Berhard sums up the situation by remarking that biologists are "exquisitely sensitive" about Darwin's theories and any attacks on them, but that Dr. Eden's challenge is "too vigorous" to be dismissed easily.[80]

SOME MYTHOLOGY

To this summing up of the views of some modern physical scientists on Darwinism and Neo-Darwinism a simple piece of mythology might be added.

A few thousand years hence our descendants carry out an archeological and geological investigation of our present civilization during which they discover the remains of automobiles dated about 1890, 1910, 1920, 1940, 1970 and 1990. The line of upward evolution of the automobile toward increasing perfection during these years becomes obvious to them. The

[79]*Ibid.*, p. 66.
[80]*Ibid.*

question is how to interpret this upward development to complexity. Why had the automobile developed so slowly over
the years instead of being invented perfect from the start?
They cannot ask the automobile designers, they no longer
exist, and no one has ever seen an automobile factory. However, they know that our generation was given to travel and
mobility. They know of the competition between the various
means of travel and transport in our age. They can even produce some studies on market research in this area.

After much study the brilliant Dr. Voorsite and his equally
erudite assistant Dr. Heindsyt, produce an all-embracing theoretical synthesis of the mass of previously incoherent facts
extant on automobiles. Our scientists find that all cars, even
mass-produced ones produced on a template, blueprint system, did in spite of everything, show slight random variations.
It is true, they were only small ones, but nevertheless variations, which obviously played an important part in the travel
pressures of our day. For certain automobile variants enjoyed
better sales than others. The public demanded certain of
them more than the previous "standard" automobiles, with
the result that more and more of the variants became produced and therefore left their "fossil" remains to the future
generation. In the end only those automobiles possessing such
variants as automatic transmission, power steering, disc brakes
and four front headlights could multiply at all. The traveling
public would not consider any car without these variations,
so that less desirable automobiles rapidly became extinct. It
came about thus that the geological formations corresponding
to 1960-70 were teeming with specimens showing power steering and automatic transmission; very few transitional specimens were to be found. Before the 1920 period, no cars with
these refinements were dug up. But those cars not developing
disc brakes, automatic windows, and rear window wipers and
heaters had died out completely by 1980, simply because the
force of buyers' selection had stopped them from being produced. Thus buyers' *selection* in a competitive society and

random variation turn out to be a totally sufficient explanation of the evolution of the car. *This undeniable fact of variation and selection in the evolution of the car was proved by all automobile geology and any competent person could satisfy himself about this by taking a visit to his nearest car geology museum.*

One other startling piece of intellectual brilliance emerged. The fixation of small variations in cars by the selective nature of the car buyers' taste renders all other theories on the evolution of automobiles entirely unnecessary. Such ideas as car designers and special buildings where entropy laws are apparently reversed and cars are designed and produced are superfluous postulates in automobile evolutionary theory. Outmoded ideas such as car designers and factories, where car synthesis instead of decay took place, where special laws of construction operated not normally seen in finished (and therefore decaying) cars, are the products of special pleading, and, on the principle of Occam's Razor, to be rejected as superfluous complicating assumptions. It suffices to say that *cars arose.* Random variation coupled with selective fixation present an entirely satisfactory total account of automobile evolution. Unfortunately, some backward people resisted the whole idea of buyers' selection and random variation as being the complete explanation of the automobile evolutionary story. These incompetents pointed out that it would be difficult to imagine transitional stages between the crash and the synchromesh gearbox leading to automatic transmission. How could such awkward transitional stages offer advantages in buyers' selection? they asked.

Dr. Voorsite argued that, on the contrary, such transitional forms of automobiles were known and did flourish in the intermediate periods, even though they never reached the population concentrations achieved by later, more perfect models. For he himself had excavated several small automobiles in the geological formations corresponding to the 1940-60 period in the wilds of Abingdon, England. Each bore the cryptic letters

MG on the radiator. The important observation he had made on these models was that some models bore a shift lever in the center of the floor, while others bore the corresponding lever on the steering column. Otherwise the models were practically identical. It is well known that all automatic transmissions bear their controls on the steering column, whereas practically all stick shifts ever discovered before the 1930 era bore their shift levers in the center of the floor. The MG models discovered were therefore quite obviously transitional automobiles between the crash gearbox, the synchromesh gearbox and the automatic transmission types; for some bore their shift levers on the floor and some on the steering column. Since it was well known that matter and metals possess an innate tendency to spontaneous synthesis up to ever more complex and therefore perfect automobiles, the postulate of design was unnecessary in explanation of the evolution of the automatic transmission in automobiles. Random variation fixed by buyers' selection produced the *appearance* of design.

In spite of all this theory, a certain Dr. Heilsam thought that random variation and buyers' selection might perhaps account for some aspects of automobile evolution, but not for all aspects. He presented some mathematical evidence against the probability of a crash gearbox becoming redesigned to an automatic one by random changes fixed by buyers' selection without an exogenous designer. He was duly informed that inspection of the evidence, particularly the geological evidence, would convince any competent person of the entire validity of the new synthetical theory. Buyers' selection and random variation *alone* gave a perfectly satisfactory explanation of *all* the observed facts of automobile evolution. No one had ever seen a car designer or car factory and apparently never would. Cars were no longer extant, designers were myths. To the informed and unprejudiced, not even a perfectly meshed gearbox was evidence of *design* but was merely proof of the universal law that a buyer would rather buy a perfectly meshed gearbox than an imperfectly meshed noisy one. Otherwise stated: random gearbox variations and perfection of meshing became fixed by the pressure of buyers' selection, so that the perfectly meshed gearbox, the synchromesh gearbox or the automatic transmission were able to leave more progeny behind them, since they found more buyers than their less fortunate badly meshed rivals, which therefore became extinct. No primitive notions of design or designers were necessary to explain the *fact* of automobile evolution.

No report on the age under review would be complete without mention of Dr. Pfortschritt's erudite research on instinct and innate behavior in fossil automobiles of the late twentieth century. Dr. Pfortschritt, together with his brilliant young assistant Dr. Hindster, reconstructed in the minutest detail a number of fossil automobiles of this period. They had been so well preserved that even the hieroglyphics on the hubcaps were in some cases readable, for they had been wrapped in sheets of transparent material evidently secreted by an extinct plant but which analyzed for $(C_2H_4)_x$. These reconstructed automobiles showed, to the amazement of all concerned, "intelligence" as well as ingrained "instincts." It was found, for example, that each car was governed by a computer brain and could navigate itself around obstacles without collision ever occurring. The cars were also capable of learning by experience, for after one mistake, ending in a brush or collision, they never collided again, there being a well-developed memory core coupled to the main computer brain. Some automobiles could get themselves out of the most hair-raising situations without any outside consultation, especially after having been involved previously in one or two minor accidents.

However, in addition to the computer brains conferring near-intelligence on these marvelous machines of the late twentieth century, the automobiles possessed, as mentioned above, well-defined, ingrained "instincts" not directly coupled to their computer brains. The instincts were part of the basic structure of the car, just as much as the doors were part of the structure. Dr. Hindster who was, in addition to his activities as Dr. Pfortschritt's assistant, a trained historian, rapidly threw light on the nature and origin of these instincts. He pointed out that they greatly resembled those characteristics described by the ancient sage of the nineteenth century Charles Darwin,[81] who had described the development of similar phenomena in insects and other animals now extinct. Dr. Hindster's explanation of instinct in the automobile of the late twentieth century has been accepted by every competent person as satisfying and complete.

The key to the sparkling explanation of instinct given by Dr. Hindster lies in the postulate that rudimentary instincts also arose by chance variation[82] and that this fact gave its possessor an advantage in the pressure of selection. Not all the progeny of the animals possessing rudimentary instinct showed it to the identical degree. Slight variations in degree were undoubtedly observed[83] upon which selection then acted to develop the instinct to a higher degree.

Dr. Pfortschritt and Dr. Hindster's great contribution to science lies, of course, in the application of Darwin's principle of random variation and selection to the automobile instincts of the late twentieth century. For, as these two scientists point out, the phenomenon of the "rpm instinct" arose by chance in a model automobile which maintained its engine rpm slightly more constant than other models regardless of its rear-wheel speed, so conferring an advantage on this model over its competitors in that reduced gasoline consumption and wear occurred. Obviously this favored the model in buyers' selection. Once this rudimentary random variation in automatic rear-wheel behavior with respect to engine speed had arisen, buyers' selection took care of the rest. Only those automobiles which possessed the ingrained instinct (for instinct it obviously is, it is definitely automatic

[81]Charles Darwin, *The Origin of Species* (New York: P. F. Collier & Son Co., 1909), p. 263.
[82]*Ibid.*, p. 267.
[83]*Ibid.*, p. 266.

and intrinsic in design, even in the youngest models investigated, and not computer brain controlled) of maintaining
relatively constant engine speed (rpm) irrespective of rear-
wheel speed, only such models possessing this valuable instinct multiplied under the pressure of buyers' selection and
therefore left more numerous progeny than other models
showing less developed capacity in this direction. Thus the
observed facts on the instinct of controlling engine speed
regardless of rear-wheel speed are fully and satisfyingly explained.

A minor scientist protested at Dr. Pfortschritt's theory,
maintaining that it did nothing to account for the complexity
of automatic transmission and its obvious design. Its relatively sudden appearance in the geological formations bearing automobiles also presented a problem. Dr. Pfortschritt
wrote a long and somewhat abstruse article in refutation of
the ignorant notions expressed by the minor scientist, showing that he obviously knew nothing at all of the all-embracing
power of buyers' selection acting on random variation in
automatic transmission which explained everything perfectly
satisfyingly to the competent person and informed mind. The
phenomenon demonstrated an *automatic method of extracting order out of chaos*,[84] *that is, design out of no design, provided they were given huge time spans to carry out the work.*

Thus all protests to this all-embracing scheme were
ignored. In fact, the protesters were all warned that they
were dependent for promotion in their jobs on the favors of
their peers, and that they would certainly find it impossible
to obtain or retain any chair in the famous universities which
graced their native country if they showed any disrespect
and incompetence in attacking established facts of science.

POSTSCRIPTUM

With regard to the supposed effectiveness of natural selection in securing the upward evolution of organisms, the

[84] See pp. 56-59, 61-72, 82, 85, 215, 216, 220, 221 of this volume.

following remarks made by Dr. William J. Tinkle are in-structive:

> . . . We do not find the kind of mutations that would be needed to initiate a more complex animal. In addition, an unwarranted assumption must be made, namely that the more complex types have an advantage in the strug-gle for existence. Daisies are considered a higher type than pines because their reproduction is more complex. Yet on abandoned farms in the Appalachian Mountains, Jack pines are crowding out daisies because the former make more shade. Among water animals, Daphnia are much more complex than Hydra, having heart, gills, alimentary canal, and big, black eyes, while Hydra is but a two-layered sack. Put the two together in a beaker of water and watch the Hydra devour the Daphnia.
>
> If animals developed specialized structures as a result of the advantage those structures confer, what shall we say about the opossum, Didelphys marsupialis, which has generalized teeth and legs and very little brain, yet increases in numbers?"
>
> . . . But this abundant marsupial has increased its range from the Middle Atlantic States into New Eng-land, and introduced into California it has become abundant on the Pacific coast. Here we have Hydra, pine, and opossum, which are not structurally complex or specialized, which should be pushed toward extinc-tion if evolution by natural selection were true. Instead of this fate they are thriving and increasing in num-bers.[85]

[85]William J. Tinkle, *Heredity, a Study in Science and the Bible* (Houston, Tex.: St. Thomas Press, 1967), p. 96.

MAN'S DESTINY

5

THE DESTINY OF MAN

Darwinism does not have much to say with respect to the future of individuals of a race, except that their chief purpose is to serve for the progress of that race as a whole. What is supposed to happen after the individual's allotted span of life is accomplished depends on whether the Darwinist is theistic or materialistic. A large number of Darwinists are materialistic and therefore believe that, with the destruction of the body, the individual is entirely finished. If life is simply and entirely an association of matter, regardless of its complexity, the dissolution of the body must be the end of the individual. The pure materialist can have neither hope nor basis for hope of existence after the dissolution of his body. Any hope there may be must lie in the development or evolution of matter in the future human race. Thus the seventy years we may have as our span of life have no purpose for the individual beyond these seventy years, which means that the holder of such beliefs will tend to become a practical nihilist in the course of time.

Few are the individuals like Father Pierre Teilhard de Chardin who can enthuse over the prospect of reaching Point Omega in the development of the race and yet retain their Darwinistic beliefs. We must only ask ourselves, however,

233

whether there is any branch of science which is purely nihilistic, and yet which has shown itself to be an expression of the truth.

NO NEW PRINCIPLES FOR SUPERRACE

Even with respect to the future development of the "superman" Darwinism has not much new to offer. For the biological destiny (Darwinism knows little else) of the superman or superrace is not going to be *qualitatively* very different from ours though *quantitatively* it may differ. For the superman or superrace is envisaged as eating, drinking, sleeping, marrying, reproducing its kind and dying, in much the same way as we do. To be sure, he will be able to eat, drink, sleep, etc., perhaps more efficiently than we. Perhaps he will work only two days a week and fly to the planets and back with ease. But no *new principles* of life or thought will have been introduced with the proposed superraces. Everything that Darwinism offers us is, of course, really an extrapolation of what we have here and now. No new directions or dimensions have been developed by Darwinists, with the possible exception of the views developed by Teilhard. And Teilhard's views on development up to Point Omega as an extension of biological evolution and cephalization are the result of a grafting of biblical prophecy onto Darwinism.

With the exception noted above, most ideas on this subject are merely an extrapolation of those we already know about, even though man may colonize the moon or the planets. Mankind now toys with the idea of war in space and on newly colonized planets, such as we already have here on earth. Mankind, in the thoughts of the space novelist, is still morally the same, even though he is a superman. What it all amounts to is an attempt in the name of "progress" to build "bigger and better elephants," but nothing basically new in thought or dimension has arisen. The development foreseen by our space and progress prophets are merely extensions or extrapolations of old ideas. But should the projected new race live nine hundred years (as long as Adam) and the standard of living become much higher than that we now know, the space novelist still views the superman as fighting, living and dying even then as we do now. And yet dying is the all-important phenomenon to which all come, men or supermen. Darwinists do not seem to be interested in what death, the common denominator in human ideas in both of the present and future races, may mean.

NO SANCTITY OF INDIVIDUAL

Of course, if death is the end, really the *end,* why bother about what happens at death and afterward? Why respect the individual at all if all is over with his death? If he dies, what of it? It is the *end,* there are no consequences to be feared. We can easily reason one step further and say that because there are plenty of individuals, in fact, too many of them, they are expendable material. And this is the conclusion to which many political devotees of Darwinism have come, and on which they have acted as policy. The Communists, Fascists and National Socialists without second thoughts sent masses of infantry into withering machine gun fire to exhaust the ammunition supplies of those slaughtering them. The masses of dead lying before their guns often blocked the field of fire. The same denial of the sanctity of the individual can still be seen in Siberian slave camps.[1] The same attitude was rampant in the Nazi extermination camps.[2] The Nazi would murder a prisoner just as nonchalantly as he would open or close a window, according to Kogon.

But we must keep steadily before us that this attitude of disrespect of the sanctity of the individual and his rights is a direct result of nihilistic beliefs. *For as a man believes so he becomes.* For such belief, life is merely an aggregation of matter. Destroy that aggregation and you have wiped out life and all its meaning. If justice is not done in this life, it

[1]Cf. John H. Noble, *I Found God in Soviet Russia* (New York: St. Martin's Press, 1966), fifteenth printing.
[2]Cf. Eugen Kogon, *Der SS-Staat* (Frankfurt/Main: Europäische Verlagsanstalt, 1964).

never will be done, according to these doctrines. So the murderer feels safe as long as he can get away with his murder in this life. He discounts the thought of retribution afterward, just so he may do as he likes now and avoid capture. As long as he can keep his enemies powerless and at his mercy, he considers himself safe. This whole attitude of mind, this lawless brutality, comes automatically from the purely materialistic doctrines with which the modern tyrant has been brainwashed.

BIOLOGICAL WORLD OPPOSES NIHILISM

And yet the biological world which surrounds us, and from which Darwin thought he learned all his lessons, speaks quite a different language from that of the above sort of nihilism— nihilism for the individual and possible salvation for the race as a whole. For in nature we find hints and rumors that bodily death is not the end of individual existence. Wherever we look in science and biology we find proof that *nothing* is ever destroyed or lost in the cycle of nature. Instead we see everywhere in nature around us great transformations of one form into another, of one form of life into another, but never the sudden total annihilation of anything. Yet the modern materialists seem to think that the death of the individual is a sudden hiatus, a sudden break, a step from existence to nonexistence. If this were truly the case it would represent a great exception to all the laws and rules of nature we know today, as we shall see later.

The grain of corn falls into the earth in order to die and to enter the state of nonexistence as a grain of corn forever. And yet nonexistence has not really been entered upon. A mighty metamorphosis takes place at this "death," but that is no hiatus, no changing of a state of existence into a state of nonexistence, for the hidden and coded order on the genetic material of the grain gives rise to the beautiful waving green plant. If we had known only the grain of corn, we would never have connected it with the plant which it has become. The caterpillar does not suggest to us the butterfly which its metamorphosis will one day produce. If we knew only the caterpillar and the butterfly as such, we could hardly be expected to connect the two. The idea of a heavy sluggish caterpillar dancing on the wind would tax our unprepared imaginations far too much. One might as well imagine pigs flying. But the improbable caterpillar metamorphosis does occur and the butterfly is derived from it. Such a metamorphosis would appear to be, on the face of things, as improbable as a pig flying. Yet it occurs.

This principle may be extended. The ovum is expelled from the ovary and starts its journey downward to meet the spermatozoon. Neither the ovum nor the sperm bear any resemblance to the human being they will jointly become. But both ovum and sperm are simply bursting with unimaginable amounts of chemical information on body and brain building, information stored for generations past on the genes. Neither the outward form of the reproductive cells nor their stored chemical information show any likeness at all to the organism which they will become, the adult human. The metamorphosis would be almost unimaginable were it not so true and observable.

METABOLISM AND INDIVIDUALITY

PERSONALITY AND EGO AS RELATED TO MATTER

Now we need to take a look at another aspect of metamorphosis. The frog is sitting on a cool wet stone. With the help of certain sugar and protein molecules in his brain and muscles, the frog obtains the energy necessary for electrical impulses (his "thoughts") and for muscular contractions (his movements in catching insects with his tongue). Nervous impulses and movements of the tongue cost energy which is supplied by oxidation of sugar and protein molecules. In the course of this oxidation the frog breathes out carbon dioxide so that a metamorphosis in the world of carbon atoms has taken place in order to supply the energy necessary for nerve impulses and muscle movements. The carbon atoms are now no longer parts of large nonvolatile sugar and protein molecules but parts of relatively simple volatile carbon dioxide molecules. The carbon atom itself has remained unchanged during this striking metamorphosis from a large nonvolatile structure to a small volatile one.

The carbon dioxide molecules exhaled by the frog are perhaps absorbed by a potato plant and, with the help of the energy of the sun, reduced photosynthetically to sugar and starch molecules which are then stored in the tuber. One fine day I eat these potatoes. I absorb and burn the starch and sugar molecules to finance with their energy my efforts in thinking and writing about metamorphosis. The same carbon atoms, the energy of which I use to finance my thoughts and movements, were used by the frog for his purposes. Yet although both the frog and I used the same carbon atoms for financing our brains with energy, neither the frog nor I have impaired in any way the exclusive nature of our personalities. So that, even though our personalities have both shared the identical material basis, this common material basis has not interfered in either case with the personality it has helped to support. Personality, as such, is not utterly dependent on matter, as such. It may "ride" on matter but it is not identical nor to be equated with matter. To be very cautious, we might say that it is the order of arrangement of matter which is more responsible for personality than mere matter itself. And order, as we have already seen, has had to be imposed exogenously on matter. It does not arise as a property of matter alone, in spite of all Teilhard assumes and teaches to the contrary.

The individuality of the frog and of its thoughts does not lie then in the identity nor even in the constancy of its material structure as such, for the latter is in constant metabolism or flux. If matter, which is common to all individuals (rather than the order imposed on matter from without) were responsible for their thought and individuality, then the thoughts of all individuals ought to become "infected" with the thoughts of other individuals, in other words, frog thoughts ought to infect my thoughts. It is well known that our entire body exchanges all its material basis of atoms and molecules about once every seven years, so that we are, materially viewed, entirely new individuals every seven years. If then matter and its properties were totally responsible for individuality, then individuality as such ought to have disappeared years ago. Yet I remain the same old person year in and year out in spite of my completely changed material basis. The fact is that I am able to impose a certain kind of order on all matter entering my body's sphere of influence and this order determines my personality and individuality. Thus life and individuality ride upon a substitutable material structure ordered by the individual just as a rider rides his horse but can change it and still remain the same rider. As we shall see later, the materialist is assuming that this order can be destroyed without trace at death with no metamorphosis accompanying it.

One can even go farther in this line of thought. My ego or personality can easily change my physical appearance, as it does, for example, when I smile when I am pleased. My ego can determine whether I get gastric or duodenal ulcers. If my ego is merely the result of the order of certain nerve impulses then obviously this order is able to impose itself on the arrangement of matter of which we partly are composed. So that my ego is capable of metamorphosing otherwise nonliving matter in its order associations. My ego can impose a certain order on matter. It assists in building or destroying a body.

WOULD NOT LIFE FOLLOW NATURE'S PATTERN?

But really the important thing about life is not only the matter of which it consists but the order which has somehow been imposed on matter to make it capable of supporting life. This order is the vital subject which concerns us.

The same problem of order confronts us at every turn in our search for origins and destinies. For even the random atom is perfectly ordered with its electrons spinning in their orbits. In fact, it is just this kind of order which makes matter what it is. Fundamentally, matter is not what the layman might regard as extremely small "chunks of solid substance," but may be regarded more accurately as wave functions liable to be found in certain orbital paths. Put crudely, we might regard matter itself as ordered wave functions in space or nothingness. But this order which we see in matter brings us to one very important conclusion relevant to our subject. Matter, which is a form of order (or energy) is indestructible. Matter may be converted into energy, according to relativity concepts, but we cannot *destroy* this order, we cannot simply make of it a hiatus. We can metamorphose matter but not destroy it, even though, basically, it consists of order.

This brings us to the main point of the argument. If life is basically an order imposed upon matter, why should it represent an exception to all the rules of nature in being destructible without trace? Metamorphosis is seen in many natural phenomena. Why should not life fall under the same heading? It consists basically of an imposed form of order. If metamorphosis can transform matter (order) into energy, why should not a metamorphosis be able to transform the order we know as life into a different form of energy (order)? Why should not the order on matter, which represents at least a part of life, be transposable by metamorphosis to an order based on a nonmaterial substrate? The consequences of this might be far-reaching if applied to all forms of life.

LACK OF OBSERVATION DOES NOT PROVE NONEXISTENCE

To say that we know nothing observable of such a process as outlined above is no proof that it is nonexistent or impossible. If order (matter) and energy (a form of matter) cannot be destroyed or created, why should we postulate that the high degree of order which we know as life is destructible? Would it not be far more reasonable to assume that life is metamorphosed rather than simply destroyed?

We have already suggested that the order which has been imposed on matter and which we call life, was imposed from extramaterial sources. For we know of no other possible origin. If this is the case, where will this extramaterial order retreat to when death parts it from the matter on which it rode? Is it reasonable to suggest that it returns to its extra-material source, there to continue as it did before combining with matter in originating life as we know it? And if this is so, is this not an alternative way of saying that life continues after death in an extramaterial form? We could substitute for the expression "extramaterial" the word "spiritual," thus meaning that life becomes naked spirit after death. Then, of course, if this retreat of life to a nonmaterial form after death could be reversed, so that the same spiritual force could re-impose order on matter then we should be talking of a resur-rection from the dead without using the language of Canaan to which we have become so accustomed.

Ancient books such as the Bible have taught us consistently for centuries that life does undergo a metamorphosis into order on a nonmaterial basis when death occurs. For what is a disembodied spirit if it is not order imposed on a non-material substrate? Even matter is a wave function imposed upon void. What objections can there be to the resurrection on purely scientific or philosophical grounds?

As a scientist I know, of course, that the order of molecules on the genes and chromosomes is subject to the laws of ther-modynamics and will evaporate in decomposition. We can prove this chemically. Entropy will increase. But if an exog-enous intelligence and technique were needed at biogenesis to order molecules into a highly improbable state, and if we have no means of scientifically defining this intelligence which has "combined" with matter to result in the order of life, who will risk maintaining that this immeasurable and immaterial essence of intelligence, vital to life's genesis, is also destroyed on pulling apart the material constituents of life at death? *If life is imparted to matter by some sort of immaterial mold or template imposing order on the material world from the immaterial world at biogenesis, who could maintain that when the material imprint of life is melted out in death, the immaterial template and "negative" of each individual life is wiped out too? If the "negative" of each individual is kept as a "template" in an immaterial form, no destruction of the material imprint is going to destroy the nonmaterial individuality.*

We do not yet know what happens at death. Death certainly causes no weight change, that is, there is no change in the mass of matter as such. And yet it is obvious that an enormous change does take place. As long as scientists are sure that life and therefore death are only material, we can rest assured they will find nothing extramaterial in either. But to deny the existence of something simply because we have no knowledge of it is scientific suicide and nihilism.

TAO

CERTAIN LAWS IN COSMOS

The continuous altering of the order in matter which we have observed in metamorphosis is a general phenomenon. In the biological world one finds certain rules which govern these metamorphic changes. As Professor C. S. Lewis points out,[3] the thinkers of antiquity were well aware of these metamorphoses in nature and recognized how general were the laws that govern them. They recognized the "way things go" or "the way the world was ordered." Moreover, they tried to conform their lives to this pattern. Certain laws and rules in the cosmos had to be observed if man was to live in peace and not destroy himself by rebelling against nature and "the way things go."

The Chinese have a special word Tao for this observation of cosmic order or the "way things go." Man has not discovered or invented this order himself; he has merely observed it as it worker. Whoever disrespects the Tao disrespects himself and the world. If he disrespects these laws, living in discord with himself, he will destroy himself. To be more concrete, the universe represents reality, the "truth." The truth is therefore Tao. The man who is a liar is at cross-

[3]C. S. Lewis, *The Abolition of Man* (New York: Macmillan Co., 1964).

purposes with the universal Tao and therefore places himself outside universal harmony. That man must of necessity wither. Or take another example. The universe is governed by law and order. The movements of the stars in heaven, the tides and the seasons all go to prove this. The anarchist or lawless one puts himself outside the universal Tao and therefore outside of universal harmony with himself and his fellows. The ancient inhabitants of India possessed an expression for a similar concept they called the Rta.

TAO AS APPLIED TO METAMORPHOSIS

Thus, if we are truthful, we place ourselves within the universal Tao or Rta. Neither of these words is used here in a purely religious sense but merely to express a concept recognized since ancient times as a reality. Let us now connect this idea with our arguments on metamorphosis. Looking at nature and at its laws of conservation of matter and energy, we remain within the Tao if we maintain *that nothing is ever really lost in nature.* This Tao teaches us that one thing, form or order, may be changed into another, but never lost. We would therefore be placing ourselves outside the Tao of nature if we assumed that matter (order) or energy could be destroyed. For the Tao teaches us to expect metamorphosis all around us but never outright destruction or loss. If total loss is ever to occur, it will have to be a special event. Indeed, the Bible teaches that God has, in fact, reserved himself this right to destroy totally,[4] just as he has the right to create.

Thus, if we stick to our principle of the Tao we shall remain inside it in assuming that the phenomenon of death observed all around us is also not a loss or a destruction but a metamorphosis. This will be the case, even though we do not yet know into what state or form life may be transformed at the metamorphosis of death. Materialistic Darwinists, on the other hand, who assert that death is the end, that afterlife

---

[4]E.g., Rev. 20.

is wishful thinking and resurrection a myth, must on this
basis be outside the Tao of nature.

It will be necessary now to develop this idea of metamorphosis a little farther. When an ovum is thrust out of the
ovary it proceeds to meet the sperm cell. When the two meet,
the mechanism is triggered which is responsible for the realization of a great metamorphosis. The two cells combine
and form one new one. Neither the individual ovum nor
sperm exist as such any longer. Those two individuals have
"died" in producing an entirely new entity.

But before the new individual can appear, there must be
the complete and absolute "death" of both constituent cells
to make the new one. And this cessation of the individuality
of each cell is the very basis of the new individual and of the
metamorphosis which forms him. The egg must forever cease
to be the egg and the sperm must yield up its individuality
as a sperm. And yet, after this death, each begins to live an
entirely new and more complete type of life in association
with the other than was conceivable for each individual cell
alone before fusion. *For the very purpose of the life of the
sperm lies in meeting the ovum and the purpose of the life
of the ovum lies only in meeting and fusing with the sperm.
This is the Tao of the biological world.*

TAO IN SPIRITUAL WORLD

The spiritual world recognizes a Tao too. It runs parallel
to what we have already indicated above. In the new birth
described in the Bible, Christ died for us and we die to ourselves as individuals in Him. His being becomes associated
with ours, and ours with his, just as the properties of the
ovum become harnessed to those of the sperm and vice versa.
There are no longer two unrelated individuals but one new
unity. When a man meets his Creator in the form of Christ,
he dies to himself. The New Testament speaks a great deal
of this meeting and its consequences. Romans 6:5-8 speaks
of a man meeting Christ in the new birth and thus dying to
himself. This type of "fusing" between a man's life and Christ's

life gives rise to the "new creature"—"Old things are passed away . . . all things are become new."[5] But to effect this "fusion" the Lord also had to die before he could be one with us and take on our complete humanity. One may object that, in his death, Jesus Christ did not lose his personality or individuality. Similarly, when a person becomes a Christian, that person does not by any means lose his individuality or ego. What makes such a convert different from what he was beforehand is the *near association* with Christ in his life, in all he does and thinks.

The analogy of conversion with fertilization is even closer when one remembers that heredity is "particulate" and not "blending." The sperm's chromosomes exist after fusion with the ovum, but what makes the new difference in the fertilized zygote is the near coupling, near association, with the particulate heredity of the ovum. In one sense the individual sperm, its chromosomes and genes, do exist as such in the zygote, as do the particles of heredity contributed by the ovum to the zygote. But being so closely associated with one another is what makes the new creature, the fertilized zygote. And they are permanently associated with one another for life and progeny. Similarly, considering conversion, we do not "blend" with Christ or he with us, so that we lose on either side our identity. We become so closely associated with him that separation is unthinkable, and the consequences are a "new creation." The new convert is a "new creation" but at the same time a "renewed old individual." His heart proximity to Christ makes him a renewed creation, yet his old individuality is not damaged or compromised.

Out of the "death" of the two contracting parties, man and Christ, the new creature, the born-again Christian, arises. This is the Tao of the spiritual world. For the purpose of the life of a man lies in meeting his Creator,[6] just as the pur-

---

[5]II Cor. 5:17.
[6]Acts 17:27.

pose of the life and existence of the ovum lies in its meeting with the sperm, and dying. If a man avoids meeting his Creator and avoids dying to himself, then that man misses the very purpose for which he was made, just as surely as an ovum misses the very purpose of its being if it misses the sperm. *The very existence of the ovum (or sperm) is meaningless and purposeless without fusion with the sperm (or ovum).*

These considerations throw light on the attitude of many so-called Christian philosophers of today toward the meaning of life. Paul Tillich has written tomes on how he deals with the whole question of the *meaninglessness* of life. He teaches that the only way open to us to escape the desperation associated with life's awful meaninglessness is to accept this meaninglessness:

> One is afraid of having lost or of having to lose the meaning of one's existence. The expression of this situation is the Existentialism of today.
> . . . the acceptance of despair is in itself faith and on the boundary line of the courage to be.
> . . . The courage to be is rooted in the God who appears when God has disappeared in the anxiety of doubt.[7]

More specifically on meaninglessness itself Tillich writes:

> The courage of despair, the experience of meaninglessness and the self-affirmation in spite of them, are manifest in the Existentialism of the twentieth century. Meaninglessness is the problem of them all. . . . The problem of meaning troubles recent existentialists even when they speak of finitude and guilt.
> . . . The decisive event which underlies the search for meaning and the despair of it in the twentieth century is the loss of God in the nineteenth century. Feuerbach explained God away in terms of the infinite desire of the human heart; Marx explained him away in terms of an

[7]Paul Tillich, *The Courage to Be* (New Haven, Conn: Yale University Press, 1952), pp. 173, 175, 190.

> ideological attempt to rise above the given reality;
> Nietzsche as a weakening of the will to live. The result
> is the pronouncement: "God is dead"—and with him the
> whole system of values and meanings in which one
> lived.[8]

As Tillich says, however, the loss of meaning to life follows
the loss of God in our lives, just as the loss of meaning for a
sperm occurs when it meets no ovum. Chemically and mor-
phologically seen, the ovum is a marvelous organism. But
even it, in all its complexity, is destined to meaninglessness,
decay and death if it does not die in fusing with its sperm to
produce the fertilized zygote. All experience shows, and philosophers such as Tillich confirm, that it is just as much a fact
that human life is as meaningless as an unfertilized ovum, if
human life does not vitally meet with Christ in forgiveness
of sins and renewal of the spirit.

THE STRUCTURE OF MAN

Our discussion of the subject of metamorphosis is, of
course, intimately bound up with the question of the destiny
of man. But in order to apply the principle of metamorphosis
to our destiny, it will be necessary to look into the question
of our total design as individuals.

MAN IS A TRINITY

The Bible gives us a good deal of teaching precisely on
this question. It says that just as God is a trinity, so also is
man (in a very different way), who is made in his image.
Though fallen man is often more like a devil than anything
else, man's basic construction of three parts, namely, of body,
soul and spirit, has remained unchanged in spite of the fall.
So that even though man is fallen, his basic structure is still
that which God gave him at creation.

When I became a graduate research student many years
ago, one of the main points of principle hammered into me

[8]*Ibid.*, p. 142.

by my professor was that I must always use the simplest working hypothesis possible until it is disproved. The simplest hypothesis may not be the correct one, but we should not take unnecessarily complicated hypotheses as working bases for experiment if a simpler one will do. This is known as "Occam's Razor." Students (and others) just love to show their learnedness by regarding all simple explanations of phenomena as naïve on principle. They usually prefer a complicated hypothesis to a simple one. Complexity is so satisfying! So we are going to apply the simplest possible explanations to the biblical teaching on the structure of man when it says that he is built of body, soul and spirit. This does not mean to imply that we understand how the trinity of body, soul and spirit in man is fused together. We know this as little as we understand how the divine Trinity is related to its parts, if we can use the term "parts" with reference to God.

God did, however, give us a report[9] on how he synthesized this human trinity when he said that he took the dust of the earth and formed a *body* out of it. That is, his mind worked on matter, presumably in a chemical way, among others, and produced an imposed order in matter resulting in a body. This was stage one in the synthesis. Then he breathed the breath or spirit of life into this body as stage two. The result of this stage two was also stage three, in which man became a living being or *soul*. Thus the combination of God's spirit of life with a material body, ordered by his intelligence, resulted in a soul or a living creature, thus giving rise to the human trinity. Man consists then of a God-given spirit in conjunction with a material body, which combination bears what we call a soul-structure.

Again this divine description lies within the natural Tao we have been discussing. For the combination of one ovum with the sperm produces a third entirely new body or individual (ego, soul). So the combination of matter (body) with spirit (God's intelligence?) gives rise to something liv-

[9]Gen. 2:7.

ing which did not exist before and is a new individual. It is, of course, difficult for us to define the exact difference between spirit and soul, both being immaterial and therefore not easily investigated by our material sciences. This difficulty of differentiating between the two corresponds with the difficulty mentioned in the Holy Scriptures concerning exactly the same problem. For, distinguishing between soul and spirit is a job only the sharpest type of "sword" can do.[10]

The way to prove scientifically that a synthesis has occurred as we thought it did, is, of course, to break the synthesis down again into its constituent parts by means of analytical processes. The Bible does just this, for it describes the breakdown or analysis of life in the death process. At death the synthesis constituting life is broken down again and this decomposition, which is the opposite process to the creation of life, is highly instructive in throwing light on the destiny of man and in explaining the purpose of the metamorphosis of death.

ANALYSIS OF DEATH PROCESS

Although one must, for reverence' sake, be reticent about analyzing the death process of our Lord, the Bible does describe this in detail for our profit. So we propose to look at the death of our Lord (with all due reverence), in order to throw light on the problem on hand.

Spirit Rendered Back to God. When it came to dying, the Lord Jesus Christ put all his earthly affairs in order and took care of his mother, who was standing at the foot of the cross. Then he bowed his head and rendered up his spirit into the Father's hands: "Father, into thy hands I commend my spirit."[11] The Creator and Sustainer of life died, and he died actively, not passively. Death to him was not something that overwhelmed him, as if he were the object of its attack. He remained the subject and gave up his spirit actively and voluntarily. The fact that he rendered up his spirit shows that he (his ego) was not identical with the spirit he (his soul or ego) dismissed.

[10]Heb. 4:12.
[11]Luke 23:46.

This first stage in the analysis of death repeated itself at Stephen's martyrdom, although the act here was passive and not active. "Lord Jesus, receive my spirit," was Stephen's dying cry.[12]

After his spirit had thus been rendered back to God, who gave it, Christ himself (that is, his soul, ego or personality) started on the journey which Christian credos call "the descent into hell." The use of the word "hell" is the result of a poor translation, for the Lord actually descended into the place of the dead, which the Hebrews called *Sheol* and which in Greek is known as *Hades*. In this place there are, according to the Bible, two "territories," the place of the lost and the place of the blessed dead. They are separated from each other by an impassable barrier.[13]

Personality Still Intact. Thus the loss of his spirit at death in no way destroyed Jesus' personality as a man after death.[14] He was "unclothed" after death in that he had put off his body (it hung on the cross), and he had given back his spirit of life to the Father. But he himself, his personality, his ego, was still perfectly intact in the place of death in spite of the lack of spirit and body.[15] That his personality or ego in death was still intact and his individuality untouched, is shown by the report of Scripture on his activity after death. For we read that he went and preached in the disembodied state (i.e., not in the flesh) to the disembodied persons in prison who, in times of old, at the time of Noah had been disobedient.[16]

This report, although much discussed and interpreted by many in perhaps quite a different way, nevertheless still gives us, if taken at its face value and as simply as possible, information on the death process. For the report supplies information

---

[12]Acts 7:59.
[13]Luke 16:22-31.
[14]Lazarus and Dives retained personal identity and conscious existence (Luke 16:22-31), as did Samuel (I Sam. 28:11-15), Moses and Elijah (Matt. 17:1-4).
[15]Cf. Rev. 6:9-11 and Paul's statement in II Cor. 5:8 and Phil. 1:23.
[16]I Peter 3:19-20, Luke 16:22-23.

on the possibilities of activity of a man after the loss of spirit
and body. That is, we are supplied with information on the
activity of the disembodied personality, both in the case of
Jesus and perhaps, to some extent, in the case of the disobedient ones who died during Noah's age. The report shows that,
though the body is no longer functional (it is dead in the
grave) and the spirit of life no longer present (it has returned to God, who gave it), the personality or soul is still
highly functional. For all the characteristics of Jesus' original
personality remained in full power during his stay in Hades.
If this were not the case, how could he have "preached," that
is, transmitted thought and thoughts to the spirits in captivity,
if either he or they had not been real intelligences, capable of
rational thought and comprehension? The whole account assumes the reality of the immaterial state after disembodiment.
Furthermore, how could he have "preached" if he had no
memory in the disembodied state? He must have been able to
call to mind the passages in Holy Scripture which he had read
and used in his earthly lifetime in order to have been able to
preach at all. For Christ always appealed to Scripture in
preaching, and referred to it as the eternal Word,[17] showing
that he regarded the Word as valid for lifetime and for eternity afterward, in other words, valid after the grave. He certainly used the Word in the grave. It all lines up with his
teaching that the Word he taught on earth will be used to
judge us in eternity, that is, after we put off our mortal bodies:
"The word that I have spoken, the same shall judge him in
the last day."[18] The same Jesus who used the Scriptures to
preach before death used them afterward for the same purpose, thus establishing (1) his continuity of personality or
ego and (2) the eternal validity of the Word of God.

Guilt Does Not Fade with Time. The same continuity
applies to the audience he spoke to there in Hades. After
death these were the same individuals, in the grave and conscious of it, who beforehand had been disobedient in ages

[17]Matt. 5:18, 24:35; Mark 13:31.
[18]John 12:48.

past. So we conclude not only the continuity of their personality after the death process, but also that personal guilt does not just fade with passage of ages afterward. They had been disobedient specifically at the time of Noah. Why should the Holy Spirit, who caused the Word to be written for us, mention the time of the disobedience, if this were without significance to us? Of course, in the grave there is probably no "passage of time" as we understand it. The grave is apparently timeless by our standards, in that matter is not the basis of its order or organization.[19] But without this continuity of personality and, indeed, of intelligence, there would have been no point in the whole report of the conversation Christ carried on with these disobedient spirits in captivity.

Thus we may conclude that the Holy Scriptures support very clearly the concept of conscious continuity of personality and intelligence after the metamorphosis we call death. In this state of metamorphosis there are, however, two distinct possibilities for each one of us: one possibility is that of being in the place of the blessed dead in "Abraham's bosom," where Lazarus was after death. The other possibility is that of being in the place of fire, where Dives was reported by Jesus himself to have been. It would seem that Jesus might have gone to both the territories in Hades to comfort the blessed and pronounce judgment upon the lost and disobedient. But it is never implied that the Lord went to hell-fire (Tartarus) which is reserved for the devil and his angels at the end of time.[20]

All the dead now are in the "unclothed" disembodied state in Hades, either in the lost or blessed estate, awaiting there the judgment of Christ on them at the resurrection morning, when they will be "reclothed" with their bodies and spirits to receive in them the recompense for the deeds done in the flesh: "For we must all appear before the judgment seat of Christ;

---

[19]Yet those in the grave "await" the resurrection and the blessed dead "await" their award. I do not profess to understand this (see Rev. 6:11).
[20]Cf. II Peter 2:4.

that every one may receive the things done in his body, according to that he hath done, whether it be good or bad."[21] The Christian comfort with respect to the dead is that Christ himself now possesses the keys of death and Hades and can thus enter at all times to be with his blessed dead who trusted him during their lifetime. They rest from their labors now in the comfort of the very presence of the Savior. In such a state of conscious blessedness they await the resurrection morning, when the death process will be reversed and they will receive a resurrection body from him.

Metamorphosis of Body Alone. But to return to the death process as described by the Scriptures in the case of the Lord. During the period he was in Hades his body lay in the grave, although without destruction. The Father had given him power to take or leave life, as he wished, so that on the third day he retook his life. His spirit returned to his material body and his soul or personality re-entered and took possession once more.

The important matter for us to remember here in this whole question of the metamorphosis of the death process (and resurrection process too) in the case of Christ, is that Christ's soul or personality remained continuous throughout. It is not suggested, of course, that the sufferings and joys of his life and death on earth did not leave any marks on his soul's make-up. They did, for it was because of his sufferings that God has now glorified him to his right hand.[22] From this point of view, his soul was certainly changed by his passage through life. But it is important for us to recognize here that the main change or metamorphosis which did take place at the death and resurrection process concerned his body alone. And it is just here, at this point, that we find so much information given us by the Scriptures particularly on the question of our own destiny.

[21]II Cor. 5:10.
[22]Heb. 2:10.

THE METAMORPHOSIS OF THE BODY AT THE RESURRECTION OF CHRIST

NO ASCERTAINABLE METAMORPHOSIS

Let us first of all sum up the ways in which there was no ascertainable metamorphosis of the body at the death and resurrection of Jesus Christ.

1. Mary seems to have recognized the tone and inflection of his voice after his resurrection when she cried out, "Rabboni."[23] Thus the voice at least retained its individuality after Christ's death.

2. The wounds of the crucifixion on hands, feet and side were still visible. Maybe the wound in his side was still open if Thomas was invited to put his hand in it.[24] Thus we may conclude that, with respect to his wounds, Christ's death and resurrection did not alter these identification marks. They remained there even after his ascension.[25]

3. After his resurrection the Lord was able to walk, eat honey and fish, drink[26] and to kindle a fire.[27] On these occasions his body was certainly not transparent. He himself said, when he found that his disciples were fearful of him, that spirits had not flesh and bones as he had.[28] Looked at purely physically he was certainly "normal" after his resurrection. So normal, in fact, that the Emmaus disciples recognized him as he broke bread at table.

FUNDAMENTAL CHANGE IN BODY

But the following points, also noted after the resurrection, tell a different story, for they show that a fundamental change in his body had taken place at his resurrection:

1. He could pass through securely locked doors.[29]

[23]John 20:16.
[24]John 20:27.
[25]Rev. 5:6.
[26]Luke 24:43.
[27]Luke 24:39.
[28]Luke 24:39.
[29]John 20:26.

2. He could disappear or reappear before their astonished eyes.[30] While the disciples watched, he was received out of their sight into heaven at the ascension.[31]

3. Although he was not present when Thomas doubted, he was nevertheless able to hear all that was said and thought on the occasion. This probably means that he was in a measure omnipresent (omniscient?) and yet at the same time a definable entity and a person, such as possesses a definite location. It may rightly be objected here that before his death the Lord showed the same faculty, so we will not insist on this difference but merely mention it for completeness.

4. The risen Lord was able·to make use of or not make use of these extra capabilities just as he wished. On the Emmaus road he disappeared before their eyes although only a few moments before he had fellowshiped with them on the way and at table. In a moment of time he could become supra-material and probably therefore omnipresent, omniscient and, as God, omnipotent. The extra properties Jesus Christ possessed were witnessed by some five hundred persons, as the Apostle Paul is careful to tell us in the Corinthian letter,[32] so that one dare not just dismiss them as mere wishful thinking.

DOES A CHRISTIAN BELIEVE MAGIC?

One might say here that the person who accepts all this about Jesus Christ is a believer in pure magic. It is certain that such properties as those described above do not fall within the bounds of materialistic science. The accusation against the Bible-believing Christian about believing in magic is, of course, dependent on one's definition of magic. In the German-speaking world the word *Zauberei* ("magic") carries with it the sense of what would be designated in some cases as black magic or occultism in the English-speaking world. We will take here as our definition the one suggested by C. S. Lewis, who said that magic is "objective efficacy which cannot

[30]Luke 24:31.
[31]Acts 1:9.
[32]I Cor. 15:6.

be further analyzed."[33] No special allusion to occultism is implied here.

Under this strict definition of magic nothing could be more "magic" than the very nature of God himself, who exists *causa sui*. Every theologian believes in this kind of "magic." So in fact does everyone who allows even the reality of extrasensory perception. In fact any scientist who allows that there are things or forces he cannot finally analyze makes a confession of belief in this type of magic. And what scientist would be so foolish as to deny the possibility of things he cannot explain? Many of the happenings of the resurrection of Jesus Christ fall into this class, and as a scientist I would be the last to deny them simply on the basis that I do not understand them. It is no use simply denying these extra properties of Christ as mythical. They are too well attested to for that. How foolish we would look if we were to deny ESP, for example, solely on the basis that it is an inexplicable phenomenon.

Thus the main weight of our argument for the metamorphosis which occurred at Christ's death and resurrection lies in the area of his body. Less seems to have occurred in the area of his soul or spirit. And it is just this point which must bear now a little further investigation in our consideration of the destiny of man.

THE METAMORPHOSIS OF MAN

The Holy Scriptures give the Bible-believing Christian two great promises, among others. The first of these promises concerns the renewal or metamorphosis of the character, ego, or soul, at and after meeting Christ in the forgiveness of sins and new birth. This renewal of the inward man, or his soul, occurs during our allotted life span of threescore years and ten, and is summed up in the well-known verse: "If any man be in Christ, he is a new creature."[34]

[33]Lewis, *Letters to Malcolm* (London: Geoffrey Bles, 1964), p. 134.
[34]II Cor. 5:17a.

BEGINS AT NEW BIRTH

This metamorphosis of the ego begins at the new birth and should continue progressively until death.[35] It is fostered by Bible reading, prayer, fellowship with other Christians and by working in God's will. The goal of this metamorphosis consists in the character of a man becoming like Christ's character. This is the start of the first great promise and leads progressively to the inward life of the Christian becoming more one with Christ's way of life. In modern language one would perhaps say that Christ's *Weltanschauung* ("philosophy of life") becomes ours.

INFECTS THE BODY

But this metamorphosis of the ego cannot remain absolutely isolated. It must spread to the other parts of the human trinity. It "infects" the body; the eyes begin to take on a new luster, the facial expression becomes different. Only that person who never experienced the new birth in the forgiveness of sins will doubt this. The Scriptures express this "infection" of the body by the metamorphosis of the ego thus: "But we all, with open face beholding as in a glass the glory of the Lord, are changed into the same image from glory to glory, even as by the spirit of the Lord."[36] The tongue begins to sing "a new song."[37] The exhausted forces of youth are renewed.[38] This means we are *psychosomatic* individuals.

INFECTS THE PSYCHE

With due conservatism we said that the metamorphosis of the ego begins to "infect" the body. But this process cannot go very far this side of the grave, for the true metamorphosis of the body takes place after the grave, or at the so-called rapture.[39] The metamorphosis of the soul in the new birth

[35]Phil. 1:6.
[36]II Cor. 3:18.
[37]Ps. 96:1-4; 98:1-3.
[38]Isa. 40:31.
[39]I Thess. 4:17.

triggers a metamorphosis of the body which cannot, however, be completed until we receive a new body later. In fact, the first, metamorphosis (of the ego), lays the foundation for the second, the metamorphosis of the body.

The Apostle Paul describes the metamorphosis of the body which awaits the Christian in the following terms:

> For we know that if our earthly house of this tabernacle were dissolved, we have a building of God, an house not made with hands, eternal in the heavens. For in this we groan, earnestly desiring to be clothed upon with our house which is from heaven: if so be that being clothed we shall not be found naked. For we that are in this tabernacle do groan, being burdened: not for that we would be unclothed, but clothed upon, that mortality might be swallowed up of life.[40]

To use modern speech, the apostle tells us that this body in which we now live is to be dissolved but that we can be glad about it all, for the Lord has already provided for us another, and better, supramaterial but not immaterial (heavenly, eternal) body to live in. He says that we all find it hard to die (become unclothed, lose our material bodies). He, the apostle, would rather not die, if that were possible; he wishes that the Lord would swallow up his mortality with immortality, thus avoiding the unpleasant process of dying and the disembodied state, in which we have neither material nor resurrection supramaterial bodies. Probably the apostle is thinking here of the words he himself wrote: "Then we which are alive and remain shall be caught up together . . . in the clouds, to meet the Lord in the air: and so shall we ever be with the Lord."[41]

Those born-again Christians who are still alive at the coming of the Lord will not have to pass through the painful and fearful process of dying, resulting in disembodiment, but their mortal bodies will be metamorphosed in the twinkling

[40]II Cor. 5:1-4.
[41]I Thess. 4:17.

of an eye into a supranatural resurrection body without an intermediate disembodied waiting period. That is, such Christians will never be "unclothed," but their mortality will be instantly swallowed up by immortality.

THE SUPRAMATERIAL KINGDOM

Flesh and blood (our present material bodies) cannot function in the new supramaterial kingdom with which God is going to renew the earth after the millenium, so they must be metamorphosed first before entering in. A caterpillar cannot function flying around on the breeze; it cannot "inherit" the kingdom of the air as a butterfly can. So to "inherit the air," the metamorphosis must take place first.

The apostle is treating the same subject of metamorphosis when he writes: "For our conversation [manner of life] is in heaven; from whence also we look for the Saviour, the Lord Jesus Christ: who shall change our vile body, that it may be fashioned like unto his glorious body, according to the working whereby he is able to subdue all things unto himself."[42]

In these verses we find the essence of the second great promise to the Christian which we mentioned above. Here we have in a nutshell the purpose of God in creating human life. Life is not meaningless, as so many great modern thinkers and philosophers, such as Paul Tillich, continually reiterate. Here is the purpose—not the meaninglessness—of life: "That mortality might be swallowed up of life. Now he that has wrought [i.e., created] us for the selfsame thing is God, who also hath given unto us the earnest of the spirit."[43] (He has guaranteed his purpose and left us a pledge of it in the form of giving us here and now his Spirit).

First, the Lord initiates, by means of the new birth, a metamorphosis of the ego. A man begins to come to himself and to recognize his true state. He experiences a hunger for righteousness, for a release from the guilt of sin and for a reinstatement before God and man. These he finds on the basis the

[42]Phil. 3:20-21.
[43]II Cor. 5:4-5.

Apostle John described: "If we say that we have no sin, we
deceive ourselves, and the truth is not in us. If we confess our
sins, he is faithful and just to forgive us our sins, and to cleanse
us from all unrighteousness. If we say that we have not sinned,
we make him a liar, and his word is not in us."[44]

Once the basis of a renewed and restored personality or ego
is assured by the new birth, the Lord directs our attention to
the question of a body to bear the renewed personality in the
renewed supramaterial new earth and new heaven. The soul
is being and has been prepared for company with the Creator
in his *milieu*. In fact, although they are physically still living
on the earth, the redeemed live there already in spirit.[45] Flesh
and blood would never be at home or indeed able to survive
in this milieu of the supramaterial world, so that they must
be metamorphosed to "inherit" such a kingdom, just as the
caterpillar must metamorphose to the butterfly before it can
take to the breeze.

But although the new supramaterial body is really new, its
structure is somehow based on the old body of flesh and blood,
just as the old caterpillar body does yield surprisingly enough
the basic structure for the new butterfly. And thus even now
our present body of flesh and blood, subject as it is to decay
and death, does belong to the Lord and is holy.[46] It is essential, therefore, that we do not think that because this body is
perishable, we can do what we like with it. Its sins and its
works are not as perishable as its material basis. Even the
physical insults we give the body or individual living cell in
this life are all recorded on the cell "memory." How, we do
not know. But every dose of ionizing radiation, for example,
is recorded. Our present physical body will be transformed
in just the same way that Jesus Christ's physical body was
transformed after his resurrection. His body carried over
with it certain of the physical marks of this life as, for example, the nail marks and the wounded side. This does not

[44]I John 1:8-10.
[45]Cf. Eph. 2:6; Heb. 12:22 ff.
[46]Cf. I Cor. 6:13, 19.

mean that nonsinful marks of illness or mutilation will be carried over in the metamorphosis (we do not expect any wooden legs in heaven!). I assume that the nail and spear marks on Christ's body constitute an exception here, since he was the "Lamb slain from the foundation of the world."

PHYSICAL PURITY

But there would seem to be a reason why the Scriptures exhort us to keep the body holy, even though it does decay, for we each shall receive our bodies back again in one form or another to receive in them the sins we have used them as agents for: "For we must all appear before the judgment seat of Christ; that every one may receive the things done in his body, according to that he hath done, whether it be good or bad."[47] One wonders what will be God's thoughts at the sight of youngsters in high school and college who are being doled out oral contraceptives so that they can join themselves to anyone willing and interested, with no "visible" consequences. Actually, of course, we do not need to wonder, for he has plainly set down his thoughts on fornication and adultery (with or without consequences).[48] We are clearly warned that he who joins himself to a prostitute sins against the holiness of his own body.[49] In fact, one passage goes as far as to maintain that anyone sinning in this way against the holiness of his own body will be shut out from the new kingdom: "For this ye know, that no whoremonger, nor unclean person, nor covetous man, which is an idolater, hath any inheritance in the kingdom of Christ and of God."[50]

The concept of bodily purity is fast becoming antique in our modern world. Even though the moderns laugh at such Victorian and Puritan ideas, the psychiatrists do tell us of the psychosomatic illnesses resulting just from promiscuity. The

[47]II Cor. 5:10.
[48]Cf. Acts 15:20, 29; 21:25; I Cor. 6:13, 18; Gal. 5:19; Eph. 5:3; Col. 3:5; I Thess. 4:3; Heb. 12:16.
[49]I Cor. 6:18.
[50]Eph. 5:5.

havoc wrought is not put away just by saying that ideas of purity are antiquated. Most girls and boys, even though they may clamor for "free love," when they marry, want to have a partner who has not given himself or herself to others in pre-marital intercourse. The discovery after marriage of pre-marital intercourse by partners can lead to serious psychic disturbances in young marriages. The psychiatrist who deals with those who have offended against their own bodily purity, often knows from the case history just where and when the seeds of these psychosomatic disturbances were sown.

No, the body is intended to be the Lord's and should not be the playground for any or every type of self-indulgence. For it is the basis of our resurrection body to be. If the basis is not in order, the superstructure built on it will show the consequences.

Recently I heard from the pulpit a statement which illus-trates the apparent ignorance of even a Christian military chaplain on this subject. He was a fine young Army chaplain who maintained the view that in the service the soldier's soul certainly does belong to the Lord and neither the State nor the Army had any claim on it whatsoever. But the body, said he, belongs to Uncle Sam, who can demand of it what he needs when he needs it. It was implied that any job could be de-manded of and carried out by a young soldier in the service of his country. As C. S. Lewis so aptly remarks,[51] it is the enemy's job to prevent people who are his dupes from read-ing any history, to cut them all off from the foregoing genera-tion, so that no one in the present generation learns any lesson from his forefathers. For it was the National Socialists and Fascists yesterday and the Communists today who teach pre-cisely the same doctrine, so forcing their slaves to commit any atrocity in the guise of serving their country. The Bible is perfectly clear that the body is the Lord's at all times, even in war, and he will hold us responsible for what we do in war or peace.

[51]Lewis, *The Screwtape Letters* (London: Geoffrey Bles, 1961), p. 122.

THE IMPORTANCE OF THE BODY

And now we must ask ourselves our last question: Why does God wish us to pay special attention to this body destined to decay? Why does he want to present it at "that day" *without fault?*[52] (This does not include "normal bodily illnesses," to which all flesh is heir, but only practices which may be classed as sinful.) What is the purpose of the redemption and transformation of the whole man—body, soul and spirit? What does the total metamorphosis signify?

The first meaning of this total metamorphosis must surely mean that our Creator loves man as a total creature—body, soul and spirit. He made all the facets of man. And loving us all, or all of us, he wishes every part of us—body, soul and spirit—to be with him where he is.[53] Why should he still be interested in such a rebellious race, and such a rebellious individual as I? That will remain forever his secret. But that the fact is so, was proved by his having become man and dying and rising for man.

But beyond this first meaning, which might seem enigmatic, the Bible informs us that the answer to this question had been hidden since the beginning of time, but that it was revealed at Christ's incarnation. Human life, looked at through the eyes of some modern philosophers like Tillich, appears to be meaningless, in fact, as meaningless as an ovum which perishes, not having met a sperm, or a sperm which perishes, not having met an ovum. They are both marvelous pieces of chemical intricacy, coded chemical information and masterpieces of concentration. Yet the sperm, ovum and human life, itself viewed alone, appear to be futile. They are short-lived, overorganized chemically and genetically for their own short lives, in fact, they are simply enigmatic as they stand alone. Only on the basis of the ovum, sperm or human life forming the substrate for a mighty, in-itself-unforeseeable metamorphosis does sense and meaning enter the picture. Meaninglessness is inevitable with the death of the unfertilized ovum,

[52]I Thess. 5:23 ff.
[53]John 17:24.

sperm, or unfulfilled human life. Life for each ovum or sperm only becomes meaningful when the genetic possibilities of the unfertilized egg or sperm become unlocked in fusion to give the fertile zygote, capable of growing into a far more glorious organism than is conceivable on the basis of a glance at the unfertilized egg alone—the healthy young man or woman in the prime of life and vigor. Who could ever compare him or her with the dying unfertilized and unfulfilled ovum?

APPROPRIATENESS FOR HIGH OFFICE

God the Father has decreed that the Lord Jesus Christ, because he died (to "fertilize" and regenerate the human race) is the most suitable Person to govern the new, metamorphosed earth and heaven he has promised to give us. Rulers over men have at most times assumed and demanded that their subjects be ready to die for them, the rulers. The God of heaven has reversed this order; he died for his subjects. Because Christ died for his subjects and loved them in spite of the mortal cost, his Father has made the following decree: "Having made known unto us the mystery of his will, according to his good pleasure which he hath purposed in himself: that in the dispensation of the fulness of times he might gather together in one all things in Christ, both which are in heaven and which are on earth; even in him."[54] Another translation renders the passage in such a way as to convey the idea that all things and authority will come under the direct supervision of Christ in the restored creation solemnly promised us.

That is the one side of the mystery of God's plan and will for the metamorphosed world ("fulness of times," "restoration of all things"). It means that Christ is going to be honored in that all administration of the new heavens and the new earth will be in his hands.

The other side to the question concerns those who have learned to love and obey him in their threescore years and

[54]Eph. 1:9-10.

ten. This may well include those we often lightly classify as "heathen," who know nothing of him by name, but have learned, according to their lights, to love mercy, do justly and walk humbly with him.[55] For may it not be the guilt of the so-called Christian that many "heathen" have never heard of him?

Many more conservative Christians may believe that a statement of this kind harbors universalism, and therefore reject it. If it did harbor universalism in reality, I would myself reject it out of hand, for I have had opportunity to observe firsthand the deadly effect of universalist doctrine on the churches in Germany and Switzerland. Universalism engenders strife, as well as killing missionary zeal, for it runs directly in the face of scriptural doctrine on eternal punishment and teaches the "second chance" after death, which are scarcely justifiable to a Christian on any count.

It is, however, generally conceded among Christians that Christ's salvation is imputed to babes and young children if they die before they reach an age of responsibility. This is believed on the basis that Christ died for such, being the Savior of children, who encouraged the little children to come to him to be blessed. Here then we have a case of a child being acceptable for salvation by imputing Christ's sacrifice to it, without the child having cooperated, *simply because it could not—in the nature of things—cooperate.* Yet Christians all believe that that child was nevertheless a sinner (its tantrums at a very early age may reveal this to any doubter, or to one who has never had much to do with small babies), yet one which is saved by grace in Christ, without the necessity of a conscious decision. It just could not make such a decision.

The question here is whether the heathen who has never even heard of the name of Christ is not in a similar position to that of our hypothetical baby. *In the nature of things, such a heathen could not make any conscious decision on Christ,*

[55]Cf. Deut. 10:12.

he does not know what to decide about. No one has ever told him. Can such a one be damned forever with hellfire because he is really in no better position to save himself by turning consciously to Christ than the small baby was? I believe it would be unthinkable that the God of heaven and earth, who will do right, would ever act this way. Since Christ died for the sins of the whole world and since the Judge of all the earth is going to do right, I believe God will impute Christ's measureless sacrifice on the cross to as many as he can with perfect justice. This is no doctrine of universalism or "second chance." It is the doctrine of salvation to all to whom Christ's sacrifice can be imputed by God to the eternal salvation of their souls. Above all this it was the *disobedient* spirits in bondage to whom Christ preached after his "descent" into Hades, not to the *unknowledgable.*[56]

By Christ's death and resurrection for me I have become Christ's property and he is my "inheritance." We belong together henceforth.[57] When I become disembodied at death (or meet Christ at his second coming) I enter a glorious inheritance and association. For my inheritance is Christ Jesus himself. All his is mine and all mine is his. If he is Heir of all things then all his redeemed are co-heirs with him of the coming glories of the renewed, restored creation. The "fertilized ovum" is growing up for this inheritance and consists of Christ associated eternally with his own. The caterpillar eats and eats green herb, so that it can be metamorphosed for the breeze—a seemingly uninteresting occupation at the time, but glorious are the consequences. So life may seem as commonplace as eating green herb but after having been "fertilized" in meeting Christ at the new birth, we assimilate the promises of God which trigger a metamorphosis. We feast on the meaning of them and put them to the test, thus obtaining the energy to grow up into Christ.[58]

[56]Cf. I Peter 3:19.
[57]Cf. Col. 1:12; Eph. 1:11.
[58]Cf. Eph. 4:15.

MAN'S DESTINY

And with this we have the key to the destiny of man within our grasp: Where Christ is, there shall his redeemed children also be.[59] God created the first man so that he needed his opposite number, his "thou." It was not good that the man be alone.[60] It is planned to make Christ the "Thou" of man and vice versa in the restoration of all things, for when he acts, redeemed man will act in perfect fellowship with him. When he praises, man will echo the praise. When he reigns, his human inheritance will reign with him: "Know ye not that we shall judge angels?"[61] "Blessed and holy is he that hath part in the first resurrection: on such the second death hath no power, but they shall be priests of God and of Christ and shall reign with him a thousand years."[62]

God in his wisdom and power as Creator has decided to involve man in his great plans for the restoration of all things. But in order for man to be able to take his part in this plan he must first receive a divine nature and method of thought to overcome the psychic and other decay inherent in the fall. He must become intimately associated with Christ. Then, when this first victory, the new birth, has been won in the regeneration of the ego, then, in order to be able to evaluate and use the new ego for eternal purposes, a new substrate for the renewed ego must be found, a substrate which stands above mortality and the other consequences of the fall. Thus man must have a new, eternal, glorious body, a "habitation" or "tabernacle," to use the biblical expressions, which matches up to the one Christ received after his death and resurrection. Man, redeemed man, is to be "like him" even bodily, just as the Scriptures predict.

To become fit to receive a new nature, our old one has to die. Dying is not exactly a self-indulgent process. It means saying no to ourselves, just as Christ said no to himself in

59Cf. John 17:24.
60Cf. Gen. 2:18.
61I Cor. 6:2-3.
62Rev. 20:6.

becoming man and leaving the Father's side. Christ's new body came as a consequence of his nature or ego. He willingly suffered death and shame and was, as a result, crowned with glory and honor. The same sequence has been taught for man ever since Christ's time. Our ego, even our redeemed ego, needs lots of discipline to become fit for the everlasting kingdom we are called to. Therefore, "We must through much tribulation enter into the kingdom of God."[63]

Thus all the trials and tribulations, conflicts and disappointments serve to prepare the renewed man for high and eternal office in a realm which is not yet conceivable to his finite, chemically controlled thinking apparatus. Man's destiny, insofar as he is redeemed of God, concerns a supramaterial world, based on the material world, but growing out of it and above it like a skyscraper towering out of the Chicago marshes, only much more so! In fact our destiny, as the redeemed of God, is so far above the present thought capacity of our limited imagination that our present human eye has not seen, nor has the mortal ear heard, nor has it ever entered into the heart of mortal man what God has prepared for those that love him.[64] Even men who do not profess Christianity have seen this possibility faintly, for Sir James Jeans writes:

> We, the only thinking beings so far as we know, in the whole universe, are to all appearances so accidental, so far removed from the main scheme of the universe, that it is *a priori* all too probable that any meaning that the universe as a whole may have would entirely transcend our terrestrial experience, and so be totally unintelligible to us. In this event, we should have had no foothold from which to start our exploration of the true meaning of the universe.[65]

[63]Acts 14:22.
[64]Cf. I Cor. 2:9.
[65]Sir James Jeans, *The Mysterious Universe* (New York: Macmillan Co., 1930), p. 136.

To bring this section to a close we quote some of the last words C. S. Lewis wrote just before his death:

> I don't say the resurrection of this body will happen at once. It may well be that this part of us sleeps in death and the intellectual soul is sent to Lenten lands where she fasts in naked spirituality. . . . Yet from that fact my hope is that we shall return and re-assume the wealth we laid down.
>
> Then the new earth and sky, the same yet not the same as these, will rise in us as we have risen in Christ. And once again, after who knows what aeons of the silence and the dark, the birds will sing out and the waters flow, and lights and shadows move across the hills and the faces of our friends laugh upon us with amazed recognition.
>
> Guesses, of course, only guesses. If they are not true, something better will be. For we know we shall be made like Him, for we shall see Him as He is.[66]

[66]Lewis, *op. cit.*, *Letters to . . .* , p. 158.

EPILOGUE

Some years ago I had the honor of holding an evangelical convocation at the University of Tübingen in Germany, the university which has produced so many Christian philosophers. During the time I was giving the addresses there, Professor Karl Heim, then dean of German theology professors, became interested in them, and as a result I was invited to his birthday party. Professor Karl Heim was already well advanced in years, but was intellectually as active as ever. Needless to say, Professor Heim's interest in and support of the campaign were a help to the success of the undertaking, since he was such a highly influential member of the faculty there.

Before the few birthday party guests had departed (Professor Heim could not at his great age stand crowds about him in his house), I requested permission to ask our aged host two questions before leaving to give my evening address. Professor Heim, who was always game for this sort of thing, aquiesced immediately.

The first question I asked was: "Do you, Professor Heim, believe that man has developed from lower animal forebears?" And the second question was: "What means can we use in order to reach the modern philosophically and scientifically trained student or graduate with the gospel of

Christ as revealed in the Old and New Testaments? Our present means do not seem to be getting very far!"

We discussed the first question for a time, when Professor Heim, with his characteristic humility, suggested I ought to discuss this question with his friend, Professor Freiherr Dr. von Huene who, as a paleontologist, was a good deal more qualified than he.

In respect to my second question Professor Heim said that the answer he would give as a result of his lifelong activity with students and academically trained people was quite simple. (I learned that even German professors of theology can be devastatingly simple at times—to my lifelong benefit.) Here is the gist of Professor Heim's answer to my question:

> The witness of the living Christ in a man's life and deportment is the strongest and the only really effective means available to reach and evangelize either the learned or the unlearned. Without this living witness in our hearts and lives we cannot evangelize either the learned or the unlearned, the technically trained or the untrained. With this testimony and witness, however, we cannot help evangelizing both. But, if learned or unlearned do happen to see such a witness of the effect the living Christ has in transforming good or bad among men, and then still do not heed it for their personal life and philosophy, we have no other means available of reaching such.

How much this reminds us of similar words spoken by Jesus Christ when he was conversing with the Pharisees of old! He said that if a man rejected the witness which Moses gave of himself (Christ), that man was incapable of being convinced of anything at all.[1] Such a man would not be capable of believing, even if someone rose from the dead and gave a firsthand report on conditions there. The point to be emphasized is, that Moses' witness of Christ is so strong and the internal evidence for the correctness of his writings so compelling, that anyone doubting Moses will doubt any truth,

[1]Cf. Luke 16:31.

no matter where it comes from or how evident its validity. Even a firsthand witness by one who has died and returned to give a firsthand report of conditions after death would not convince the man who doubts Moses' witness in the Holy Scriptures. Such a person is incapable of conviction on anything (German, *ueberzeugungsunfähig*).

In order to be able to understand the destiny of man, we must be able to believe the testimony of God as laid down in the Scripture (substantiated by the testimony of fallen nature). We cannot, however, believe God's testimony about anything except we believe first his testimony about ourselves, in other words, that we are naturally alienated from him. Once the question of our alienation from him has been regulated and righted, the rest follows as surely as day follows night. As Tillich says, modern man has lost God, and with him has lost the purpose and meaning of life. We lost God when we lost the sure testimony of him in the Scriptures. If we recover the Scriptures as the sure testimony of things unseen (which they profess to be), we shall recover God and at the same time recover life's meaning. This is the reason for the writing of this book. Science (so-called) has been misused for a hundred years to invalidate the testimony of God in the Scriptures (particularly the argument from design). The biblical story of creation has been laughed out of court, and chance and natural selection have been put in its place. Huxley and others have reiterated *ad nauseam* that God is now an unnecessary concept. But science, real science, knows that a prime cause (or mover) is now just as necessary as in the days before "modern" science. The testimony of the Bible is still just as valid today as is the testimony of the living Christ in a living man.

But, if one prefers not to take the Book seriously for regulating one's personal life, the Book will mean nothing to us from the point of view of ultimate destiny either. *We cannot think biblically if we do not act biblically.* If we all, according to our lights, get right with our Creator by repentance toward him followed by his forgiveness, more enlightenment will surely follow, for the substance of faith is progressive.

Meanwhile, the sure promise of God remains:

> For, behold, I create new heavens and a new earth: and the former shall not be remembered, nor come into mind. But be ye glad and rejoice for ever in that which I create: for, behold, I create Jerusalem a rejoicing, and her people a joy. And I will rejoice in Jerusalem, and joy in my people: and the voice of weeping shall be no more heard in her, nor the voice of crying. There shall be no more thence an infant of days, nor an old man that hath not filled his days: for the child shall die an hundred years old. . . . And it shall come to pass, that before they call, I will answer; and while they are yet speaking, I will hear. The wolf and the lamb shall feed together, and the lion shall eat straw like the bullock. . . . They shall not hurt nor destroy in all my holy mountain, saith the LORD.[2]

Just threescore years and ten are allotted us to prepare for that which eye has not seen, nor ear heard, and to get ready for that which has never entered the heart of man—the everlasting joys of a fulfilled destiny.

[2]Isa. 65:17-25.

APPENDIX

I. *Analysis of the Theistic Evolutionary Theories Propounded by Professor Rohrbach in His Books (and in Lectures Circulated by Tape Recordings).*

THEISTIC EVOLUTIONARY THESES

The original German edition of the present volume contains an appendix, a part of which gives a detailed analysis of the views of one of Germany's foremost theistic evolutionists, Dr. Hans Rohrbach, Professor of Mathematics at the University of Mainz, Western Germany. Although there are a number of theistic evolutionists in the United States and in the English-speaking world today, we have taken Professor Rohrbach's views as an example simply because he figures in the original German edition of the present volume. His views will reflect those of a large number of Anglo-Saxon theistic evolutionists. This is the justification for a shortened analysis of the main points dealt with in the original book.

The following literature serves as the basis of this analysis:

1. *Naturwissenschaft und Gotteserkenntnis,* Evg. Akademie, Mannheim, 6. Auflage, Germany, 1965.

2. *Naturwissenschaft und Glaubensbekenntnis,* Evg. Akademie, Mannheim, 2. erweiterte Auflage, Germany, 1965.

3. *Die Biblischen Wunder, Biblischer Schöpfungsbericht, Weltbild der Bibel und die Moderne Naturwissenschaft*, Evg. Akademie, Mannheim, Germany, 1965.

Professor Rohrbach discerns two separate and different reports in the biblical account of creation. He believes that these two accounts differ fundamentally from each other. The first report speaks, according to Dr. Rohrbach, of the slow evolutionary process through millions of years, during which man emerges from an animal ancestry by Darwinian natural selection and chance mutation.

The second report in Genesis 2 which Dr. Rohrbach distinguishes, describes events in the Garden of Eden. It does not describe the *biological evolution* of man according to Darwin, but rather his *spiritual election or calling out from among the animals* to become the chosen man of God and the father of modern man. *This second point means, in the last analysis, that Adam existed biologically as an animal organism before he was called spiritually by God (in the second biblical report on creation).* This proposition we must now examine.

Theistic evolutionists in Germany and Switzerland, among them Dr. Rohrbach, cite the following reasons for their views:

1. Cain murdered Abel and afterward was afraid that anyone who found him would kill him. So God marked him to avoid this happening. Theistic evolutionists say, therefore, that this proves conclusively that other humans existed at this time, of whom Cain was afraid. These other humans must have been of a para-Adamic race.

2. Cain later built a city. How, asks Dr. Rohrbach, could he have done this if other humans besides himself, Adam and Eve, were not present to help him build? This is taken as further evidence of a para-Adamic race living at the same time as Adam and in contact with him, though Dr. Rohrbach does not, so far as I am aware, use the term "para-Adamic."

3. Cain took himself a wife. He must have taken her, say the theistic evolutionists, from the para-Adamic races living round about him.

Thus, having deduced the existence of other humans at the time of Adam, it is a short step to conclude that God took Adam out of this race, maybe as a child, and breathed the breath of life into him, so making a man, a spiritual human being, out of an animal. This means that the report of Genesis 2 really describes the calling out of Adam from existing animal stock.

To counter these propositions from the orthodox point of view the following should be taken into consideration: At the time of the scriptural report in question, there were obviously (and really) other humans present on earth besides Adam, Eve and Cain. Otherwise Cain would not have feared them and otherwise he could not have built his city with them. And where, otherwise, could the poor man have found his wife? Thus, the conclusion of theistic evolutionists that other humans besides Adam, Eve and Cain were present at this time is perfectly reasonable and orthodox. The difference between orthodox teaching and that of the theistic evolutionists lies, of course, in the nature of the assumed origin of these other humans. Were they of a para-Adamic race, or were they other offspring from Adam's and Eve's marriage?

Professor Rohrbach teaches that these para-Adamic men were biologically but *not spiritually* related to Adam. In fact these para-Adamic beings are not the sons or daughters of Adam and Eve in Dr. Rohrbach's view. Orthodox belief holds that Eve is the mother of *all* the living.[1] Professor Rohrbach thus concludes that Cain's wife was a para-Adamic and not a daughter of Adam. And it is with such para-Adamic races that Cain is postulated to have built this city.

This means that theistic evolutionists of the above shade of opinion teach that Adam was biologically not the first man. They think that at the time God breathed the breath of life into Adam (until then a para-Adamite) there existed many similar "men," who had evolved through millions of years from lower animals by the principles laid down by Darwin. These para-Adamic races were actually animals, in

[1]Gen. 3:20.

their view (just as today's men are), but they were not the
"elected ones" to become men, in the spiritual sense, by receiving the breath of life.

*But the important point to remember in these theistic
evolutionary deductions is that the para-Adamic races are
postulated as being biologically of the identical race and
species as modern man. For Cain is said to have married one
and to have had fertile children by her, which settles forever
the question of species. Cain and the para-Adamites on this
basis must have been of one biological species.* So *biologically*
Adam is postulated by this type of theistic evolutionist as not
being the first man. Only spiritually is this priority conceded
to him.

The para-Adamic races, although biologically fully human,
are believed by Dr. Rohrbach as having "turned away" from
the knowledge of God and his revelation. Therefore they
were not the "elect." Dr. Rohrbach does not think that such
beings as the para-Adamites could actually have sinned or
"fallen" since they had never received any light or law to
fall from. The orthodox believer must surely reply that,
according to the Scriptures, any turning away from divine
revelation, be it in the form of the Scriptures themselves *or in
nature,* would in itself be a dire sin.[2]

This line of thought must lead to a position where theistic
evolutionists believe that the creation or evolution of man
biologically must have taken place long before Adam's appearance. For evolution is postulated as having turned up
the human species, biologically speaking, long before Adam.
Then, if the para-Adamites turned away from God's revelation before Adam's time, they, according to Romans 1:19-20,
must have fallen too, long before Adam. It all simply results
in pushing the creation and fall of man back into pre-Adamic
times, which the present author at least finds intellectually
and theologically less than satisfactory. For it solves no problems.

[2]Cf. Rom. 1:19-20.

According to Dr. Rohrbach, these para-Adamites all perished in the deluge at the time of Noah. It was to these "other men" that Christ went and preached the gospel after his crucifixion[3] and it is on this basis that Dr. Rohrbach proceeds to justify the Apostle Paul's statement that through Adam's sin, death entered the world,[4] and not through a pre-Adamite fall. All the para-Adamites are postulated as having died in the deluge, leaving only true sons of Adam on earth, through whom it could therefore be said that sin entered the world, according to Pauline doctrine. Which all really concedes that the para-Adamic races were in fact *punished* in the flood, and that for a fall, in which, according to theistic evolutionists of this persuasion, they were never involved!

Similarly, the statement that Eve is the mother of all living is justified on the basis that all other human beings other than her progeny were liquidated at the flood. But here again it must be pointed out that if Seth took a para-Adamic wife, then Eve is not the sole mother of all living. The para-Adamites outside Adam would be part of our human ancestry today, for Seth's progeny did not all die in the flood. If Cain took a para-Adamic wife, why should not Seth have taken one too? But if both Seth and Cain took para-Adamic wives, why would God go to all the bother of a tricky dissection of a rib from Adam's side and then carry out some difficult tissue culture with it to build up a wife for Adam out of his own flesh? Why did he not take a para-Adamic woman for Adam, if it was all right to do so? And how does one account for the necessity of the rib out of Adam's side to make a woman on the basis of theistic evolution? I have never yet heard of any real theistic evolutionist solution to this *operation* as such. If God had to make Eve by resorting to such catastrophic creational methods, why did he produce Adam the long evolutionary way? We may well the more insist on this question when we read in Genesis that he did make Adam by a catastrophic creational method too. It is up to the

[3]Cf. Rom. 5:12.
[4]Cf. I Peter 3:19-20.

creative evolutionist to tell us why he adopted different methods in the two instances.

The whole concept of the para-Adamic races being wiped out in the flood so as to make Eve the mother of all who are now living, rests on a rather shaky basis. For if both Seth and Cain took para-Adamic wives, then there is now no "pure" Adamic human race left. We are all mongrels derived from Adam and Eve and para-Adamic races. As such, according to the theory under discussion, we ought all to have died in the flood with our father Noah, who must also have been a mongrel.

But if Seth took a daughter of Adam to wife, why should not Cain have done likewise? For Adam lived 130 years and begat Seth, after which event he lived a further 800 years begetting sons and daughters.[5] If both Seth and Cain took Adam's daughters to wife, then the whole concept of para-Adamic races to supply wives and neighbors with whom to build cities, or to flee from, becomes superfluous. And surely, if Abraham, at a much later date, could have taken Sarai his half sister, with no poor genetical or eugenical consequences, Adam's generation could have done likewise with even less likelihood of trouble.

As to the problem of the rapid multiplication of the human race in antediluvian times, consider the following: If each family had six children (and there is evidence that they had, in fact, many more) and lived the many hundreds of years (which they did), their period of fertility for the production of children being spread over these long years, one is driven to the conclusion that there may have existed at least 258 million people seventeen generations (each generation being calculated as ninety years—probably much too long and therefore giving a much too conservative answer) after Adam, and 774 million inhabitants eighteen generations after him, calculated on the same basis.

There being on this basis an ample supply of Adam and

[5] Gen. 5:3-4.

Eve's progeny on earth shortly after Eve started to bear children, the difficulties raised by the theistic evolutionists turn out to be nebulous. For further information on this subject see Whitcomb and Morris.[6]

SOME FURTHER CONSEQUENCES OF THEISTIC EVOLUTIONARY VIEWS

1. It is not the view of the present writer that the proposed distinction of two different creation accounts can be justified on any grounds. Both describe different aspects of the same event.[7]

2. Theistic evolutionists often maintain that the idea of biological evolution is not foreign to the Scriptures. They point out, as does Dr. Rohrbach, that Noah produced Shem, Ham and Japheth, from whom all the different human races are reported to have been derived. This is supposed to prove that evolution has taken place in the development of the human race since Noah's time and described in the Scriptures.

But evolution postulates as a main thesis that one species develops into another. A *conditio sine qua non* of Darwinism is the instability and infinite mutability of species. The Bible reports that all the different human races came from Noah, which however, has nothing whatsoever to do with the concept of Darwinian evolution. For in this development described in the Scriptures no new species was ever in question. All human races are, of course, mutually fertile and belong therefore to the same species. The mutation of one species into another which is not mutually fertile is the basis of Darwinian evolution.

It is, of course, well known that variations within species do take place and that some of these variations are inheritable. If two such variants become separated by sea water,

    [6]Henry Morris and John C. Whitcomb, *The Genesis Flood* (Philadelphia: Presbyterian & Reformed Publishing Co., 1961), pp. 25-26.
    [7]Kenneth A. Kitchen, *Ancient Orient and Old Testament* (Chicago: Inter-Varsity Press, 1966), pp. 116-17.

mountains or other conditions of habitat, the two variants will stop interbreeding and the differences may become greater as the years go by. Darwin cites many cases of this, for example, the Galapagos ground finches Geospiza magnirostris, G. fortis, Camarhynchus parvulus and Certhidea olivacea.[8]

It is one thing to note such variation and explain its occurrence in the finches. For such variations can be accounted for by relatively small changes and reshuffling in the genes and chromosomes. But it is surely an entirely different matter to believe that the genes and chromosomes of an amoeba could be reshuffled and modified by chance and natural selection to produce an elephant, man or tomato. Yet this is what the evolutionist asks us to believe. It would be easy to believe that one General Motors automobile could be modified into another but an entirely different matter to modify a Chevrolet into a seagoing submarine.

3. Theistic evolutionists do not seem to teach that the material and biological world was altered much when their para-Adamic Adam became a human Adam by receiving the breath of God. Nor do they teach that the biological world was much altered by the "fall" of Adam. The Scriptures do, however, teach that a huge difference arose in biology before and after the fall. In fact, most theistic evolutionists seem to teach that the biological laws (which are assumed to govern their postulated evolutionary processes) continued to exist after the fall, as they had beforehand. Dr. Rohrbach thinks that evolutionary processes before the "election" or "call" of Adam were the same as those afterward. Thus, through long ages of millions of years, before and after the fall, biological development is assumed to have continued unchanged at a slow and steady rate.

Adam is assumed to have been removed from this evolutionary world by being taken into a protected garden where

[8]Sir Gavin de Beer, *Charles Darwin* (Garden City, N.Y.: Doubleday & Co., Inc., 1964), p. 83.

the breath of God fell upon him. After the fall, he and Eve are supposed to have been removed from this protection. Natural selection and chance mutation would have again come into operation, so that development according to evolutionary principles would have restarted.

As far as I am aware, Dr. Rohrbach does not mention whether, in his view, aging and decay took place outside the garden but not inside. The raising of such a problem would be highly significant for theistic evolutionists in general. For, according to Scripture, sin and death (aging and decay) entered *the world* as we know it only after Adam's fall. So that before the fall the whole world (inside and outside the garden) must have been a paradise without sin and decay. Before the fall there was no law of death in the whole animal creation.[9] The world became subjected to vanity (decay) at the fall, but this subjection is only temporary. One day it will be removed and paradise on earth will return. Acts 3:21 and many other scriptures promise this same restoration of paradise on earth, lost at the time of the fall.

Now, if a *restoration* of paradise, with no sin or death, is promised, it means that paradise was, in fact, *once existent on earth at the time of Adam's creation.* Theistic evolutionists do not treat this single fact fundamentally. If they did they would find that they would immediately have to abandon many concepts and aspects of theistic evolution, as taught today and harnessed to Darwinian evolution. This is for the following reasons: According to the biblical concept, nature as we know it today is fallen. It fell at the time of Adam, and with it the facts of decay, aging, illness and, in general, the principles of the second law of thermodynamics were introduced. Thus, before the fall there would have been in nature no question of natural selection involving pain and death in the struggle for existence. For in an entirely harmonious paradisiacal nature there could have been no mortal struggle for existence. *And if there was before Adam's fall no*

[9]Rom. 8:20.

*struggle for existence and therefore no natural selection, how
could there have been, before the fall, an upward evolution
according to the Darwinian concept? The very mechanism
of Darwinian evolution must have been lacking in a paradise.
And if upward evolution in such a paradise before the fall
was lacking, how could higher plants and animals and even
a para-Adamic race have been evolved at all?*

Thus it can never be correct to imagine that the world
before the fall closely resembled the world as we know it now
after the fall. The whole of creation, both in and out of the
garden, must have been a paradise if Adam introduced death
to the creation. From where would the sin or incompleteness
in creation have come without a fall? This ought to be fundamentally treated by all theistic evolutionists, especially if they
subscribe, or claim to subscribe, to the authority of all Holy
Scripture. For Holy Scripture speaks of a paradise in all
nature into which sin entered by Adam. And all Scripture,
both in the Old and New Testaments, solemnly promises a
return of these conditions to all nature at or after the second
coming of Christ. To deny the paradise of Eden at the beginning of creation is to question the paradise of God promised us by Scripture at the time of the "restoration of all
things."[10]

These facts alone cut the ground from under the very concept of the mechanism of the proposed Darwinistic evolution.
How could it yield pre- and para-Adamic races in a paradise
before Adam? And since Adam must be relatively young,
geologically speaking, the same consideration cuts out Darwinistic evolutionary mechanisms for any ages before Adam
(which were supposed to have delivered us the evolutionary
raw material for Adam). Dr. Rohrbach and his theistic evolutionary supporters are overdue in providing us some reasonable way out of these very serious difficulties in their theories, if they wish us to listen to them further.

[10]Acts 3:21.

4. These difficulties in the way of theistic evolution are only augmented by the following facts:

a. The Scriptures inform us that Adam and Eve and all animals were vegetarians before the fall:

> And God said, Behold, I have given you every [green] herb bearing seed, which is upon the face of all the earth, and every tree, in the which is the fruit of a tree yielding seed: to you it shall be for meat [food]. And to every beast of the earth, and to every fowl of the air, and to every thing that creepeth upon the earth, wherein there is life, I have given every green herb for meat: and it was so.[11]

Thus all men, animals, creeping things and even birds were vegetarians (notice how specific the text is) before the fall of Adam. This means that the metabolism of our present carnivores and omnivores, as well as their dental and intestinal tract anatomy and biochemistry, must have vastly changed since then.

Bernard Ramm seems to miss the entire point of the Messianic promises stemming from the original paradise of Eden when he writes: "To insist that all carnivora were originally vegetarian is another preposterous proposition. Why such huge teeth and sharp claws?"[12] Surely nobody is suggesting that the dentition (or the claws) of the lion were such while it "ate straw like the ox," or that such dentition will do for the millenium when he will, according to prophecy, revert to the same mode of life. The point which the Scriptures seem to be making (and which uniformitarians such as Dr. Ramm would appear, at heart, to deny) is that originally at creation and finally at the restoration the nature of man and animals was and will be so different from what it is now, that even the outward biology at creation and at the restoration will suit this inward nature. To deny that this was so at

[11]Gen. 1:29-30.
[12]Bernard Ramm, *The Christian View of Science and Scripture* (Grand Rapids: Wm. B. Eerdmans Publishing Co., 1954), p. 209.

creation is to deny the historicity of the Genesis account
(which Dr. Ramm attempts to avoid by calling the latter
"prescientific"), and to deny that a restoration is promised
us, is to deny the value of prophecy with regard to historicity
(which some try to get around by denying that there will be
a literal millennium or literal restoration). The Scriptures
indicate that the fall was the trigger for unprecedented biological changes in both man and the whole kingdom of life.
To maintain that there have not been these changes is to
reveal that one is, at heart, a uniformitarian. To maintain
that no restoration is to come, is to demonstrate that one
makes the prophetic promises of God of none effect. To believe and to teach (as Dr. Ramm does[13]) that only man
reaped death as the result and wages of sin is to destroy the
teaching of Romans and other parts of the New Testament
to the effect that the whole creation fell as a result of Adam's
fall: "The *whole creation* groaneth and travaileth in pain together until now waiting for the adoption, to wit, the redemption [from the consequences of the fall] of our body."[14]

b. This change in metabolism and anatomy must have been
accompanied by a radical change in habits and behavior. For
only after the flood did animals begin to fear man.[15] Before
men began to feed on animals, the animals obviously would
not fear that man would make his next meal out of them.
Nor did animals fear other animals, for the same reason.

c. It looks as if the whole process of reproduction was also
altered at or after the fall. In any case, pain in childbirth is
spoken of as a "sorrow" after the fall. Perhaps the whole
process would have been different if paradise had not been
lost.[16]

C. S. Lewis in his *The Problem of Pain* points these changes
out in his chapter entitled "The Fall of Man,"[17] when he

[13]*Ibid.*, p. 206 (citing Dawson).
[14]Rom. 8:22.
[15]Gen. 9:1-5.
[16]Gen. 3:16.
[17]C. S. Lewis, *The Problem of Pain* (New York: Macmillan Co., 1948),
pp. 70-71.

suggests that the fall brought with it a "change of species."
Lewis says:

> The process was not, I conceive, comparable to mere
> deterioration as it may now occur in a human individ-
> ual; it was loss of status as a *species*. What man lost by
> the fall was his original specific nature. . . . This condi-
> tion was transmitted by heredity to all later generations,
> for it was not simply what biologists call an acquired
> variation; it was the emergence of a new kind of man—
> a new species, never made by God, had sinned its way
> into existence. . . . It was a radical alteration of his con-
> stitution.

We are trying to point out that this radical change of
species occurred at the fall and was seen not only in Adam
and Eve, but in the serpent too. For although we may not
know the precise historical and metaphysical meaning of the
changes which took place after the temptation in the serpent's
species, yet it is clear that they were even outwardly very far-
reaching. For, after the temptation and fall of Adam the
serpent is condemned to crawling on his belly and eating dust
—whatever that may mean metaphorically. Practically it
meant that the use of limbs was henceforth denied to him,
so that we are obviously dealing with a loss of species in the
serpent's case too. What forms the parallel losses of species
may have taken in the rest of creation after Adam's and the
serpent's loss of species we are not told beyond the details
concerned with teeth, claws, vegetarianism and predatory
nature all arising after Eden. It does seem most important
to emphasize the huge changes occurring in all the biological
world as a direct consequence of the fall and that the changes
involved catastrophic loss of species.

But it would not be sufficient to mention only this loss of
species at the fall without mentioning the regaining of species
at the restitution of all things mentioned in Acts 3:21. At the
time of the restitution of all things the features lost by Adam
at the fall will be recovered, together with the resurrection

body Christ is even now preparing for his disciples. Adam, before the fall, had perfect and spontaneous access to God and the spiritual realm in apparently the same way that Christ's disciples will experience the same on regaining Adam's lost status at the change occurring with Christ's return to the earth. The last Adam, who is a quickening Spirit, certainly belongs to a new race of man—and so do those who are his regenerated people.

The above considerations lead us a step further. If the vast changes in species in Adam, in the serpent and the animals took place at the fall of Adam, this fact must bring with it the consequence that before Adam's fall none of these species showed the consequences of the fall. This means, of course, that the fall must have had universal consequences. For it to have had universal consequences the total creation (even the part of it outside Eden) must have been paradisiacal. For if the paradise of God had been restricted to Eden alone, then the rest of the world outside Eden could not have been a paradise, but a jungle in which the lethal struggle for existence had always gone on—even before the fall. This means that the consequences of the fall (jungles) had always existed in the world outside Eden and that Eden was an exception, an island in the midst of a raging ocean.

But, if the world outside Eden was already a jungle before Eden was created, how could it have fallen with Adam? It had already fallen before Adam in becoming a jungle. If it was already red in tooth and claw before Adam's fall, no change could have taken place at the fall. We are informed, however, that an enormous change did, in fact, take place in all creation. So we conclude that paradise, before the fall, was universal and not restricted to Eden. This effectively rules out Darwinian evolution before Eden.

Perhaps a majority of orthodox Christians think rather differently on these somewhat speculative matters, particularly in view of modern geological opinions. C. S. Lewis, for example, believes that Satan caused the fall of the animal

kingdom long before Adam arrived on the scene.[18] Lewis
believes that Adam was intended to be the "redeemer" of the
already fallen kingdom of nature. Thus, carnivorousness
existed, in Lewis' opinion, long before Adam.

To justify this opinion in the face of the scriptures we
have already discussed (that the fall entered the kingdom of
nature, and not only man's kingdom, via Adam) Lewis makes
use of a means often used by modern theologians. He maintains that Christ humbled himself to share, as man, the current superstitions of his time: "Thus, if our Lord had committed Himself to any scientific or historical statement which
we knew to be untrue, this would not disturb my faith in His
deity."[19] This method of avoiding the consequences of the
statements of the Scriptures on historical matters is not one
that the present author would like to envisage. He feels sure
that a proportion of orthodox believers will be inclined to
agree with him on this point.

   d. If the consumption of flesh had been permitted in paradise, death would have been introduced thereby. But the
death of animals was first introduced after paradise was lost,
and not to provide food but as a source of clothing and a
sacrifice for sin.[20] Man did not eat this flesh (that was fit only
for an offering to God) until Noah's time, after the flood: ·

> And God blessed Noah and his sons, and said unto them,
> Be fruitful, and multiply, and replenish the earth. And
> the fear of you and the dread of you shall be upon every
> beast of the earth, and upon every fowl of the air, and
> upon all that moveth upon the earth, and upon all the
> fishes of the sea; into your hand are they delivered.
> Every moving thing that liveth shall be meat for you;
> even as the green herb have I given you all things. But
> flesh with the life thereof, which is [in] the blood thereof,
> shall ye not eat.[21]

[18]*Ibid.*, pp. 121-24.
[19]*Ibid.*, p. 122.
[20]Gen. 3:21.
[21]Gen. 9:1-5.

e. It has often been asked how Noah managed to entice all the animals into the ark. Would they not have attacked each other or feared Noah? The foregoing considerations throw light on this question.

Since no animal at that time feared being made a meal of by Adam or by any other animal, there was automatically quite a different relationship than at present between man and animals, and between animal and animal. The peace of paradise died slowly (in spite of the activities of Cain's off-spring) even after the fall, and nature only became really "red in tooth and claw" after the flood. Thus the consequences of the fall were progressive. In fact the Bible teaches that the animals at the time of the flood went willingly and of their own volition into the ark, as though they sensed the impending catastrophe,[22] just as sea gulls today fly inland well before the storm breaks.

f. It is obvious that the Scriptures view the death of a plant quite differently from the death of an animal. Plant food was allowed and even commanded in the garden and after-ward. Eating a piece of fruit (in Eden) did not necessarily mean the death of the whole plant but merely of part of its reproductive organs. The death of an animal, whose life is in its blood, was a very different matter. It was permitted, after the deluge, to provide food. Thus it was consistent with the laws of paradise that plants should die in it to provide food, but not that animal blood should be shed to provide nourishment for other animals or for man.

The Bible does not go into the difficulty of distinguishing between plant and animal life in the microbiological world. It is only fairly recently that modern science has discovered this border line between plant and animal life. But the Scriptures make abundantly clear just what was meant by "plant" and "animal": "And to every beast of the earth, and to every fowl of the air, and to every thing that creepeth upon the earth, wherein there is life, I have given every green herb for

[22]Gen. 7:9.

meat."[23] "Every moving thing that liveth shall be meat for you; even as the green herb have I given you all things. But flesh with the life thereof, which is the blood thereof, shall ye not eat."[24]

Christians today often forget that this primeval restriction on the eating of blood set up in Genesis 9 has never been removed to this day. On the contrary, the New Testament reiterates the same command: "For it seemed good to the Holy Ghost, and to us, to lay upon you no greater burden than these necessary things; that ye abstain from meats offered to idols, and from blood, and from things strangled, and from fornication: from which if ye keep yourselves, ye shall do well."[25]

Thus from a practical point of view the new animal food which was allowed after the flood, was concerned with the flesh of higher animals, possessed of blood which was shed on slaughtering. This type of death was introduced after the fall, first as a sacrifice for sin and then as a new source of food. But it was never part of the economy of paradise.

To summarize, we may conclude that theistic evolutionary ideas, and attempts to couple them with the principles of evolutionary Darwinism, do not take adequate account of the fundamental changes in the biology and metabolism of nature which took place in man and animals according to Holy Scripture after the fall; and that before the fall nature was a paradise where no pain, death, decay, aging, carnivores nor omnivores were known. Before the fall there was a relationship between man and animals quite different from that which we know today, which is based largely on fear.

Although we cannot conceive of a paradisiacal nature today nor imagine its beauty and perfection (since even in our thinking we are dominated by the second law of thermodynamics), we have no valid reason for rejecting the biblical picture given of nature in the past—and its promise for the

[23]Gen. 1:30.
[24]Gen. 9:3-4.
[25]Acts 15:28-29.

future, in the restoration. It would be intellectual suicide simply to reject everything we cannot comprehend just on the basis that we cannot comprehend. But such a paradisiacal nature precludes the very mechanism of Darwin's supposed evolutionary concepts. There would be no natural selection and struggle for existence in paradise. Therefore the paradisiacal conditions before the fall of Adam would at the same time remove the possibility of the previous evolution of higher organisms before Adam appeared. How then could Adam have been derived from a stock of higher animals formed by previous evolutionary processes, if the evolutionary mechanism for forming such a stock (death, natural selection, struggle, etc.) was not and could not have been present in the paradisiacal conditions existing throughout the world before Adam and the fall?

How then can theistic evolution be coupled with Darwinistic evolution if the basic mechanism of the latter is precluded before the fall of Adam? For it is precisely in the period before the fall that the major part of this theistic evolution is postulated to have occurred.

g. There is one further consequence of theistic evolutionary ideas which is, as far as I know, seldom recognized. It is the relationship between theistic evolution and a-millennialism.

It is well known that in recent years conservative Christians, especially in the United Kingdom and British Commonwealth, have been swinging progressively to the a-millennial interpretation of scriptural prophecy. This has, no doubt, been due in some measure to the direct personal influence of certain popular preachers who are of this persuasion themselves. But what is often not realized is the fact that theistic evolution in itself, apart from the personal influence of preachers, does contain the seeds of a-millennialism. If one is a theistic evolutionist, a logical extension of this view of past history, biologically speaking, leads to the a-millennial view of future history.

The reason for this is, of course, that the biblical millennium is a "restoration of all things," a return to earth of conditions as they were before the fall of creation through Adam.[26] If, now, one accepts the doctrine that sin and death really did enter the creation by Adam, there can have been none of either on earth before his fall (which means incidentally, that we can expect no fossil evidence of the paradisiacal state and therefore no scientific evidence for it). It follows that removal of sin and the other consequences of the fall will allow a paradise to return to earth once more. But theistic evolution does not allow for a universal paradise before Adam lived, because a paradise could not have worked by struggle for existence, a natural selection and/or mutation (since a mutation is in reality a decomposition, a decay in chromosomal order in most cases). This has the consequence that theistic evolutionists must deny a universal paradise before Adam. And if they deny this, then they must logically deny the restoration of paradise at the end of time. Thus the denial of the first chapters of Genesis leads naturally to a denial of the final chapters of the Bible promising a paradise on earth, as it was at the beginning. Which all goes to show how important it is not to deny or distort any part of Scripture, for if one does, other parts will also surely become distorted. The whole Scripture has a unity which cannot be disturbed.

II. Note on *The Order of the Living—Evolutionary Theory and Belief in God*, by Dr. Rudolf Frey.[1]

This book was published by Dr. Hans Bürki, the leader of the Inter-Varsity Christian Fellowship movement in German-speaking Switzerland, in collaboration with the Brockhaus Verlag, one of the few publishing houses left in Germany which still adheres to scriptural truth. The publication was reviewed in the original German edition of this book and is mentioned here to bring to the notice of English-speaking

[26]Heb. 3:21.
[1]Rudolf Frey, *Die Ordnung des Lebendigen und Schöpferglaube* (Wuppertal, Germany: R. Brockhaus Verlag, 1964).

readers the thoroughgoing theistic evolutionary doctrine, coupled with straightforward Darwinism, which is generally taught in European Christian circles, even in organizations coupled wth American evangelical organizations.

Dr. Frey's book teaches that organic evolution, as an explanation of life as we see it today, is a fact to be reckoned with in theological doctrinal formulations. That Darwinism is an accepted fact is the *Leitmotif* ("main theme") of the book. We must shape our theology accordingly or we shall not be educated persons. However, Dr. Frey does point out some of the difficulties of Darwinism and is perfectly honest intellectually. He does notice, for example, the absence of "missing links" in paleontology. He also says that science does not yet know for certain the entire cause and mechanism of evolution. "Life and the living is for the biologist just as much unexplained as matter and energy is for the physicist."[2] "Even if man should synthesize life, we still have not explained the spirit [*Geist*] of the scientist who is behind the synthetic homunculus."[3]

Students in the German-speaking world have little literature which deals with questions on current biological trends and treats them from a scientific and/or biblical point of view.

III. *Dinosaur and Human Tracks in the Cretaceous (Paluxy River, Texas)*.

As already mentioned,[1] human tracks have been found in a Cretaceous formation in Texas. Dr. R. T. Bird reported on such tracks in his article entitled "Thunder in His Footsteps"[2] and reproduced photographs of them.

If it could be conclusively proved that modern man had lived at the same time as the giant saurians, scientists would be forced to rethink the whole presently accepted evolution-

[2]*Ibid.*, p. 16.
[3]*Ibid.*, p. 19.
[1]*Natural History* (May, 1939), pp. 96 ff.
[2]*Ibid.*, pp. 255 ff.

ary Darwinistic concept. One well-documented factual observation of this sort would rob the theory of the huge time spans regarded as a *conditio sine qua non* for evolution to have occurred. It is conceded that modern man is geologically speaking young or recent, and that he arose not more than one to ten million years ago depending on which scientist is speaking. Before this time, hominides of various types are supposed to have existed, which were, however, by no stretch of the imagination *Homo sapiens*. According to modern evolutionary theory, therefore, man could not possibly have lived as long ago as fifty million years, let alone 100 to 120 million years, which latter time brings us, according to Darwinians, to the age of the saurians, the giant reptiles. It is postulated by evolutionists that the whole realm of animal life 120 million years ago was not developed sufficiently to have brought forth a hominide or a modern man. In their view, at the time of the giant reptiles, many millions of years were needed before the animal kingdom could have evolved modern man.

On this basis it would be simply incompatible and impossible for an evolutionist to imagine a modern man living contemporaneously with the giant lizards. One London biologist, when this possibility was discussed in his presence (of man tracks and brontosaurus tracks having been found in the same formation) remarked that a single such find would provide sound reason for renouncing all evolutionary theory. He was a convinced evolutionist.

Dr. Bird reports in his article in *Natural History* that he he saw in a small shop in the South in the States, pieces of rock for sale which contained imprints of human tracks. The rock fragments, which had been taken from the Paluxy Riverbed in Glen Rose, Texas, showed well-formed footprints about fifteen inches long and about six to seven inches wide at the widest spot. They showed five well-formed toe prints and a normal instep and heel. They could thus not have been the tracks of the giant cave bear, but were too big for the footprints of a normal modern man.

Dr. Bird was at first of the opinion that these tracks were forgeries, for they were perfect in every detail. But he was informed that there were more footprints of the same type *in situ* in the Paluxy River bed, from which the tracks, which were for sale, had been taken. And Dr. Bird says that he was told at the same time that nearby there were dinosaur tracks too. Such astounding nonsense sent Dr. Bird straight to Glen Rose to see for himself.

First he visited James Ryals, whose farm lay on the Paluxy River and who knew well all the tracks in the neighborhood. At first Dr. Bird could not persuade Mr. Ryals to show him the tracks in question. The price Mr. Ryals had obtained for tracks he had previously dug out himself, had been too low. But Mr. Ryals did confirm that there had been a whole chain of such human tracks which had been washed out, in a recent flood there. A few water-eroded tracks were still to be seen, but they lay under the level of the river water. Mr. Ryals then showed Dr. Bird these latter tracks, which were about the same size as those he had seen on sale in the shop and which had also come from Glen Rose. Dr. Bird confirms in his article that he spoke with at least a dozen persons in Glen Rose who had personally seen the chain of human tracks before the local flood. Dr. Bird photographed the tracks he saw himself and published them in the article cited above, mentioning at the same time the beautiful dinosaur and brontosaur tracks in the same Cretaceous formation. He also illustrated the latter with photographs.

The author himself saw some really impressive brontosaur tracks in Glen Rose at the same site and photographed them. These are reproduced herewith (see Figs. 13, 14, 15, 16).

In the autumn of 1965 an experienced American geologist Dr. C. L. Burdick wrote me that he intended to go to Glen Rose to search for the human footstep chain that Ryals and many others in Glen Rose had seen, but which had been washed farther downstream with tons of rocks in a flood. The bend in the river, where these washed-out rocks had accumulated, was well known, so that he hoped to be able to sort them out with earth-moving machinery, thus recovering, if possible undamaged, some of the lost human tracks. I was invited to take part in a preliminary prospecting at the site and willingly accepted the invitation.

Glen Rose is a small town about sixty miles south of Dallas and Fort Worth in Texas. In the half-dried-up bed of the Paluxy River south of Glen Rose may be seen, on both sides, Cretaceous formations bearing innumerable tracks of dinosaurs of various types. Some tracks, especially those of a brontosaur, are exceedingly clear and well preserved. Some tyrannosaurus footprints are also almost perfect. Figures 11-16 show photographs taken at Glen Rose.

In a tributary stream bed, which was completely dried up at the time, I saw innumerable dinosaur tracks of all types, which looked as if they had been formed recently. These footprints were very often superimposed on each other and it looked as if a bunch of giant reptiles had been squabbling with one another over some booty. This mass of footprints runs straight into the stream bank, but we could not investigate further without moving masses of earth lying over the formation. All these tracks helped to confirm the Glen Rose formations as being Cretaceous (about 120 million years old according to the standard time scale).

Not far from the area just described we found a track about thirty-eight centimeters long and fifteen centimeters wide which pierced the chalk layer right into the blue clay layer beneath. The body borne by these feet was obviously heavy to have sunk in so far. For this reason no toe or heel prints were to be seen. But otherwise the tracks were of the identical shape and size of those which Dr. Bird describes (Figs. 17 and 18). Figure 19 shows the length of the stride of the creature—a biped walking upright—which made the tracks about three yards long. If it was of the same species as the one which made the tracks which Dr. Bird observed (and this is neither proved nor suggested as being proved) the toes, foot arch and heel might have shown it to have been human, although a giant human.

For those who take the Bible seriously, the matter of the huge dimensions of these tracks found by Dr. Bird is not difficult to solve, for the Holy Scriptures speak of giants on earth both before and after the flood. Genesis 6:4 and Numbers 13:33 speak of the "Nephilim, the sons of Enak" or "the fallen ones." In Deuteronomy (2:11, 20; 3:11, 13), Joshua (12:4; 13:12; 15:8; 17:16) and I Chronicles (20:4, 6, 8) are reports on the *rapha*, the giants or the "terrible ones," who lived at these times. Second Samuel (21:16, 18, 20, 22) speaks also of the *rapha* or the "terrible ones." We know that Goliath was also a giant (I Sam. 17). If the above tracks are those of a giant or giants, they simply confirm the reliability of the Holy Scriptures in these historical and biological matters. But for the geologist this does not solve the problem of the age of the formation in which these tracks have been found.

We can summarize the findings at Glen Rose as follows:

1. In Cretaceous formations (which are estimated to be about 120 million years old) which show numerous brontosaur and dinosaur tracks, giant human tracks have been found and photographed by Dr. Bird and other geologists. Most of these giant human tracks have now been removed from the riverbed and sold or otherwise dispersed. One such track may still be seen, set in concrete, outside a small hotel in Glen Rose. The giant human tracks have perfectly clear toe, heel and arch imprints. The holes in the riverbed from which the tracks were taken by collectors, together with the remains of Dr. Bird's excavations, were still visible in the autumn of 1965, when the author was on the site. Dr. Bird spoke with at least a dozen people in Glen Rose who had personally seen the chain of perfect man tracks *in situ* before a flood washed them out.

2. The writer personally saw some water-eroded footprints the same size and shape as those photographed by Dr. Bird, which are apparently human. He also saw some other footprints of about the same dimensions as those reported by Dr. Bird but with no toe prints due to the track having passed through the chalk layer into the blue clay beneath.

3. Although the layers which carried the detailed giant human tracks seen by Dr. Bird have now been washed away by a flood, the possibility of finding some of them in the rocks heaped up by the floodwaters at a bend slightly downstream, should be considered.

4. Dr. Bird and others who have investigated these giant, apparently human, tracks would have been ready to recognize them as human if the theory of evolution had not made such recognition "impossible." On account of this "impossibility" Dr. Bird asked Mr. Ryals very carefully[3] whether he knew of any human tracks in the Paluxy River:

> Even the possibility of such an association [between dinosaurs and man] seemed incredible . . . but to my surprise he [Ryals] said: "Oh, you mean the man tracks! Why sure, there used to be a whole trail of them above the fourth crossing before the river washed them out."
> . . . I smiled. No man had ever existed in the Age of Reptiles.

Thus pure theoretical prejudice prevented Dr. Bird from recognizing some exceedingly important geological evidence.

Present plans call for further investigations at Glen Rose.

IV. *Constancy of Species*

One of the foundation concepts of evolution is the unlimited mutability of species. One generation is distinguished from the previous one by small changes which summate in the course of thousands of years producing a new species. The new species are supposed to be better fitted to their environment by the effects of natural selection than the old ones. Thus, the new species are supposed to be more effective in the struggle for existence than the old ones. The evolutionary ladder of life is presumed to have been climbed by one species moving slowly up into a higher one.

But this idea does not fit a number of the observed facts in

---

[3]See Roland T. Bird, "Thunder in His Footsteps," *Natural History* (May, 1939), pp. 255, 257.

the biology of numerous plants and animals. For some species have remained practically unchanged for periods of years reckoned today in millions. The following short and incomplete list is intended to give an idea of the relative immutability of species observed in a number of cases:

PLANTS

1. Plants of the *equisetum* type are reckoned by modern botanists to be hundreds of millions of years old and are still in some species unchanged.

2. *Psiotale* is considered to be a primitive plant which has kept its original form unchanged for long ages amounting to millions of years.

3. The maidenhair-tree (ginko) is supposed to be a "living fossil" by modern botanists, who reckon it to have remained practically unchanged since very primitive times.

This list of primitive plants existing in substantially unchanged form for very long times could easily be lengthened.

ANIMALS

The constancy of at least some species was brought to public attention with the discovery of living *coelacanthus* specimens from East Africa. This species was previously known only as a fossil thought to be scores of millions of years old. Today it has turned up living in substantially unaltered form. Other types which may be considered to show the same lack of change are listed below:

1. Certain types of cockroach (German, *Schabe*) existed in the same form 250 million years ago as today, according to modern geological time reckoning.[1]

2. The black ant (*Formica fusca*) has been found in formations which are reckoned to be 70 million years old.[2]

3. Dragonflies have been found in formations reckoned to be 170 million years old.[3]

[1] Cf. "Insects in Amber," *Scientific American* (Nov., 1951), p. 57.
[2] Cf. *ibid.*, p. 58.
[3] Cf. *Science Digest* (May, 1961), p. 6.

4. In 1950 a deep-sea mollusk (*Neopilina galathea*) was found off the coast of Central America at a depth of three kilometers. It is closely related to the trilobites. The trilobites are considered to be among the earliest inhabitants of the earth, that is, 350 million years old. They are reckoned to have become extinct 280 million years ago. But it has been found that close relatives are still alive today.[4]

5. The Tuatara (*Sphenodon*) is today found exclusively on a small island near New Zealand. The nearest relative of this animal is found in the European Jurassic formations of 150 million years ago. Today the Tuatara closely resembles these relatives.[5]

This list is of necessity incomplete.

V. *Human Tracks in the Carboniferous*

As already mentioned (see pp. 139-142), human tracks have been found in Carboniferous formations. W. G. Burroughs, Professor of Geology at Berea College, Kentucky, chose the name *Phenanthropus mirabilis* for the creatures which left these tracks.

The tracks are in formations considered to be Upper Carboniferous (250 million years old) and show five toes and an arch which is unquestionably human. The tracks are 9½ inches long and 4.1 inches broad at the heel. The width at the forward end of the track, by the toes, was 6 inches. The being that left the tracks was a biped that walked uprightly like a human.[1] Well-known authorities such as Professor C. W. Gilmore of the Smithsonian Institution collaborated in working out this problem, which therefore guarantees considerable reliability. *Antiquities* published photographs of the tracks and said that similar ones had been found in Carboniferous formations in Pennsylvania and Missouri. The Missouri tracks look exceedingly human and resemble those of Southeast Asian aborigines.

[4]Cf. Bentley Glass, *Science* (July 26, 1957), p. 158.
[5]Cf. Charles M. Bogert, *Scientific Monthly* (March, 1953), p. 167.
[1]Cf. *Antiquities* (May 10, 1938).

VI. *The Implications of Evolution,* by G. A. Kerkut, Professor of Physiology and Biochemistry, the University of Southampton, England.

Dr. G. A. Kerkut is professor at Southampton University, England, where he lectures in comparative biochemistry and physiology. He is executive editor of the scientific journal known as *Comparative Biochemistry and Physiology,* published by the Pergamon Press, Oxford, New York and Paris.

In 1960 Dr. Kerkut dropped somewhat of a bombshell in the scientific world by publication of the above cited work which attacks the commonly accepted bases of Darwinian evolution.

Dr. Kerkut does not mention particularly the religious implications of the theory of evolution, and he seems to be a mild evolutionist himself. He does examine the whole theory scientifically from the standpoint of comparative physiology and biochemistry and comes to the conclusion, from this approach, that the scientific evidence for the evolution of life from a common primitive stock is often completely nebulous.

Dr. Kerkut, in the second chapter of the above work, summarizes admirably the seven basic assumptions of evolution as follows:

1. The first assumption is that nonliving things have given rise to living material, in other words, spontaneous generation has occurred.

2. The second assumption is that spontaneous generation occurred only once. The other assumptions all issue from this second one.

3. The third assumption is that viruses, bacteria, plants and animals are all interrelated.

4. The fourth assumption is that Protozoa gave rise to Metazoa.

5. The fifth assumption is that the various invertebrate phyla are interrelated.

6. The sixth assumption is that the invertebrates gave rise to the vertebrates.

7. The seventh assumption is that within the vertebrates the fish gave rise to the amphibia, the amphibia to the reptiles, and the reptiles to the birds and mammals. Sometimes the latter is expressed by saying that modern amphibia and reptiles had a common ancestral stock.

Dr. Kerkut makes his first point in showing that these seven basic assumptions are in no case capable in a single instance of experimental verification. Dr. Kerkut's book is, in essence, an analysis for or against the evidence for these assumptions and by the time one has finished reading the book one wonders how anyone could ever have had the temerity to make seven such assumptions.

Dr. Kerkut points out that the evidence that life arose only once is indeed uncertain. And yet evolutionary theory seems to spend no end of time assuming that this is the case. If it were not the case, and life did arise separately at different times, then all life forms would not necessarily be genetically related. Evolutionists spend a lot of time fighting for the proposition that all life is related genetically, which would not be a fact if life arose more than once.

It is further pointed out that biochemists and comparative physiologists usually assume that all protoplasm possesses the same fundamental biochemistry. But in point of fact the biochemistry of protoplasm varies enormously, and there are many different biochemical mechanisms for carrying out any given reaction. The common possession of a specific blood pigment does not indicate a close phylogenetic relationship. If it did we would have to take *Daphnia* out of the Crustacea because it possesses hemoglobin. It would also be necessary to place the root nodules of leguminous plants with the vertebrates because they both contain hemoglobin. Similarly because nettle stings contain acetylcholine, 5-hydroxytryptamine and histamine the nettle ought on the above principle to be related to the mammals![1] After similar reasoning Kerkut

[1] G. A. Kerkut, *The Implications of Evolution* (London: Pergamon Press, 1960), pp. 8-9.

points out that it is premature to claim that the "universal" accounts of the glycolysis and citric cycles is proof of the common origin of life from one source. The evidence does not exclude the possibility that living things today may be of very different origins.[2]

Dr. Kerkut concludes that if life did arise separately and on several different occasions, then one would expect a large number of distinct groups of animals and plants whose relationships and affinities would be difficult to determine. Which, as Kerkut points out, is close to what we observe in fact. It should be pointed out that this view may, with certain extensions and reservations, be applied to scriptural teaching on the mechanisms of the creation of life.

Kerkut cites A. Lwoff[3] to show that evolution from a physiological point of view might not even be progressive but rather retrogressive. Lwoff states that the most primitive protozoa must have been self-supporting (autotrophic), with little or no food requirements. As evolution took place, the cells lost their synthetic ability and became more dependent on other cells, in other words, they regressed physiologically. Kerkut points out the fallacies in Lwoff's argument.[4]

Kerkut's analysis of the so-called evolution of the horse[5] is instructive. He calls it, rather derisively, the evolution of the story of the evolution of the horse and it is well worth the reader's time to study it. "At present, however, it is a matter of faith that the textbook pictures are true, or even that they are the best representations of the truth that are available to us."[6]

As a result of all this, the book concludes that there is little evidence for evolution's first assumption (spontaneous biogenesis) and that we have no indications at present that autobiogenesis takes place. The second assumption is pronounced

[2]*Ibid.*, p. 13.
[3]A. Lwoff, *L'Evolution Physiologique* (Paris: Herrmann, 1944).
[4]Kerkut, *op. cit.*, p. 30.
[5]*Ibid.*, p. 144.
[6]*Ibid.*, p. 148.

to be a matter of faith or belief rather than proof based on evidence. With regard to the third assumption, we have no definite evidence about the way in which the viruses, bacteria or protozoa are related. The fourth assumption is merely interesting—that protozoa gave rise to metazoa. Other schemes are possible. Under the fifth assumption the evidence for the affinities of the majority of invertebrates is tenuous and circumstantial, in Dr. Kerkut's view.

With respect to the sixth assumption, not discussed in Dr. Kerkut's book, the reader is referred by Dr. Kerkut to the work of Neal and Rand.[7] Dr. Kerkut points out that speculatively the vertebrates have been derived from the annelids, nemerteans, hemichordates and the urochordates. Thus, the theories of the origins of vertebrates are highly heterogeneous. Kerkut believes that as good a case can be made out for the origin of the vertebrates from among the urochordates, in which the *sessile ascidian* is considered to be the basic form, as for the *tadpole form* as the basis.

The sixth basic assumption is summed up with the words of Berrill: "In a sense this account [of the evolution and derivation] of vertebrates is science fiction."[8]

With reference to the seventh assumption, it is on this that most of the work of early modern evolutionists has been based. Kerkut writes:

> We are on somewhat stronger ground with the seventh assumption—namely that the fish, amphibia, reptiles, birds and mammals are interrelated. There is fossil evidence to help us here, though many of the key transitions are not well documented and we have as yet to obtain a satisfactory method of dating the fossils. *The dating is of the utmost importance, for until we find a reliable method of dating the fossils, we shall not be able to tell if the first amphibians arose after the first choanichthian or whether the first reptile arose from*

[7]H. V. Neal and H. W. Rand, *Comparative Anatomy* (London: Blakiston, 1943).
[8]*Ibid.*, p. 153.

the first amphibian. The evidence we have at present is insufficient to allow us to decide the answer to these problems.[9]

It is interesting to note that such an independent and well-known observer as Dr. Kerkut does not, by implication, take the index-fossil method of dating very seriously (cf. pp. 127-31). Dr. Kerkut wants something far more precise, and rightly so.

Dr. Kerkut believes that the amphibia, reptiles and mammals appear to be polyphyletic, that is, that they arose from many scattered stocks and are not derived simply from one basic ancestral pair of animals or group. According to Kerkut, we also have to decide whether in view of the above, the various differences in species we observe are due to one species splitting into two and not to two species being in the process of merging into one.[10]

The seven main assumptions on which Darwinism is based are summed up by Dr. Kerkut with the following words: "In effect, much of the evolution of the major groups of animals has to be taken on trust."[11] This sounds different from the statements as to evolution being "a fact", about which we hear so much.

One or two of Kerkut's general remarks will bear repetition here, since his book is not easily available to the general public:

> It seems at times as if many of our modern writers on evolution have had their views by some sort of revelation and they base their opinions on the evolution of life from the simplest form to the most complex, entirely on the nature of specific and intra-specific evolution. . . . it is premature, not to say arrogant, on our part if we make any dogmatic assertion as to the mode of evolution of the major branches of the animal kingdom.
>
> . . . It may be distressing for some readers to discover that so much in zoology is open to doubt, but this in effect indicates the vast amount of work that remains

[9]*Ibid.*
[10]*Ibid.*, p. 154.
[11]*Ibid.*

to be done. . . . Much of what we learn today are only
half truths or less and the students of tomorrow will not
be bothered by many of the phlogistons that now tor-
ment our brains.[12]

It is important to realize that progress is made especially
when half-truths are rejected. Kerkut says, in fact, that one
of the chief factors hindering the development of zoology today is the fact that presently accepted half-truths cause mental
blocks, preventing our assimilation of a true, clear picture:

> Everything will seem simple and straightforward once
> it has been explained. Why then cannot we see some of
> these solutions now? . . . One reason is often that an
> incorrect idea or "fact" is accepted and takes the place
> of the correct one. . . . Most students become acquainted
> with many of the current concepts in biology while still
> at school and at an age when most people are, on the
> whole, uncritical. Then, when they come to study the
> subject in more detail, they have in their minds several
> half truths and misconceptions, which tend to prevent
> them from coming to a fresh appraisal of the situation. In
> addition, with the uniform pattern of education most
> students tend to have the same sort of educational back-
> ground and so in conversation and discussion they ac-
> cept common fallacies and agree on matters based on
> these fallacies.[13]

Dr. Kerkut, himself an evolutionist, concludes his valuable
critique of the seven basic assumptions of the General Theory
of Organic Evolution, with the suggestion that it would be a
good thing to encourage students to study "scientific heresies"
to avoid "having scientists brought up in a type of mental
straightjacket.[14] He obviously refers not only to the present
teaching of evolution in schools and universities but also to
the whole development of education on strictly conformist
lines as seen in England and particularly in the United States
today.

[12]*Ibid.*, p. 155.
[13]*Ibid.*, pp. 155-56.
[14]*Ibid.*, p. 157.

Finally:

> This theory . . . can be called the General Theory of Evolution and the evidence that supports it is not sufficiently strong to allow us to consider it as anything more than a working hypothesis . . . the answer [to the problem of evolution] will be found by future experimental work and not by dogmatic assertions that the General Theory of Evolution must be correct because there is nothing else that will satisfactorily take its place.[15]

In view of the above, one can only ask oneself why evangelical Christians and others bother to try to harmonize their own particular beliefs with a mere working hypothesis for which there is so little real scientific evidence of an experimental nature. It is, as someone has remarked with respect to cosmology, a fact that the person who becomes wedded to the scientific cosmology of one generation will find himself widowed in the next. The same consequences will surely follow any wedding to any sort of working hypotheses. Tomorrow they will be outdated. But to be continually "widowed" does tend to make the poor "widows" look ridiculous. For it shows a profound lack of knowledge of the history of science, together with a lack of grip on the great foundations and fundamentals of the Christian doctrines which have stood the test of centuries.

But over and above all this comes the fact that the experimental evidence for the working hypothesis of evolution is tenuous. One wonders if experimental proof of its untruth will be so easily forthcoming, since it is not founded on experiment in the first place. The reader is referred to Dr. Kerkut's book itself for a useful bibliography on the subject of the General Theory of Evolution and the origin of life.

VII. *Note on the Views of Claude Lévi-Strauss*

Dr. Claude Lévi-Strauss, Professor of Social Anthropology at the Collège de France, Paris, is one of France's foremost

[15]*Ibid.*

intellectuals of today[1] who has devoted his career and some seven books to the proposition that all men, including the so-called primitive tribes and aboriginals, are intellectually equal and do not show stages in an evolution of the mind. He maintains, too, with respect to the development of the mind, that today's philosophers do not show "progress," but that the minds of all men have been at an equal level of development for some one million years. Today's philosophies such as reflected in TV and hydrogen bombs, are not thought to show a higher intellectual capacity than mankind's earliest brainstorms.

Dr. Lévi-Strauss' ideas have, in France at least, deposed those of existentialist Jean-Paul Sartre. Lévi-Strauss' views on anthropology are already offered in courses at Cambridge University, England, an honor which usually does not come until after death of the author. Three of his books have already been translated into English.[2] Two others are shortly to follow: *Kinship Systems* and *The Raw and the Cooked*.

It has been generally assumed, in biological circles to date, that man's mind has climbed the evolutionary tree in much the same way as his body. Thus, in the stages of the development of the mind, the Old Stone Age, the New Stone Age, the Copper, Bronze and Iron ages are all distinguished in popular scientific thought today. Lévi-Strauss rejects all this evolutionary system of thought as nonsense and wishful thinking, and shows that the human intellect has been fully operative ever since human society was created.

During Lévi-Strauss' stay in Brazil at the University of Sao Paulo, he investigated primitive Indian tribes, expecting to find ignorance and primitiveness in frozen patterns of the past. He found instead that the so-called primitive people, in their own environment, were his intellectual peers. The great arts of civilization such as pottery, weaving, agriculture and the

---

[1]See review in *Time* magazine (June 30, 1967), p. 34.
[2]*Structural Anthropology* (New York: Basic Books, 1963), *Totemism* (Boston: Beacon Press, 1963); *A World on the Wane* (New York: Criterion Books, 1961).

domestication of animals were all established during the
Stone Age. Since then they have only been improved.

Lévi-Strauss does not believe that man is perfectible; what
man is, he already has been. Evolution, he maintains, has
not taken place in the development of the mind of man—the
whole idea is a will-o'-the-wisp. Communication is basic to
society, and even writing itself has a function apart from its
actual message. On this basis, provided by Lévi-Strauss, a
new school of fiction has arisen in France which consults
man's subconscious intellectual infrastructure, rather than
the rules of literary composition.

Roland Barthes is one of the spokesmen of this new movement in France. He believes that even criticism, written by
a critic, is a criticism in itself of that critic, which, incidentally, book reviewers might take profoundly to heart.

To conclude, Lévi-Strauss says that he does not believe in
God, but neither does he believe in man.

VIII. *Post Scriptum*

A number of friends active in youth and student work have
suggested that the author republish and supplement his article
written many years ago entitled *Die Problematik der Deszendenzlehre* ("Problems in the Theory of Evolution").[1]

During the period since the publishing of that article a
great deal of progress has been made in this area of thought.
It gives the author satisfaction to note that his main thesis in
this article still holds firm, if not firmer, as a result of this
progress. A number of new areas not covered by the original
short article have had to be taken into account in the present
publication.

The text of the present volume is based on the revised contents of the author's book[2] which appeared in Germany and
Switzerland in 1966. It is the author's hope that the line of

---

[1]A. E. Wilder Smith, *Die Problematik der Deszendenzlehre* (Wuppertal-
Vohwinkel, Germany: Brockhaus-Verlag, 1949).
[2]A. E. Wilder Smith, *Herkunft und Zukunft des Menschen* (Giessen and
Basel: Brunnen Verlag, 1966).

thought followed may help to clarify the issues of the scientific controversy on evolution still being waged, and that it may also provide a sound basis for facing up to the modern attitude to God and faith in God in general, and biblical faith in Christ in particular. It is not generally realized, perhaps, that Professor Bultmann's theology is often based on a completely antiquated view of science. Bultmann stumbles at problems which stumbled Victorian science, causing it to oppose orthodox Christianity. Much of his theology, with respect to science, is today totally passé. Theologians and men of faith should be made aware of this.

It is, of course, perfectly clear to the present author that scientific knowledge cannot, in itself, produce faith, not to mention faith in divine revelation. But removal of some scientific misunderstandings, particularly with reference to biological evolution and its consequences on faith in the historicity of parts of the Old Testament, may help us to see more clearly through the fogs and mists of some kinds of pronouncements made in the name of science, especially by those concerned with the evolutionary views of the origin of life and the Genesis account. An evaluation of the real scientific worth of some of these loud pronouncements may help us to arrive at a clearer position with respect to biblical teaching and faith.

Biblical faith is often represented today in newspaper and magazine reports as being utterly impossible for an enlightened scientific intellectual. Many students are kept from even considering the teachings of Christ by the threat of being considered medieval and nonintellectual if they do. The author of a series of valuable lectures on these subjects, a chaplain to Queen Elizabeth of England, was heckled recently in print and in person at the University of Oxford, England, to such an extent that his lectures were canceled. His views were called medieval. This same threat was used against students wishing to go and hear the worthy theologian. The Genesis account of the creation, of Adam and Eve, of the flood, of the

Tower of Babel, of Jonah, etc., were held up to ridicule (or demythologization) before the students in the name of so-called science, on the basis that no intelligent, educated person could possibly believe their historical veracity today. The Genesis account of creation is either demythologized, harmonized with evolutionary thought, or held up as an example of discarded and outmoded religious thought.

No scientist can be asked to believe in nonsense, of course. I could not believe that Jonah swallowed the whale. That would be plain nonsense. But belief that the whale (or fish) swallowed Jonah falls into an entirely different category. It is not of necessity nonsense.

In the foregoing pages the author has endeavored to examine and compare both the present-day evolutionary teaching on the origin of life and the biblical teaching of Genesis, to ascertain just how far they are mutually compatible, and whether difficulties, or even nonsense, would be involved in believing either account. The reader must judge which account involves more belief in myths or nonsense.

There is, however, another most important aspect to this inquiry: If Christ himself believed in Adam and Eve as physically and literally the first human pair in the Garden of Eden, in the serpent and the fall, then we shall get into difficulties, if we are Christians, the moment we call these accounts nonsensical, from a scientific point of view, or mythological, from a theological aspect. And our real trouble will be with the confession and claim of Jesus Christ to be one with the Father and, in fact, God, who therefore himself believed these accounts. The basic difficulty for modern theologians is, of course, that Jesus claimed to be God (in John 17, for example) and yet believed quite obviously in the biblical account of creation, Noah, the Tower of Babel, etc., just as they stand. In fact, he called his own word (and therefore beliefs), eternal and refers to it as the basis on which the last judgment will be decided.[3] If Christ was wrong, if he held a

[3]John 12:48.

false *Weltanschauung,* then his whole claim as Messiah and God, the only begotten of the Father, must fall with his wrong views.

It is for this reason, obviously, that modern theology has been teaching us with the zeal of despair for the past fifty years that Christians must abandon the world picture of the Bible, or lose their Christianity. According to them, the biblical world view is hopelessly wrong and out of date. We are told that Jesus' world views were merely a concession to the hearers of his times. But then, Jesus made no concessions on other popular subjects such as hypocrisy, covetousness and sexual sins.

Modern theology has been maneuvered into the position of finding that scientists have proved the *Weltanschauung* of the Bible to be wrong and that therefore Christ was wrong and therefore not the God-Man. They have tried unsuccessfully to dissociate Jesus from his own views, preferring those of a Victorian sort of science to his own. Now that they recognize that there is, in their view, not much left to save in Christ's teaching, they are discarding him altogether. The result is a Christianity without Christ, and even a theology without God. It is well known that Germany has a number of clergymen who are avowed atheists today. And there are plenty of "God is dead" theologians all over the modern world. All this is merely a result of allowing our ship of faith to have been torpedoed by a "science" which is being continually outdated in its forward march to truth. Victorian science has robbed many a Bultmann-type theologian, even in his student days, of any confidence in the message of Christ as revealed in Scripture. This book is an attempt to prevent our younger (and maybe older) students from being frightened out of looking to the revelation of God in the Scriptures on the basis that they are outmoded. The experience of many Christians has been that serious study and daily application of the Scriptures bring with them the promise mentioned in Psalm 119:97-99, "O how love I thy law! It is my meditation all the day. Thou through thy commandments hast made me wiser than mine enemies: for they are ever with me. I have more understanding than all my teachers: for thy testimonies are my meditation."

GLOSSARY

Abiogenesis. Origination of living organisms from non-living matter; spontaneous generation.

Archebiopoiesis. The original or first formation of a living organism from lifeless matter.

Abiogenically. Pertaining to abiogenesis.

Algorithm. a) The art of calculating by means of nine figures and zero. b) The art of calculating with any species of notation, as of fractions, surds, proportions, etc. c) A deterministic set of rules for computing the solution to a set of problems.

Biogenesis. The development of living organisms or a theory of the same.

Biopoiesis. The creation or making of life from non-living material.

Carnivore. Flesh or meat-eating animal (or plant).

Coacervate. a) To pile up; to collect into a mass or crowd. b) A concentration of substances (proteins, etc.) supposed by some (Bungenberg de Jong) to be a percursor of living material from lifeless matter.

Catalysis. Acceleration of a reaction by a substance which may be recovered unchanged at the end of the reaction.

Cephalization. Tendency to the development and domination of the head and nervous functions in animal and human organisms; localization of important functions in the head.

Endergonic. Requiring or absorbing energy.

Entropy. A measure of the unavailable energy in a thermodynamic system.

Enzyme. A substance catalyzing specific chemical transformations in plants and animals.

Eobiont. Primitive living organism (hypothetical).

Esterases. Enzymes that form or split esters.

Eugenical. Concerning improvement of inborn hereditary qualities; race improvement.

Exogenous. Produced from without.

Gene. A cell entity concerned with the transmission, development or determination of heredity.

Genetic code. The information code determining heredity.

Hiatus. A gap, chasm or break in a manuscript.

Hominid. Resembling the *Hominidae;* manlike.

Hormone. A chemical messenger in the body, producing a specific effect from its source; an internal secretion.

Hydrosphere. The aqueous envelope of the earth; oceans, lakes, rivers, streams, underground waters and aqueous vapor in the atmosphere.

Index fossil. Any impression or trace of an animal or plant from past geological ages which is assumed to indicate the age of the formation in which it occurs.

Kinetic energy. Energy of motion.

Lithosphere. The solid part of the earth.

Logos. The word; creative, revelatory thought; often used to refer to the second Person of the Trinity.

Macromolecule. Large complex molecule.

Macromutation. Large mutation or change.

Marsupial. Having a pouch for carrying the young; pertaining to the *Marsupiala.*

Mechanomorphic. Of the form of a machine or mechanism.

Micromutaion. Small mutation or change.

Mutation. A change; a sudden variation in the hereditary code.

Metamorphosis. Change of form, structure or substance; a striking alteration of appearance.

Nihilism. The doctrine that no reality exists (nihil—nothing).

Occam's razor. System whereby all unnecessary hypotheses are eliminated.

Omnivores. Plants or animals which eat anything available.

Ontogeny. The life history or development of the individual organism.

Otto cycle. A four stroke cycle for internal combustion engines.

Oxidases. Enzymes that oxidize chemical substances.

Paleontology. The science dealing with the life of past geological ages and founded upon the study of fossils.

Pantheism. The doctrine that the whole of the universe is God.

Peptides, polypeptides. Combinations of two or more amino acids, the amino group of one acid being combined with the carboxyl of another.

Phlogiston. The hypothetical principle of fire regarded as a material substance.

Photosynthesis. Synthesis of chemical compounds using radiant energy (light) as the source of energy.

Phylogeny. The race history of an animal or plant.

Polyphyletic. Derived from more than one original type or race.

Psychosomatic. Pertaining to the interaction of psychic (of the soul) and somatic (of the body) phenomena.

Quantum. Quantity; amount; elemental unit of energy according to the quantum theory.

Racemate. A mixture of the dextro and laevo rotary forms of optical isomers.

Rta. An Indian system of doctrine.

Stereoisomers. Isomers differing only in arrangement of atoms or groups in space.

Spereospecificity. Chemical specificity of action dependent on stereo isomerism.

Symbiosis. Living together of two organisms in a mutually advantageous association.

Tao. Figuratively, the course of nature, the absolute, the cosmic order; hence Truth or right conduct (Chinese philosophy).

Template. A gauge, pattern or mold used as a guide to the form of the work to be executed.

Thermodynamics. Science treating the mechanical action or relation of heat.

Trilobites. A group of (extinct) marine arthropods constituting the group *Trilobita.*

Uniformitarianism. The doctrine that existing processes are sufficient to account for all past geological changes.

Universalism. The doctrine that all men will be saved or rescued to holiness and happiness.

Vestigial organs. Small, degenerate or imperfectly developed organs which have been more fully developed in an earlier stage of the individual or in a past generation.

Zygote. Fertilized ovum or egg.

GENERAL INDEX

BIBLIOGRAPHY

DE BEER, GAVIN. *Charles Darwin.* N.Y.: Doubleday & Co., 1964
BERNAL, J. D. *The Origin of Life.* London: Weidenfeld & Nicholson, 1967
BLUM, HAROLD F. *Time's Arrow and Evolution.* Princeton, N.J.: Princeton
    University Press, 1955
CLARK, R. E. D. *Darwin, Before and After.* Chicago: Moody Press, 1967
DARWIN, CHARLES. *Origin of Species.* New York: P. F. Collier & Son, 1909
DARWIN, FRANCIS. *Life and Letters of Charles Darwin.* New York: D. Ap-
    pleton, 1898
DIXON, MALCOLM, and WEBB, E. C. *Enzymes.* New York: Academic Press,
    1964
VON ENCELN, O. D. and KASTER, K. E. *Geology.* New York: McGraw-Hill,
    1952
ENOCH, H. *Evolution or Creation.* Madras: Union of Evangelical Students
    of India, 1966
FRAIR, WAYNE. and DAVIES, P. WILLIAM. *The Case for Creation.* Chicago:
    Moody Press, 1967
GOSSE, PHILIP HENRY. *Omphalos, An Attempt to Untie the Geological Knot.*
    1857
HAMILTON, FLOYD E. *The Basis of Evolutionary Faith.* London: Jas. Clark
    & Co. 1931
HEIDEL, ALEXANDER. *The Gilgamesh Epic and Old Testament Parallels.* Chi-
    cago: University of Chicago Press, 1946

For Journals and articles see footnotes.

HITLER, ADOLPH. *Mein Kampf.* München: Verlag Franz Eher Nachfolger, 1933
HOWELLS, WILLIAM. *Mankind in the Making.* N.Y.: Doubleday & Co., 1959
HOYLE, FRED. *Galaxies, Nuclei and Quasars,* N.Y.: Harper & Co., 1965
VON HUENE, FREIHERR. *Die Erschaffung des Menschen.* Frankfurt/Main: Anker Verlag, n.d.
———. *Weg und Werk Gottes in der Natur.* Siegen-Leipzig: Wilhelm Schneider Verlag, n.d.
HUXLEY, JULIAN. *Evolution: The Modern Synthesis.* London: Allen & Unwin, 1942
———. *Evolution After Darwin.* Chicago: University of Chicago Press, 1960
JEANS, SIR JAMES. *The Mysterious Universe.* New York: Macmillan Co., 1930
KERKUT, G. A. *The Implications of Evolution.* London: Pergamon Press, 1960
KITCHEN, K. A. *Ancient Orient and Old Testament.* Chicago: Inter Varsity Press, 1966
KOGON, EUGEN. *Der SS-Staat.* Frankfurt/Main: Europäische Verlagsanstalt, 1964
LEWIS, C. S. *Letters to Malcolm.* London: Geoffrey Bles, 1964
———. *The Problem of Pain.* New York: Macmillan Co., 1948
———. *The Screwtape Letters.* London: Geoffrey Bles, 1961
MIXTER, RUSSELL L. *Evolution and Christian Thought Today.* Grand Rapids: Wm. B. Eerdmans Publishing Co., 1959
MORRIS, HENRY, and WHITCOMB, JOHN C. *The Genesis Flood.* Philadelphia: The Presbyterian & Reformed Publishing Co., 1961
MORRIS, HENRY. *The Twilight of Evolution.* Nutley, N.J.: Presbyterian & Reformed Publishing Co., 1964
NEAL, H. V. and RAND, H. W. *Comparative Anatomy.* London: Blakiston, 1943
OPARIN, A. I. *Origin of Life.* New York: Macmillan Co., 1938.
OPARIN, A. I., and FESENKOV, V. *Life in the Universe,* New York: Twayne, 1961
OVERMAN, RICHARD. *Evolution and the Christian Doctrine of Creation.* Philadelphia: Westminster Press, 1967
POLLOCK, J. C. *The Christians from Siberia.* London: Hodder & Stoughton, 1964
RAMM, BERNARD. *The Christian View of Science and Scripture.* Grand Rapids: Wm. B. Eerdmans Publishing Co., 1954
REHWINKEL, ALFRED M. *The Flood in the Light of the Bible, Geology and Archaeology.* St. Louis: Concordia Publishing House, 1957
ROHRBACH, HANS. *Naturwissenschaft und Gotteserkenntnis.* Mannheim: Evg. Akademie, 1965
SMITH, A. E. WILDER. *Die Problematik der Deszendenzlehre.* Wuppertal-Vohwinkel: Brockhaus-Verlag, 1949
———. *Herkunft und Zukunft des Menschen.* Giessen and Basel: Brunnen Verlag, 1966
———. *Why Does God Allow It?* Eastbourne: Victory Press, 1960
TEILHARD DE CHARDIN, PIERRE. *The Phenomenon of Man.* New York: Harper & Row, 1964
TINKLE, WILLIAM J. *Heredity: A Study in Science and the Bible.* Houston: St. Thomas Press, 1967
TILLICH, PAUL. *The Courage to Be.* New Haven: Yale University Press, 1952
VELIKOVSKY, IMMANUEL. *Worlds in Collision.* New York: Macmillan Co., 1950
WADDINGTON, C. H. *Science and Ethics.* London: Allen & Unwin, 1942
ZIMMERMAN, JOHN, and KLOTZ, J. W. et al. *Darwin, Evolution and Creation.* St. Louis: Concordia Publishing House, 1959